THE
DRAMATIC TECHNIQUE OF
ANTOINE DE
MONTCHRESTIEN

THE
DRAMATIC TECHNIQUE OF
ANTOINE DE MONTCHRESTIEN

Rhetoric and Style in
French Renaissance Tragedy

RICHARD GRIFFITHS

FELLOW OF BRASENOSE COLLEGE
OXFORD

OXFORD
AT THE CLARENDON PRESS
1970

Oxford University Press, Ely House, London W. 1

GLASGOW   NEW YORK   TORONTO   MELBOURNE   WELLINGTON
CAPE TOWN   SALISBURY   IBADAN   NAIROBI   DAR ES SALAAM   LUSAKA   ADDIS ABABA
BOMBAY   CALCUTTA   MADRAS   KARACHI   LAHORE   DACCA
KUALA LUMPUR   SINGAPORE   HONG KONG   TOKYO

PRINTED IN GREAT BRITAIN

Más csak levelenként kapja a borostyánt
Neked egész koszorút kell adni.

Preface

THIS is the study of one man's dramatic aims, and of the extent to which he achieved them. It has, however, a much wider interest. Montchrestien is in many ways a dramatist typical of Renaissance tragedy. Though he comes late in the history of that genre, his lateness does not lead to distortion and exaggeration of the intentions of the form, such as one finds in certain of his contemporaries. His works remain in the purest line of Renaissance Tragedy, and any exaggerations, stylistic or otherwise, which occur in them are rather logical if extreme results of Renaissance dramatic practice than imperfections or distortions.

Montchrestien, then, provides a perfect case for an examination of Renaissance dramatic aims and practice; and it has been my intention, while studying him in this light, to draw attention to his relation to the other dramatists of the late sixteenth century, and to those aspects of his work in which he differs from certain of them. In doing so, I have naturally been led into producing something in the nature of a tentative 'dramaturgy' of the century. In the process much stress has been laid upon the importance of rhetorical training in the formation of Renaissance literature. In many ways Montchrestien reaches one of the highest points in the rhetorical tradition of tragedy.

Thirty years after the publication of Montchrestien's last tragedy, *Hector*, in 1604, a new genre was to come into being. After an interregnum filled with irregular tragedies and tragi-comedies, regular tragedy was coming into its own again. But it was regular tragedy of a vastly different kind. The great fault of many literary critics has been to see Renaissance tragedy as a mere forerunner of the tragedy of the Classical Age, similar in kind but inferior in substance. Renaissance tragedy is, however, a genre of its own type, which reached its own kind of excellence, first in Garnier and then in Montchrestien.

Even those critics who have gauged correctly the difference between the two forms of tragedy have tended to ascribe to Montchrestien, because of his lateness, certain attributes (particularly in the fields of style, language, and imitation), which are rather more of the seventeenth century. Though Montchrestien's language and imagery developed naturally with those of his contemporaries, it must be stressed that his poetic language, his style, and his methods of composition are, like those of other authors of the reign of Henri IV, in the tradition of the Renaissance. These problems are discussed in my chapters on 'Imitation' and 'Style', and in the Appendix on M. Lebègue's 'Malherbe' theory,

Starting with a discussion of some general aspects of Renaissance tragedy, this book continues with an examination of Montchrestien's methods of Imitation. The Renaissance tragedian's lack of concern with what the seventeenth century, and indeed we ourselves, would consider to be certain necessary dramatic attitudes is highlighted; and Montchrestien's primary concern with literary matters, rather than with religious and political content, is shown to differentiate him from many other tragedians of the time, though he is in fact thereby rather closer to Renaissance dramatic intention. There follows a close examination of the structure of Montchrestien's drama, starting with the various types of 'set piece', and concluding with a study of his style, that part of the poet's stock-in-trade to which the whole art of Renaissance tragedy was subservient. In the process, the problem of the way in which the plays were intended to be staged is touched upon.

Montchrestien's life, though much of it may seem to have little relation to his work, is of sufficient interest to warrant a place here: it also illustrates the problem of his religion, and the small effect his religious ideas (if any) had on his work. Two Appendices study the problems raised by M. Lebègue with regard to the changes between the editions of Montchrestien's plays.

It may appear surprising that there is no section upon dramatic theory as such. The influence of the theoretical writers is, however, a questionable one. On general matters pertaining to tragedy there, is on the whole, agreement between theorists and dramatists, and attention has been drawn to these cases in the text. Theorists were rarely practising dramatists, however; only one major dramatist produced an extensive theoretical work, Jean de la Taille, and this work, the Preface to his *Saül le furieux*, was probably written eleven years after his plays, which differ from its requirements in certain respects. Occasionally one gets the impression that the theoretical writers are imitating other theorists, while the dramatists are imitating the classical dramatists. Certainly it has seemed for present purposes better to study dramatic practice, and to draw attention to dramatic 'theory' only where it coincides with that practice.

Other critics whose works have helped the production of this volume are acknowledged in the text or in footnotes. I should like here, however, to say how useful M. Jacques Schérer's book, *La Dramaturgie classique*, has been in clarifying my ideas on seventeenth-century dramatic forms, and the works of Father Ong, Miss Tuve, and Mr. D. Lemen Clark for the stimulus they gave to my study of rhetoric.

The work for this volume was originally undertaken under the guidance of the late Mr. Donald Beves; and I should like to record here my heartfelt gratitude for his generous advice, encouragement, and hospitality. An even greater debt is owed to Dr. Robert Bolgar, discussions with whom set me off on many profitable lines of thought, and whose unstinting advice was invaluable.

My thanks are due to many people for help of various kinds, often in the form of profitable conversations upon aspects of sixteenth-century literature in France and abroad. They include Professor Alan Boase, Professor Charles Brink, Dr. Grahame Castor, Dr. Terence Cave, Dr. Dorothy Coleman, Professor Leonard Forster, Professor Gilbert Gadoffre, Dr. Kathleen Hall, Mr. Frank Higman, Dr. Gillian Jondorf, Dr. Richard Ladborough, Professor H. W. Lawton, Professor Raymond Lebègue, Professor Ian McFarlane, Dr. Odette de Mourgues, Father Walter J. Ong, S.J., Dr. Anne Righter, Professor Jacques Schérer, the late Professor Albert-Marie Schmidt, Mr. Christopher Smith, the late M. Jean Tremblot de la Croix, and Mr. Brian Vickers.

I should also like to express my gratitude, for the opportunities they provided for the research upon which this volume is based, to the Provost and Fellows of King's College, Cambridge, the Master and Fellows of Selwyn College, Cambridge, and the Principal and Fellows of Brasenose College, Oxford.

For permission to reproduce parts of my articles, 'The Influence of Formulary Rhetoric upon French Renaissance Tragedy' (*M.L.R.* lix, 2 April 1964), 'Les Sentences et le "but moral" dans les tragédies de Montchrestien' (*R.S.H.* 105, janvier–mars 1962), and 'Some Uses of Petrarchan Imagery in Sixteenth-Century France' (*F.S.* xviii, 4 October 1964), I would like to thank the editors of the *Modern Language Review*, the *Revue des sciences humaines*, and *French Studies*.

Contents

Abbreviations

In *Sophonisbe* (ed. Fries) A = 1596 edition
                             B = 1601 edition
                             C = 1604 edition

In *Aman* and *Les Lacènes* A = 1601 edition
  (ed. Seiver and Calkins) B = 1604 edition

Arsenal	Bibliothèque de l'Arsenal
Biens.	Bienséances
B.M.	British Museum
B. Nat.	Bibliothèque Nationale
D. et I.	*Deffense et illustration de la langue françoyse*
Diss.	Dissertation
Doctrine	Brunot: *La Doctrine de Malherbe*
edn.	edition
F.S.	*French Studies*
Inst.	Bibliothèque de l'Institut
L. H. des I.	*Les Huguenots des Isles*
M.F.	*Mercure François*
M.L.N.	*Modern Language Notes*
M.L.R.	*Modern Language Review*
Morph.	Morphologie
P. de J.	Petit de Julleville's edition (1891) of Montchrestien's plays
P.M.L.A.	Publications of the Modern Language Association
Priv.	Privilège
Rép.	Répétition
R.H.L.F.	*Revue d'Histoire Littéraire de la France*
R.S.H.	*Revue des Sciences Humaines*
s.d.	sans date
s.l.n.d.	sans lieu ni date
v.l.	vers liminaires
vocab.	vocabulaire
Z.fr.Spr.L.	*Zeitschrift für französische Sprache und Litteratur*

1. Montchrestien's Life

FOR all readers of the post-Romantic era it requires a tremendous effort to view the literature of preceding centuries with anything approaching understanding. Western literature has been imbued, for almost two centuries, with certain critical preconceptions which make a proper appreciation of what was written before that era extremely difficult. One can make judgements based upon nineteenth- or twentieth-century practice, and these judgements may in one sense be valid; if one presumes the main value of literature to consist in the bearing it may have upon our own lives, then an appreciation of an author which may, in his own terms, be untrue, may nevertheless be of worth. Yet there exists another way of looking at the literature of former centuries; it consists of an attempt to place oneself in the position of both author and audience, and to understand the aims of one, and the demands of the other. This is as important a pursuit as the former; indeed, it may fulfil the purposes of the former, for a proper understanding of the intent of an author may bring us an even fuller understanding of our own problems. At the same time, this historical approach will in many cases provide us with a far more satisfactory aesthetic experience, in that through our understanding of the conventions and requirements of the age we shall be able to appreciate more fully the achievement of the authors concerned.

The path to such knowledge is uncertain and treacherous, the results often fragmentary. One cannot hope to recapture in its entirety the experience of others; the most one can do is to recreate some of the conditions of that experience. No era is more elusive, in this respect, than the Renaissance. The work of many scholars has brought us a knowledge not only of most of the basic principles underlying Renaissance literary creation but also of many details of the literary practice of the era. Nevertheless, whole areas of this practice still remain uncertain and uncharted. This book is an attempt to chart one confined area of French Renaissance literature—the French tragic theatre of the sixteenth century.

Only an examination on these lines could show us the complete difference in nature between sixteenth- and seventeenth-century French tragedy. Only such an examination could show us that, taken on its own terms, sixteenth-century tragedy attains its own form of excellence, and that, far from being an ill-conceived attempt at French classical tragedy which fails in not fully achieving the aims of a Racine, it is in fact, in the works of Garnier and Montchrestien, one of the best examples of the adaptation of Renaissance rhetoric to literature.

This drama is 'non-dramatic' in modern terms; yet it remains essentially a dramatic form. The emotions and moods depicted by the speeches could perhaps be expressed in individual poems, as they were in the prosopopœic exercises of the rhetoricians. But their ideal place is in the mouths of individual characters in individual situations, and the rhetoric of which they are formed is a spoken rhetoric, made to be declaimed. Whatever the form of representation, even if these plays are merely read aloud, they are more than a string of 'elegies'. In the best authors there is a continual, planned design into which these speeches fit. Light succeeds dark, sorrow succeeds joy, anger succeeds calm. The plot of a play of this type is the skeleton upon which the author sets his 'set pieces', just as each 'set piece' is the skeleton which he clothes with flesh in the form of the 'flowers' of his style.

Montchrestien is in most respects a typical example of this theatrical form. His lateness does not appear to affect the 'regular' nature of his dramatic creation, except in the case of the play *David*. He eschews the political or religious preoccupations of certain of his fellow dramatists, but this only serves to highlight even more his literary aims. He is one of the last voices of the Renaissance theatre in France, and one of the best.

Like so many writers of his period, Montchrestien appears to reflect in his works very little of the events of his life. Indeed, the plays were all written in his early youth, at the outset of his career. But an examination of his life will help us in certain ways, by providing information for a setting of his works in the context of their times; at the same time, the detachment of the works from a personal involvement on the part of the author will become even more clear.

There is still little known about the strange and eventful life of Antoine de Montchrestien; and what is known is often seemingly contradictory. Many of the sources of information are of doubtful reliability; the *Mercure François* above all, of which Petit de Julleville so rightly says: 'On ne peut accepter qu'avec une certaine défiance un récit qui émane d'un adversaire politique et religieux, naturellement acharné contre un insurgé vaincu; mais en l'absence de tous autres documents, nous sommes bien forcés de nous servir de ceux que nous possédons.'[1]

More documents have been discovered since the time of Petit de Julleville. Some corroborate the *Mercure*, others contradict it; the fact remains that the *Mercure* itself certainly presents the facts in the most unfavourable way. This, then, is a source of which one must be wary.

Tragedian, poet, scholar, economist, cutler, factory-owner, merchant ship-owner, town governor, *chicaneur*, duellist, rebel, Montchrestien is so many-sided that at times we feel that the historical facts must refer to several people of the same name. His career is punctuated by long and inexplicable gaps of silence. All that can be said with certainty is that he was a man of humanist education (this is clear from his works); and that he was a man of action, rather unscrupulous in his means of obtaining power and money.

Antoine de Montchrestien was born in Falaise, probably in the year 1575 or 1576.[2] Both Malherbe and the *Mercure François* inform us that his true name was Mauchrestien, and that he was the son of an apothecary. Nothing was known of his father's family or origins, says the *Mercure*; yet the name of Montchrestien's cousin, 'le sieur des Ventes',[3] which is mentioned by Malherbe, the *Mercure*, and Montchrestien's servant Pierre Paris, seems to indicate that his family had some connection with the nobility.

His father and mother died while he was still a child, and he was put in the care of a neighbour, 'le sieur de sainct André Bernier'. He cannot have been entirely destitute, as the *Mercure* would attempt to suggest: 'Apres le decez de sondit pere, le Procureur du Roy à Falaize, fit assigner les voisins pour eslire un Tuteur audit Anthoine fils; et faute de toute autre alliance, le sieur de sainct André Bernier, comme proche voisin fut condamné en Justice d'en prendre la tutelle, *en laquelle, pour le peu de biens qu'il y auoit, il ne fit aucune formalite ny inuentaire.*'[4]

---

[1] *Les Tragédies de Montchrestien*, 1891, Introduction, p. vii.

[2] Both Petit de Julleville and Funck-Brentano come to this conclusion on the evidence of the portrait in the presumed 1601 edition of the tragedies. This portrait is marked AET. XXV; however, this is not conclusive proof, for the edition may be later than 1601 (cf. the 1603 edition of *L' Escossoise*, which bears the same *privilège* and *permis d'imprimer*), or the portrait may have been drawn some time before the edition appeared.

[3] *Interrogatoire de Paris*, reproduced in Leboitteux's *Les Huguenots des Isles*, p. 28. Petit de Julleville denies that the 'Les Ventes' mentioned by Malherbe and Funck-Brentano was any relation of Montchrestien's; but he did not have at his disposal this extra evidence, which explicitly mentions Les Ventes as 'Cousin de Montchrestien'.

[4] *M.F.*, t. vii, p. 815. My italics.

The falsity of this picture is demonstrated by a later statement made by the *Mercure* itself: 'Estant deuenu chicaneur, il attaqua son Tuteur, luy demanda compte, et le plaida tellement qu'il fut contrainct d'accorder auec luy, et luy donner mille liures.'[1]

The lack of inventory made by his guardian does not therefore reflect on his own penury, but on the guardian's honesty.

Soon Montchrestien went to the university, as a companion to two brothers, Jacques and François Thézart, barons de Tournebu des Essarts, who lived near Falaise, in the château de Tournebu. 'Anthoine estant grandelet et d'un esprit vif, il fut pris pour suiure au College et seruir les sieurs de Tournebu, et des Essars freres.'[2]

He does not seem to have been treated like a servant, but rather as a companion: 'Deuenu aagé de 20 ans, il apprend auec ses maistres à tirer des armes, à monter à cheval, et en hantant les nobles il faict le noble, le vaillant, le hardy et l'homme de querelle pour se porter sur le pré . . .'[3]

His situation would, in fact, seem to have been that of a member of a noble youth's *familia* at the university. Hastings Rashdall describes the life of a young noble at the university as being very similar to what he was used to at home; he would live in a hostel of his own with a numerous *familia*, 'including poorer but well-born youths who dressed like him and acted as his *socii* or humble companions',[4] and with a chaplain and a private tutor, besides the ordinary servants.

The Thézart brothers must have been about the same age as Montchrestien; they were almost certainly born between the years 1570 and 1577.[5] At the death of their father François Thézart, in 1582, they, and their sister Suzanne, were left in the care of their mother, Jehane de Monchy, who later married Raoul (or Paul) de Briqueville.

Montchrestien was to remain in contact with this family throughout his life,[6] and many years later, in 1618, he married Suzanne Thézart.

---

[1] *M.F.*, t. vii, p. 815.   [2] Ibid.   [3] Ibid.

[4] *The Universities of Europe in the Middle Ages* (ed. Powicke and Emden), vol. 3, pp. 404–5.

[5] 'Les deux fils, mineurs à la mort de leur père, lui succédèrent dans la baronnie, sans qu'il y ait eu de partage entre eux: de 1587 à 1590, on les trouve comme sous-âge; de 1597 à 1603, comme barons de Tournebu.' (Charles de Fierville, 'Histoire généalogique de la maison et de la baronnie de Tournebu', in the *Mémoires de la Société des Antiquaires de Normandie*, 3e série, 6e volume.)

In Larousse's *Grand Dictionnaire Universel* we find that from the 14th century onwards, the age of majority in Normandy was 20 years.

[6] Some evidence of this is provided by the following documents:

(a) '29 des mêmes mois et an (*juillet 1611*) procuration donnée par le même (noble

At what age did he go to university? The age for admittance was far lower than it is nowadays, and Rashdall states the usual age to have been between thirteen and sixteen.[1] Twenty was the minimum age for the mastership, and the full course in arts lasted seven years.

Caen was the university nearest to his home; and it is almost certain that he went there, because the *vers liminaires* to his first play are almost all by eminent figures at this university. It had been founded originally by the English in opposition to the University of Paris, but even after the departure of the English it remained an important centre of learning. Here Montchrestien would have been trained, during his arts course, in, among other things, the arts of logic and rhetoric. His plays attest the fact that Montchrestien must have had the thorough Humanist education of his time.

At the University, the *Mercure* informs us, 'il estudie, il s'adonne à la Poësie Françoise, fait bien des vers'.[2]

One of the first examples of his poetic talent must be the poem *Susane ou la Chasteté*, which, though first published in 1601, must have been written before 1596.[3] This poem is dedicated to Suzanne Thézart. Montchrestien addresses her respectfully, telling her: 'Vous égallés en chasteté celle qui m'en a fourni l'argument.'[4] It was she who gave him 'la volonté de l'entreprendre, et le courage de l'acheuer'.[4] Her soul 'seruoit d'objet à mon esprit, il la regardoit de fois à autre cependant que ma main trauailloit au tableau'.[5]

Suzanne was married to Léonard Hamon, sieur de l'Isle, in about 1598.

It must have been towards the end of his university career that Montchrestien published his first play, *Sophonisbe*, in 1596. By the year 1599 he seems to have left Caen.[6]

---

homme Antoine de Montchrestien, sieur de Vatteville) pour agir contre le baron de Tournebu.' (By this time François was dead, and Jacques Thézart held the title.)

(*b*) 'Lundi des fêtes de Pasques *4 avril 1616*, en l'Escriptoire… 600 livres qu'il (Montchrestien) a affermé luy estre deubz et desquels s'est pour luy oblige Me. Jacques Thezard, chevalier, seigneur et baron de Tournebu, pour les causes estans en certain compte fait et arrestés entre eulx devant les tabellions de Rouen, le 16 juillet dernier passé.' (Actes communiqués par Ch. de Robillard de Beaurepaire, *Bulletin de la Commission des Antiquités de la Seine-Inférieure*, t. vii, pp. 369 ff., 1888.)

[1] Op. cit., vol. 3, pp. 352–3.   [2] *M.F.*, t. vii, p. 814.

[3] Two of the *poésies liminaires* to the 1596 edition of *Sophonisbe*, Montchrestien's first published work (those of I. B. Buissonnière and I. D. M. Sieur du Parc), mention a poem on the subject of Susane.

[4] Dedication to 1601 edition of *Susane*.   [5] Dedication to 1604 edition of *Susane*.

[6] His 1599 *Derniers vers*, and his subsequent works, are printed in Rouen, where also most of his friends of the time seem to have lived.

The play is dedicated to Madame de la Vérune, wife of the governor of Caen, and we learn that it has already been performed in her presence: 'Il vous pleut prendre la peine d'asister à la representation de céte Tragedie, vous le prendrés encor', s'il vous plaist, de la lire.'[1]

The *vers liminaires* to this edition show Montchrestien to have been acquainted with many of the prominent figures in the world of scholarship at Caen University. Jacques de Cahaignes, *professeur du roy en medecine*, Claude Colin du Prignon, *professeur royal de littérature grecque*[2] and *professeur ès arts*, Pierre des Rues, *docteur ès droits* and *curé* of Saint-Julien de Caen, and Jacques du Buisson, *docteur en théologie* and *curé* of Bretheville, were all rectors of the University at one time or other, and *doyens* of their faculties. Estienne Le Fanu and Jacques le Paulmier, both praised by Cahaignes for their erudition, belonged very much to university circles. The praises showered on Montchrestien by these men suggest that he may have impressed them as an outstanding pupil. He is well received in the academic world of his elders, be they doctors, lawyers, or theologians. Some of them were themselves poets of reasonable competence.

By the time Montchrestien had reached the age of twenty, the *Mercure* tells us, he had taken on the noble title of 'de Vatteville': 'En hantant les nobles il faict le noble, le vaillant, le hardy et l'homme de querelle pour se porter sur le pré, et se fait appeler Vatteville, mais de terre ny de fief de Vatteville, non dicitur tit. de feudis.'[3]

An attack was made upon him at about this time by a certain Baron de Gouville. The full reasons for the enmity between the two men are not known: 'Ayant fait querelle contre le Baron de Gouville, en une rencontre que ce Baron accompagné d'un sien beaufrere et d'un soldat eut avec luy, il met la main à l'espée, se defend mais ces trois contre un le laisserent pour mort.'[4]

But Montchrestien recovered, and opened a lawsuit against the Baron, who was forced to pay him damages: 'De ce rencontre ayant fait plainte, l'affaire cousta audit Baron et à son beaufrere plus de douze mil liures, dont il s'empluma, et commença à faire l'homme de moyens.'[5]

---

[1] *Dédication* of 1596 *Sophonisbe*.

[2] Were these two 'professeurs royaux' attached at any time to the Collège de France, or was their title an honorary one? Cahaignes is not mentioned in Lefranc's *Histoire du Collège de France*, but Claude Colin is mentioned as follows: 'Henri IV ... par arrêt du 21 avril [1592], choisit deux lecteurs pour le grec: François Parent, principal du collège de Navarre, et Claude Colin, principal du collège de Caen. Ce dernier ne semble pas avoir professé, car il n'est plus question de lui par la suite. (Goujet ne le compte pas au nombre des professeurs.)' (Lefranc, pp. 228–9.)

[3] *M.F.*, t. vii, pp. 814–15.

[4] Ibid., p. 815.

[5] Ibid.

As the *Mercure* goes on to say, this incident obviously aroused his appetite for lawsuits, for soon we find him successfully claiming 'mille liures' from his tutor. In later years he acted for Suzanne Thézart in a lawsuit against her husband, Léonard Hamon: 'Il fut depuis fort blasmé d'auoir esté le soliciteur du proces qu'une Damoiselle de bonne maison auoit contre son mary qui estoit Gentil-homme riche, mais imbecile de corps et d'esprit: et auoit pensé essuyé ce blasme en l'espousant clandestinement après le decez de son mary: mais ce mariage luy fut debatu apres la mort de ceste femme.'[1]

Probably as a result of these lawsuits, by 1603 Montchrestien was to become rich enough to buy various properties at 'Anbleville, vicomté de Falaise' (probably the modern Damblainville).[2]

The first sign we have of Montchrestien's new title 'de Vatteville'[3] is in a slim volume of poetry published in 1599 by Raphaël du Petit Val, the Rouen printer, entitled *Les Derniers Propos, avec le Tombeau de feu noble dame Barbe Guiffart, femme de Messire Claude Groulart Cheualier, Conseiller du Roy en ses Conseils d'Estat et Priué, et premier President en sa Court de Parlement de Rouen.*[4] This volume is signed 'A. M. Sr. D. V.', and contains five of the poems later to be included in the 1601 edition of the tragedies,[5] but in a completely different form; it also includes two poems which do not exist outside this 1599 edition.[6]

By this time Montchrestien had possibly already moved to Rouen. This volume marks his first acquaintance with Rouen celebrities; by the time of the 1601 edition of the tragedies this acquaintance will have been extended even further. Where his friends at Caen had been mainly scholars, those at Rouen include lawyers and politicians, Groulart himself being one of the great figures of the political life of the time, and Louis Bretel, sieur de Gremonville et de Lanquetot, being another president of the *parlement* of Rouen.

[1] Ibid.

[2] See Acte of 13 September 1612, at Rouen (in *Bulletin de la Commission des Antiquités de la Seine-Inférieure*, t. vii, pp. 369 ff.: '. . . Certains contrats passez entre ledit sieur de Montchrestien et le dit maître Nicolas, tant pour lui que pour M⁰. Jehan Hemon, son frere, par devant les tabellions de Fallaise, les 14ᵉ jour de septembre et 6 octobre 1603 et 27 fevrier 1604, touchant la vente faite par ledit sieur Hemon audit sieur de Montchrestien de plusieurs maisons et héritages assis en la par. d'Anbleville, vicomté de Falaise.' Unfortunately the Falaise *tabellionages* for the two years in question were destroyed in the Normandy landings in 1944.   [3] Or 'De Vasteville'.

[4] This edition has until now remained entirely unknown to Montchrestien scholars and biographers.

[5] 'Les Derniers Propos', 'Tombeau', 'Stances', 'Complainte de la Ville de Rouen', 'Sonnet'.

[6] 'Stances à Monseigneur le premier President', 'Stances à mes Demoiselles ses filles'.

The 1601 edition, printed in Rouen, and dedicated to the Prince de Condé, contains five tragedies, *L'Escossoise ou le Desastre*, *La Cartaginoise ou la Liberté* (a new version of the 1596 *Sophonisbe*, 'qui reuient sur le Theatre vestue d'un habit neuf et mieux seant à sa grandeur que celuy dont auparavant ie l'auois accommodée'),[1] *Les Lacènes ou la Constance*, *David ou l'Adultère*, and *Aman ou la Vanité*. It also includes the long poem *Susane ou la Chasteté*, several short pieces in poetry and prose, and a *Bergerie* (a pastoral play written in both poetry and prose) preceded by some sonnets.

In this same year, 1601, we hear the first rumblings of a diplomatic incident caused by Montchrestien's play *L'Escossoise*, which has as its subject the death of Mary Stuart. A letter of 17 March 1601,[2] from Sir Ralph Winwood to Cecil, refers to a performance of this play[2] in Paris, and his own complaints to the Chancellor about it. Villeroy ordered 'punishment of that which is past, and . . . future Remedy'.[3] This banning of the play seems to have been fairly rigorously carried out, for in a letter of 21 June 1603 from M. de Beauharnais, *lieutenant général* at Orléans, to the Chancellor Pompone de Bellièvre, we find that he has been enquiring after the comedians who had recently acted the play in his town; also that he has found the book,[4] which he encloses with the letter.[5]

---

[1] 'Au Lecteur', before *La Cartaginoise*.

[2] This first letter does not expressly refer to Montchrestien. But, as Miss F. A. Yates points out in her article 'Some new light on *L'Écossaise* of Antoine de Montchrestien' (*M.L.R.* (1927), 285–97), the similarity of information to that in later letters shows it to be referring to Montchrestien's play.

[3] 'Since the beginning of Lent, certain base Comedians have publicklie plaied in this Towne the Tragedy of the late Queen of Scottes. The King being then at Verneuil, I had no other recourse but to the Chancellor; who upon my complaint was very sensible of that so lewde an Indiscretion, and in my hearing gave an especiall charge to the Lieutenant Civill, (to whose Duty the provisions for such Disorder doth appertaine), to have a care, both that this Folly should be punished, and that the like hereafter should not be committed. Since, Monsieur de Villeroy (upon the Notice which I gave him) doth promise that he will give order both for the Punishment of that which is past, and for future Remedy.' (Sir Ralph Winwood, *Memorials*, 1725, i. 398.) Quoted by F. A. Yates, art. cit. p. 286.

[4] The details show that it is definitely Montchrestien's play.

[5] 'Monseigneur — Pour obéir à vos commandemens, je me suis tres soigneusement enquis quelz estoient ces comédiens qui avoient joué en cete ville, depuis deux mois ou environ, une tragédie sur la mort de la feue royne d'Ecosse, et n'ay peu aprandre autre chose, sinon que le chef de leur compaignie se nomme La Vallée, et qu'ilz sont partis de cete ville depuis ung mois ou six sepmaines, sans que j'aye peu scavoir où ilz sont allez. Mais j'ay tant faict, que j'ay recouvré ung livre de tragédies, la premiere desquelles, nommée *L'Escossoise* aultrement *Le Desastre*, est celle mesme qu'ilz ont représentée, ainsi qu'il m'a este asseuré par gens d'honneur qui y ont assisté. Je vous envoye, Monseigneur, ce livre, très marry que je ne puis obéir entièrement à ce que vous m'avez commandé, et

On 13 February 1604 another letter from Paris to London shows us that the incident was not yet closed. Parry, the English ambassador, tells Cecil that the play has been performed again, that the players have been imprisoned and the book suppressed, and that the author and the printer are being searched for.[1]

The suppression of the written play does not seem to have been as thorough as that of the performances; in 1603 another edition of the plays appeared at Rouen, and in 1604 a completely revised edition appeared,[2] in which all the plays have been changed almost line by line, and a new play, *Hector*, has been added; it was issued with a new *privilège du roy*, dated 10 April 1604.[3]

This last fact would seem to invalidate Miss Yates's theory that Montchrestien's swift departure to England some time in the following year was caused by the *Escossoise* incident.[4] It is possible that the *Mercure* is right in attributing his flight to a duel: '. . . S'estant trouué en un rencontre accusé de auoir tué traistreusement le fils du sieur de Grichy Moynnes prez Bayeux en feignant de luy demander la vie, il s'en alla en Angleterre, crainte d'estre pendu . . .'[5]

In his poem *Au Roy*, asking pardon,[6] Montchrestien, too, refers to the 'eschaffaut' that awaits him. As Joly points out, he seems to deny

supplie Dieu le Créateur vous donner, Monseigneur, heureuse yssue de tous vos desirs et vous conserver en longue vie pour le repos de ce royaume. A Orléans, ce XXI juin 1603, Vostre très humble serviteur, Beauharnois, lieutenant général à Orléans.' Quoted by L. Auvray, *R.H.L.F.* (1897), 89–91.

[1] 'The Comedians, ye heretofore sd., bn. prohibited to represent on stadge ye Tragedy of ye death of ye k. mother, adventured this weeke to act it again publickly. But ye k. counsel advised of it, caused them ye next morning to be apprehended and imprisoned, where they yeat remayn: besides ye booke is suppressed, and the author and ye printer inquired after to tast of ye same cupp. The k. shewed hymself very highly offended, and hath commanded very rigorous punishment to be done on them al.' (P.R.O., *State Papers, Foreign, France*, 51.) Quoted by F. A. Yates, art. cit. p. 287.

[2] This edition consists of *Hector, La Reine d'Escosse, La Cartaginoise, Les Lacènes, David, Aman*, and *Susane*. But the *Bergerie* and the smaller poems have disappeared.

[3] Probably the prosecutions were initiated for the sake of the English, and therefore only for show, i.e. the performances were stopped, but editions allowed to continue.

[4] 'Is it not possible that this affair may have been at the bottom of Montchrestien's hasty departure into England which biographers, following the *Mercure François*, have hitherto attributed solely to his having killed the son of the Sieur de Grichy-Moinnes in a duel.' Art. cit., p. 288.)

[5] *M.F.*, t. vii, pp. 815–16.

[6] There is one copy of this poem, bound with the arms of Henri IV (i.e. probably the copy he presented to the King), in the Bibliothèque Nationale. The poem was reprinted in the *Parnasse des plus excellens poetes de ce temps*, Paris, Mathieu Guillemot, 1607. (Until now Montchrestien scholars have only mentioned the 1618 edition of the Parnasse—but a 1607 edition exists at the Bibliothèque de l'Institut.)

the opprobrium cast on him for treachery, when he refers to 'l'innocence de mœurs, compagnon de mes jours', and asks:

> Puniroit-on ma faute, ains plustot mon malheur,
> Puis que mon plus grand crime est ma seule valeur.[1]

By the time of his departure to England Montchrestien has decided
to give up dramatic writing altogether. In the new 'Dédication' to
Condé which heads the 1604 edition of his plays he excuses their
insufficiency, and says he is thinking of turning to more serious
matters.[2] Can he be speaking of the '*Pseaumes de David, en rithme*', or
the '*histoire de Normandie*' which the *Mercure* describes him as having
worked at? Or is he already thinking of his great work on political
economy, which did not appear until eleven years later?

Though he gave up writing plays at this time, there is reason to
believe that he still occasionally wrote small poems. Two such poems
appear at the head of a posthumous collection by a Dominican nun,
Sœur Anne de Marquets, which appeared in Paris in 1605.[3]

The date of Montchrestien's departure to England is not known;
but he was most probably in that country by 8 March 1605.[4] The next
six years are a blank period in our knowledge of Montchrestien's life;
all we know is that during this time he probably went from England to
Holland at one stage. In this absence a new edition of his tragedies was
printed at Nyort in 1606, based on the 1604 edition, but so badly done
that it was almost certainly a pirated edition.

When he returned we do not know;[5] but he was back in France by

---

[1] *Au Roy*, p. 4.

[2] 'S'il m'estoit possible de les dégager totalement du public, ce me seroit un grand
contentement, et par mon propre consentement elles seroient desormais plustot suprimées
qui reimprimées: Car la grandeur de vostre nom demande quelque chose plus sérieuse et
mon humeur de maintenant est plus portée à un autre sujet d'escrire.'

[3] *Sonets spirituels de feüe tres-vertueuse et tres-docte Dame Sr. Anne de Marquets
Religieuse à Poissi, sur les dimanches et principales solennitez de l'Année*, Paris, Claude
Morel, 1605.

[4] Funck-Brentano calculates this date from a passage in the *Traicté de l'œconomie
politique* where Montchrestien remarks, when mentioning a cargo of cloth which had been
seized at Rouen: 'A bon droit, disait-on publiquement à Londres sur le bruit qui en vint.'
James I had complained about the incident to Henri IV, and the French king's reply was
dated 8 March 1605.

[5] His return presents yet another mystery. The *Mercure* says: '. . . Entr'autres il desdia
L'Escossoise au Roy de la grande Bretagne, ce qui luy sauua la vie; . . . il s'en alla en
Angleterre, crainte d'estre pendu iusques à ce que sa M. de la grande Bretagne obtint du
feu Roy Henri IV sa grace.' Misled by this passage, some eighteenth-century critics
placed the date of *L'Escossoise* later than 1605, which is, of course, ridiculous. Also,
would James be likely to be sufficiently pleased by a play he had sought to have banned,
to ask for the author's reinstatement?

23 July 1611, for in two legal documents drawn up at Rouen on 23 and 29 July we find him described as 'noble homme Antoine de Montchrestien, demeurant en la ville d'Oussune sur Loire'.[1]

Oussone-sur-Loire is undoubtedly the town where, on his return from France, Montchrestien set up a factory to makes knives and cutlery. The *Mercure* says:

> S'estant retiré vers la forest d'Orleans, et puis à Chastillon-sur-Loire, il trauailla à faire de l'acier et en faire faire des lancettes, cousteaux, canivets et autres instruments qu'il venoit vendre à Paris: et pource il se logea en la ruë de la Harpe chez un taillandier, et demeura quelques années en cest estat, grandement soupçonné de faire de la fausse monnoye.[2]

Oussone, being 'vers la forest d'Orleans' and near Châtillon, must have been the first location for the factory.

This new venture may seem extraordinary, in relation to his previous life; but from this time onwards Montchrestien is almost entirely concerned with commercial ventures. His interest in economics, which he is to voice in his *Traicté de l'œconomie politique* in 1615, may have been aroused by the sight of the prosperity of England and Holland.

But one must not think that he founded his factory purely in order to put his economic theories into practice, and to lead the way in helping France's economy. As in most of his activities, he was hoping to make money for himself by this enterprise; the personal note in some of his entreaties to the King in the *Traicté* show this very clearly.[3] But the factory was unsuccessful, mainly owing to the market's being flooded by cheap articles from abroad; Montchrestien's ideas on political economy seem to stem from this failure.

The last we hear of Montchrestien's connection with Oussone is in September 1612, when, in a legal document drawn up at Rouen, he is still described as '*demeurant* à Oussune-sur-Loire', though '*estant logé* de present en ceste ville, par Saint-Estienne la grand Église'. In this document he is selling his property at Anbleville.[4]

---

[1] 'Actes communiqués à la commission des antiquités de la Seine-Inférieure par Charles de Robillard de Beaurepaire', *Bulletin de la Commission*, t. vii, pp. 369 ff.

[2] *M.F.*, t. vii, p. 816.

[3] e.g. 'Ne laissez point esteindre le feu de la forge; il est plus aisé de le conseruer, que de le r'allumer s'il estoit mort.... Faites nous donc ioüissans du fruict de nostre industrie; c'est à dire, rendez nous à nous mesmes. Faites nous valoir ce que nous valons.... Et que font cependant nos Artizans beaucoup meilleurs et plus fidelles (que les étrangers)? Ils chomment et languissent de faim. ... On n'a iamais veu l'incommodité de ceux qui manient les Arts de la forge si grande, comme à présent ... voire (ils) se voyent quasi tous contrains de quitter le trauail.' (*Traicté de l'œconomie politique*, 'Des Manufactures', pp. 73–8.)

[4] Acte of 13 September 1612, *Bulletin de la Commission des Antiquités de la Seine-Inférieure*, t. vii, pp. 369 ff.

Some time between this date and 4 April 1616 he seems to have left Oussone, and returned to live in Rouen, for in a new legal document of that date, concerned with various financial dealings with Jacques Thézart, Montchrestien is described as '*demeurant* en la paroisse Saint-Lô de Rouen',[1] whereas previously he has been '*demeurant* à Oussune-sur-Loire, *estant logé* de present en ceste ville . . .'. Some of the financial dealings referred to had taken place on 16 July 1615, so it is possible that Montchrestien was already living in Rouen at that date.

It was in 1615 that his great economic work appeared, the *Traicté de l'œconomie politique*,[2] published by Jean Osmont of Rouen. This book, dedicated and addressed 'Au Roy et à la Reyne Mere du Roy', is a plea for France's manufacturers, who are faced by ruin owing to the lack of economic organization on a national basis. The country is going gradually to ruin economically, mainly through neglect of skilled trades,[3] through lack of check upon foreign products, and through difficulties of trade in foreign countries. The solution is drastic, and original for the time: the government must place restrictions on foreign imports, subsidize the home industries, and set the French manufacturer and merchant at least on an equal, and preferably on a better, footing than his foreign counterpart. The titles of the main sections of the book show clearly what Montchrestien considered to be the important features of national economics; they also reflect, to a certain extent, his past experience and future plans: 'Des Manufactures' reflects his experience as a manufacturer, and gives vent to the grievances of this important class; 'Du Commerce' and 'De la Navigation' look forward to his future ventures in maritime matters; 'De l'Exemple et des Soins Principaux du Prince' shows the importance he places on the Royal power to organize the national economy.

Between the years 1617 and 1619 we find evidence of Montchrestien taking an interest in shipping. On 11 February and 22 September 1617 legal documents show him borrowing money to pay off the sailors of a ship called *Le Régent*.[4] About two years later, the *Mercure* informs us, he wished to '. . . faire un embarquement suiuant ses inconstances

---

[1] Acte of 4 April 1616, *Bulletin de la Commission des Antiquités de la Seine-Inférieure*, t. vii, pp. 369 ff.

[2] Though Brunet mentions a 1614 edition, this seems unlikely in view of the phrase, on p. 114 of the section 'Du Commerce', 'en l'année dernière 1614 au mois de Novembre ou Décembre.'

[3] He notes that France, through religious intolerance, has driven out some of her most skilled craftsmen.

[4] *Bulletin de la Commission*, t. vii, pp. 369–71.

ordinaires, et en eut un procez à Rouen contre le sieur de Pont-Pierre pour un nauire'.[1]

At his wedding two of the witnesses were connected with the Admiralty, one being *Intendant*, the other *Lieutenant Général*.

At this wedding, which took place in Paris on 31 January 1618, he married his childhood companion 'Dame Suzanne Thézart, Vefue de feu Messire Léonard Hamon, viuant Sr. de l'Isle, fille de deffunctz Messire François Thézart, viuant Sieur Baron des Essartz et de Tournebu, et de Dame Jehanne de Monchy, sa femme, d'autre part'.[2] Was this marriage a result of the lasting fidelity of his love? Or was it, as Malingre would have us believe,[3] due solely to ambition? Suzanne's riches would certainly be of great help to a man whose ventures seem to have met with such lack of success.

It is interesting that the wedding took place in Paris, for there are other things which point to an extended stay by Montchrestien in Paris at this time. No doubt he must have known the city quite well from his frequent stays in the Rue de la Harpe at the time of his venture at Oussone.

Malherbe, writing from Paris in August 1618 to his cousin, M. du Bouillon Malherbe, and mentioning some information he had received about a book possessed by Monsieur de Cagny,[4] says: 'Un nommé M. de Montchrestien est celui de qui je le tenois, et qui le m'a dit, non une fois ou deux, mais une douzaine.'[5]

This is written in a tone as of a recent event; and certainly it would

---

[1] *M.F.*, t. vii, pp. 816–17.

[2] Montchrestien's marriage contract, quoted by Lachevre, *R.H.L.F.* (1918), 452. The witnesses, described as 'amys commungs des dites partyes', were: (*a*) *Messire Jean Villemaille, Seigneur et Marquis de la Flosselière*, Protestant nobleman from Poitou, to whom Montchrestien was to send one of his followers the day before his death. (See *L.H. des I.*, p. 28.) (*b*) *Nicolas Sanguin, escuyer, Sr. de Pierrelee, et de Mont, Intendant de l'Admiraulté*, who is presumably the same Nicolas Sanguin who wrote *vers liminaires* to the Catholic *recueil* by Sœur Anne de Marquets, at the same time as Montchrestien, in 1605. (*c*) *Noble homme Mę Guillaume Martin, Conseiller du Roy et lieutenant général de l'Admiraulté de France*. These three acquaintances were both noble and powerful; Montchrestien appears to have been, as always, well connected.

[3] Referring to Montchrestien's part in the rebellion of 1621, Malingre says: 'La naissance ne le pouuoit pas porter à de si hauts desseins, mais son esprit et son courage luy ayant fait espouser *une Dame riche* de l'une des bonnes Maisons de Normandie, et son ambition propre et capable de tout entreprendre, luy promettoient assurément, que si les affaires de ce party prosperoient, il y auroit bonne part.' (Malingre: *Histoires tragiques de nostre temps (par le sieur de Saint Lazare Historiographe)*, Paris 1635, p. 811.) My italics.

[4] M. de Cagny was one of the people visited by Montchrestien in his 1621 Normandy campaign. See 'Interrogatoire de Paris' (*L. H. des I*, p. 27).

[5] Malherbe, Letter to M. du Bouillon Malherbe, 'ce 2ᵉ d'aout 1618'. (*Œuvres*, ed. Lalanne, t. iv, pp. 43–4.)

seem unlikely that (as M. Lebègue would suggest) he was referring to his stay in Caen in 1598 and 1599. It is corroborated by a letter from Malherbe to Peiresc at the time of Montchrestien's death in 1621: 'Vous le pouvez avoir vu à la suite du conseil,[1] *il y a, ce me semble, deux ou trois ans.* . . . Je me trompe ou il donna en ce même temps-là un livre in-4° de sa façon, assez gros, à Monsieur le garde des sceaux, et me semble que le sujet de son livre étoit du commerce, ou de quelque chose pareille.'[2]

In the same year, 1618, a sonnet signed 'MON CHRESTIEN', at the head of the *Œuvres poetiques du sieur Daudiguier*, could, if it is indeed by Montchrestien, point to some contact with Paris literary circles at that time.[3]

Soon after this, possibly owing to the support of influential friends such as Martin and Sanguin, Montchrestien became governor of Châtillon-sur-Loire. His servant, Pierre Paris, later described him as 'vivant de son bien et revenu'.[4] However, after the death of his wife, which soon occurred, her family (i.e. Jacques Thézart) disputed Montchrestien's claim to her money and property.[5] This is probably the cause for Montchrestien's later poverty; the *Mercure* describes him, in 1621, as being 'pas des plus aisez des biens de ce monde'.[6]

This, then, was Montchrestien's situation at the outbreak of the Huguenot revolt in 1621. The reasons for his joining this revolt we shall never know; everyone disagrees as to whether they were religious or ambitious. Certainly many other people fought on the side of the rebels for political or ambitious reasons.

This revolt, admittedly, was more specifically Huguenot in character than the other revolts of the previous ten years, i.e. the first ten years

[1] I do not believe this to mean that he was a *conseiller du Roy*, as some of his biographers would have us believe: surely some other mention of the title would have come down to us? He was probably waiting to present some demand to the counsellors, perhaps to present his book to Du Vair, perhaps in connection with his maritime interests, perhaps even to request some post such as he subsequently received. Certainly he numbered M[e]. Guillaume Martin, a *conseiller du Roy*, among his close friends.

[2] Malherbe, Letter to Peiresc, '14e d'octobre, 1621'. (*Œuvres*, ed. Lalanne, t. iii, p. 557.) My italics.

[3] D'Audiguier was quite a famous poet at the time. The *Grande Encyclopédie* says of him: 'Ses ouvrages, tombés aujourd'hui dans l'oubli, ne laissèrent pas d'avoir assez de réputation en leur temps, pour être de ceux où l'Académie française décida qu'elle irait chercher les exemples de la langue.' He had been one of the large literary circle gathered around Marguerite de Valois until her death in 1615.

[4] '. . . domicilié en la ville de Châtillon-sur-Loire, province de Berry, où il vivait de son bien et revenu, faisant profession de la religion prétendue Réformée, de la quelle ville il avait été gouverneur, sous Monseigneur le prince de Condey . . .' (*L.H. des I.*, p. 26.) The question of his religion will be discussed later. Malingre also describes him as governor of Châtillon.   [5] *M.F.*, t. vii, p. 815.   [6] Ibid., pp. 801–2.

of Louis XIII's reign, had been. Previously the concern of the Princes with the incompetence and maladministration of succeeding governments had on the whole been the mainspring for action. Though the League of Princes in 1614 had included a Huguenot such as Bouillon, he appears to have acted less for religious than for political reasons.

Huguenot worries at the Regency's *rapprochement* with Spain, and its rejection of France's former Protestant and independent allies, however, led to a certain community of interest with the Princes in their rejection of the policies of the government. So in the 1615 rebellion one is not surprised to see the Protestants, under Rohan, rallying in force to the cause. It was Rohan and the Protestants who roused rebellion in Guyenne, Languedoc, and the Cévennes, and tried to stop the royal progress to Spain for the marriages which were to cement agreement between the two nations. It was Rohan, and Condé, who, with Poitou in their hands, blocked the path northward for the royal party. In the subsequent negotiations, however, Protestant interests were almost completely ignored.

The inconstancy of alliances is shown by the fact that in the 1616–17 rebellion Rohan fought with the *royal* troops against the dissidents Nevers, Bouillon, and Longueville (Condé being in prison). The King's sudden taking of power from the Queen Mother, however, meant certain reversals of alliance, and in the 1620 rising we find Rohan as one of the dissidents, together with Longueville, Vendôme, Épernon, Mayenne, and the rest of the Queen Mother's party.

Now the specifically Huguenot rising sparked off at the end of 1620 and beginning of 1621 was far more religious in origin than any of the others we have been describing. It was set off, above all, by the King's actions in Béarn, for example his restitution of Church property which had been owned by Protestants for about half a century. When the demands formulated in La Rochelle in December 1620—(a) fulfilment of the conditions of the Edict of Nantes and (b) restoration of former conditions in Béarn—were refused by the King, the Protestants divided France into eight military provinces, and prepared for battle. Rohan headed the rising; but for once there were few outstanding figures beside him. Protestants such as Bouillon and Lesdiguières took no part; other former dissidents of whom Rohan had at times been a companion and at times an opponent, fought for the King: Condé, Mayenne, Épernon.

While this revolt thus differs from previous ones, however, this is not to say that motives were necessarily simple. In a decade of rebellion, people had made their fortunes both in victory and in defeat; the Protestants had chosen sides and shown themselves to be good allies, and now many dissidents of various kinds joined *them* in their rebellion without necessarily changing their views. Montchrestien could have joined the cause for one of many reasons: he may have been a Protestant; he may have been politically ambitious; as an economist he may have been exasperated by the incompetence of the government; or he may have fought as a mercenary for money.

Whatever the cause, in May 1621 he joined the rebellion,[1] setting out from Châtillon to relieve the besieged town of Jargeau, further down the Loire. Unfortunately, before he arrived the town capitulated to the Comte de Saint Paul, and the citizens agreed to leave the town the next day. Montchrestien, with 200 men, entered the town by river on the morning of 23 May, but was unable to get the inhabitants to break the treaty, so left the town once more with his little band, which now numbered about 400 men.

From Jargeau he went straight to Sancerre, and took over the town. But there were internal dissensions, which grew when the Prince de Condé[2] appeared before the walls, on 28 May, with 4,500 men. Condé, taking advantage of this, called some of the leading citizens to him, and tried to persuade them to give up the town. Then he had an interview with Montchrestien himself, in which he stressed the weakness of his position, and said that the citizens of Sancerre were prepared to betray him, and lay all the blame for the rebellion on his shoulders. On 29 May Montchrestien capitulated, and was granted a month to find a place of safety.

He is said to have been given a great deal of money to give up the town.[3] His ambitions may have been far greater, however; on leaving the town he is said to have wept, crying: 'Quelle fortune ie perds par la meschanceté des traistres de là dedans qui m'ont vendu!'[4]

---

[1] The King's forces having taken the field in April.

[2] The same to whom Montchrestien had dedicated his plays.

[3] The *Mercure* claims that Condé gave him 6,000 francs. Various critics have mistrusted this statement, but it is corroborated by the statement of Montchrestien's servant, Pierre Paris, made after his master's death. At the first interrogation we are informed that: 'Paris croit que son maître toucha de l'argent pour sortir de Sancerre.' At the second interrogation he said: 'Et alla le dit sieur de Montchrestien, trouver mon dit seigneur le Prince, par son commandement, et le Prince lui donna libéralement mil écus pour lui rendre la ville de Sancerre en l'obeissance du Roi.' (*L. H. des I.*, p. 27.)

[4] 'Et adiousta, que Monsieur le Prince avoit pris Sancerre avec un fantosme, et qu'il s'estonnoit comme il estoit venu en l'esprit d'un homme de songer à prendre auec des paroles la plus forte place de France pour ce qui est de la situation.' (*M.F.*, t. vii, p. 383.)

Montchrestien took very little heed of the warning he had received, for in July he invested the town of Sully; here he was besieged by the Comte de Saint-Paul and the Maréchal de Vitry, but it took the arrival of the Prince de Condé to force him once more to capitulate, on 19 July.

Again he was set free; obviously he decided that the Loire was no longer a favourable field of operations, for after a short visit to Paris he went straight to La Rochelle, the headquarters of the insurrection. Here he stayed for only fifteen days, but in the course of this time he received commissions, dated 9 August, from the council at La Rochelle, sending him into Maine and Normandy, 'tant pour lever des regimens de pied que des compagnies de chevau-légers'. Obviously it was felt that Montchrestien would have local knowledge in Normandy.

For over a month he diligently visited people in this area, 'tant de ladite religion que d'autres de leur cabale . . .',[1] helping to organize an armed uprising. The rendezvous for all their forces had been arranged for 11 October, in the Forêt d'Andeine.

By the beginning of October this area began to fill with groups of armed men. Anxiety was growing in Caen, as we can see in one of Malherbe's letters:

> On nous a tantôt dit qu'il y avoit deux mille hommes, tantôt huit cents; chacun se dépêchoit d'en conter selon sa peur ou selon son desir. On y envoya de cette ville un espion, qui rapporta qu'ils pouvoient estre cent cinquante ou environ, et que leur retraite étoit en une forêt nommée la forêt d'Andaine assez près d'Alençon, et s'en alloient vivre par troupes dans les lieux circonvoisines, mais qu'ils se promettoient bien d'être en peu de jours un beaucoup plus grand nombre, et qu'ils avoient dessein sur Falaise, Argentan, Domfront et Alençon.[2]

Montchrestien and a few companions left the forest as one of the 'troupes' who went to live in the 'lieux circonvoisines'. After about a week of wanderings they ended up, on the night of 7 October, in an inn at Les Tourailles, a small village near Athis. While they ate their dinner, the innkeeper, Pierre Lemancel, who did not know Montchrestien, but believed his guests to be some of the rebels who were causing so much trouble in the neighbourhood, sent a message to the local squire about them.

Claude Turgot des Tourailles, whose château was about a quarter of

---

[1] This statement would support my view of the mixed support for the Huguenot rebellion.

[2] Malherbe, Letter to Peiresc, Caen, 14 October 1621. (*Œuvres*, ed. Lalanne, t. iii, p. 556.)

a league away, came quickly 'avec quinze ou vingt mousquetaires'.[1] Just after midnight, one of Montchrestien's companions was later to attest, the rebels heard a noise outside the house. They had gone to bed fully clothed, and now took hold of their weapons to defend themselves.

Someone called for their names, and Montchrestien shouted that his was Champeaux. It was replied, however, that it was generally believed that he was the Montchrestien who was trying to raise troops against the King. Montchrestien denied this, and came out with his companions, firing as they came. In the resulting mêlée Montchrestien was killed, and all the others fled, except his servant Pierre Paris, who was wounded and captured, and eventually forced to give the evidence on which much of our knowledge of these events is based.

Montchrestien's corpse was taken to Domfront, to be tried, and on 12 October the following sentence was given against it:

. . . Le corps dudit sera cejourd'hui, trois heures de relevée, traîné sur une claie, en la place de la Brière, près cette ville, lieu accoutumé à faire les exécutions criminelles, et là, sur un échafaud, ses membres brisés sur un gril en la forme et manière accoutumes; puis sondit corps brûlé et réduit en cendres, et les cendres jetées au vent par l'exécuteur des sentences criminelles . . .[2]

This sentence was carried out to the letter; the *parlement* of Rouen also demanded Montchrestien's body for trial, but too late; it had already ceased to exist. The rebellion in Normandy dissolved at the news of Montchrestien's death: 'Tant y a que par sa mort nous croyons être en repos en Normandie', says Malherbe.[3]

Montchrestien's life thus ended in ignominy. The apparently disreputable nature of his life and end may be one of the reasons why so little is known of his career. People would have been fairly guarded when mentioning his name (Malherbe, for example, was far less willing to acknowledge his acquaintance after he had become a rebel).

However, he was still regarded as a great tragedian. In 1621 the *Mercure* recognized him as 'un des bons Poëtes tragiques de son temps'.[4] In 1627 a new edition of his works appeared at Rouen, published by Pierre and Martin la Motte.[5] His works were soon to be

---

[1] *L. H. des I.*, p. 29.   [2] Ibid., p. 36.
[3] Malherbe, Letter to Peiresc, Caen, 14 October 1621.   [4] *M.F.*, t. vii, p. 815.
[5] This edition, though it closely follows that of 1601 (and thus omits *Hector*), contains the 1604 versions of the 'Dédication' to Condé ('. . . *Hector* que ie fay marcher a leur teste . . .') and of the 'Stances a luy mesme'.

included in the general scorn felt by the French seventeenth century
for the poetry of the sixteenth century, and thus were not reprinted
until the late nineteenth century.

As far as Montchrestien's life is concerned, the *Mercure* seems to
have been right in referring to his 'humeur tres-inconstante et legere'.[1]
He had innumerable different careers, but in two of them he left lasting
proof of his genius: his tragedies are some of the greatest produced by
the Renaissance theatre, and his work on political economy, which
could stand on its own as an example of literary style, also foreshadowed
many later economic theories.

* * *

Montchrestien's Religion

'. . . On n'est pas parvenu jusqu'ici à résoudre l'énigme autour de
Montchrestien. On ne saurait préciser s'il était protestant ou catholique',
writes Seidmann.[2]

No agreement has ever been reached upon this matter. Lanson,
Willner, Loukovitch, and Funck-Brentano believe Montchrestien to
have been a Catholic, while Petit de Julleville and Seiver see him as a
Protestant. Lebègue, after stating many of the contradictions to be
found in the life and works of this mysterious author, confines himself
to saying:

Nous renonçons à résoudre cette enigme; constatons simplement que dans ses
drames il exprimait volontiers des sentiments chrétiens, que les adeptes des
deux religions pouvaient approuver. Il évitait de faire du prosélytisme pour
l'une d'elles; tout en ménageant les catholiques, il devait avoir une préférence
pour le protestantisme.[3]

For various reasons, clues as to Montchrestien's religion do not
appear in his plays; but outside evidence tends to point to a different
solution from that propounded by Lebègue. There is very little sign
of a 'préférence pour le protestantisme', and certain indications that in
the earlier part of his life he may have been a Catholic, even if not a
particularly devout one.

For the purposes of investigation, let us divide Montchrestien's life
into three periods: (*a*) His university years and his career as a tragedian,

---

[1] *M.F.*, t. vii, p. 816.
[2] 'La Bible dans les tragédies religieuses de Garnier et Montchrestien', unpublished
Sorbonne D.U.P. thesis, p. 94.
[3] *La Tragédie française de la Renaissance*, p. 69.

ending in 1604. (*b*) From 1604 until his marriage in 1618. (*c*) From 1618 until his death in 1621.

(a) *1575–1604*

Little can be gained from a scrutiny of Montchrestien's acquaintances in these years, or indeed at any time of his life; for they include both Catholics and Protestants. Whether this denotes tolerance, or merely indifference towards religious matters, it is difficult to say.

The Thézarts, his early companions, were of a well-known Protestant family;[1] on the other hand, two of his acquaintances at Caen University were Catholic priests, Pierre des Rues and Jacques du Buisson. The latter, a Doctor of Theology, exhorts Montchrestien to turn his pen to religious works (a thing he would be unlikely to suggest to a Protestant).[2]

At Rouen, Loys de Bretel, sieur de Languetot, was fanatically anti-Protestant.[3] Claude Groulart had once been a Protestant, but had abjured Calvinism on returning to France from his studies in Geneva.

Moreover, little can be gained from a study of the plays themselves. In accordance with better sixteenth-century dramatic practice, Montchrestien avoids anything extraneous to the plot of his plays. These plays themselves are written on a particular subject because of that subject's suitability for a classically tragic situation (e.g. *hybris*, the fall of the proud man, in *Aman*, and the destruction of man by the passions of love in *David*). The Bible is used as just one more source among many; Montchrestien appears to have had no religious reason for using it.

Religious passages in these plays are therefore incidental to the plot. Mardochée and Nathan are expected to speak in the manner of prophets; and as such, they are given the full benefit of such set pieces as extended prayers and monologues. Many of the religious statements come straight from the Bible (e.g. Mardochée's prayers, from the Apocrypha and from Psalm 79), while others are there merely as remarks that would be expected of the characters, and cannot be taken as the opinions of the author.

[1] See Cahaignes and Fierville. Also, in the *Rôle des principaux gentilhommes de la généralité de Caen, accompagné de notes secrètes*, drawn up in 1640, Jacques Thézart is referred to as 'viel homme, ... philosophe stoïque, huguenot ...' (Archives du Calvados, Don Abbé Larue, 1939.) Suzanne Thézart, Montchrestien's wife, is known to have been a Protestant.   [2] In his 'Sonnet liminaire' to *Sophonisbe* (1596).

[3] Floquet tells us (*Histoire du Parlement de Normandie*, t. iv, p. 85) that he protested against 'l'enregistrement imposé par Henri IV d'un édit de 1577 en faveur des protestants' and that 'le roi en éprouva du ressentiment'.

The same is true of *La Reine d'Escosse*. The two queens, who are treated in a completely unbiased way by the author, each express the ideas that one would expect of their different religions: Elizabeth talks against Catholicism, and Mary refers to Protestantism as 'la folle opinion d'une rance hérésie'.[1] It is hard to say whether the choice of this Catholic queen as the subject for a tragedy would point to some sympathy with the Catholic religion, as Lanson and Loukovitch claim; after all, Schiller appears even more Catholic than Montchrestien in his play *Maria Stuart*. The observation made by Lanson and Lebègue, that there are no Saints, nor the Virgin Mary, in Queen Mary's vision of heaven proves nothing in the opposite direction.

The conception of grace expressed in the 'Avis au Lecteur' to *David* and in Nathan's first speech in the same play, to which Lanson, Lebègue, and Seidmann draw attention, saying that it states the doctrine of predestination, does in fact do nothing of the kind. Loukovitch is completely justified in saying that there is nothing dogmatic in this conception of grace, but that it is the general idea of divine assistance.

The idea of original sin is not a specifically Protestant idea:

> Que le vice est commun à nous, malheureux hommes! . . .
> Monarque tout puissant, sans ta divine grace
> L'homme fait tousiours mal quelque chose qu'il face . . .[2]

Nor is the conception of man's dependence on God's grace: 'Que l'homme est misérable si Dieu l'abandonne à luy mesme. . . . Comme sans la grace de Dieu il ne pouvoit vouloir ny faire aucun bien, sans son assistance il ne peut vouloir ny faire que tout mal.'[3]

In fact, the view expressed by Montchrestien has little connection with Calvinism: 'Le pecheur qui s'afflige de la connoissance de son péché est en chemin de salut: celuy qui endort son ame d'une profonde letargie et *ne se reveille point à la voix de l'Eternel*, minute lui-mesme sa reprobation.'[4]

We know that Montchrestien used a Protestant Bible for his plays, and that it was almost certainly the translation of Olivétan.[5] But, at the

---

[1] *La Reine d'Escosse*; *P. de J.*, p. 92.
[2] *David*; *P. de J.*, p. 229.
[3] 'Avis au Lecteur', *P. de J.*, p. 304.   [4] Ibid.
[5] At the end of *Aman* Psalm 124 is used; in Catholic Bibles, the *Vulgate*, and the translation of Lefèvre d'Étaples, this psalm is numbered 123. Of the Protestant translations, Olivétan's is the nearest to Montchrestien's text. (See Seidmann.) The use of the *Apocrypha* does not rule out the use of a Protestant Bible, for the *Apocrypha* was printed separately at the end of such Bibles. Rivaudeau, a Protestant author, also makes use of the *Apocrypha* in his *Aman*.

time of writing these plays, when he was much in the company of the Protestant Thézarts, Montchrestien may have found this Bible the nearest French translation to hand.

In this period, very little can be gathered of Montchrestien's religious opinions. His plays give one an impression of pagan humanism, the subjects being chosen for their tragic suitability, and religious sentiments being added where necessary to the plot or character.

(b) *1604–1618*

Though the plays give us so little idea of Montchrestien's religious opinions, in 1605 there appeared two poems, on the evidence of which Lachèvre claims: 'Quoi qu'il en soit, l'orthodoxie du Montchrestien de 1605 n'est pas douteuse, catholique il était et né catholique.'[1]

The poems in question are *vers liminaires* to a collection of poems by a Dominican nun, Sœur Anne de Marquets,[2] who had died in 1588, and whose works were now being published for the first time. The *vers liminaires* in question are: (i) *Stanses* ('Comme a peu ceste Vierge enfanter des enfans . . .'), signed A. de Mont; (ii) The unfinished poem which comes before this, unsigned, *Elegie sur les œuvres de feüe Madame de-Marquets* ('Si David revivoit . . .').

The reasons for thinking these poems to be by Montchrestien are as follows:

First, the signature; in the bibliography of Lanson, and in the catalogue of the Bibliothèque Nationale, there is no other author of this period[3] to whom this signature could apply. Yet the style of the poem is that of an accomplished poet.

Second, another of the writers of *vers liminaires* to this edition, Nicholas Sanguin, sieur de Pierrelée, was one of the witnesses to Montchrestien's marriage in 1618, and must therefore have been known to him.

On this evidence, the second poem would seem a probable product of Montchrestien's pen; but what of the first, unsigned one?

It seems to be written in very much the same style as the second poem, and to fit in very well with one's view of Montchrestien's

---

[1] F. Lachèvre, 'Antoine de Montchrestien, sa religion, son mariage', *R.H.L.F.* (1918).

[2] *Sonets sprituels de feüe tres-vertueuse et tres-docte Dame Sr. Anne de Marquets, Religieuse à Poissi, sur les Dimanches et principales solemnitez de l'Année.* A Mme. de Fresne. A Paris, chez Claude Morel . . . MDCV . . .

[3] The poems must have been written some time between the death of Sœur Anne de Marquets on 11 May 1588 and the year of their publication, 1605.

poetry. This in itself would be no kind of evidence, however, were it not for a reference in the first poem which points directly to one of the facts we know about Montchrestien: the *Mercure François* informs us that 'à ses heures de loisir il a aussi traduict les Pseaumes de David en rithme'.[1] Written in 1621, this statement is borne out by the fact that the translations of three psalms are included in his plays. Now we read in the last five lines of this 1605 poem:

> Je me promettois bien avant que de cognoistre
> Les traicts vrément divins que ces vers font paroistre,
> D'imiter les chansons du Prophete Royal,
> Mais or' les congnoissant ie me suis desloyal:
> Tout ravy de les voir, ie desdy ma promesse . . .

For all these reasons it seems possible that at least the second of these poems is by Montchrestien, if not both. The collection of poems they introduce is extremely Catholic in nature, being a series of verses appropriate to the different feasts in the Church calendar.

After a silence of ten years, Montchrestien, in his next published work, the *Traicté de l'œconomie politique*, gives us a certain amount of information about his religious ideas at the time. Many subjects having no vital link with economics are mentioned in this work, in certain digressions. Religion is treated at various points in the work, and the general impression emerges of a lukewarm Catholic, with decided views upon religious tolerance.

The work is, of course, dedicated to a Catholic king; this might account for many of the more open Catholic (and Gallican) sentiments expressed.

But far more than being a Catholic, Montchrestien shows himself a patriot, who puts the interests of his country before everything. This explains his Gallican views with relation to the temporal power of the Church: 'Demeurez tousiours constant en cette resolution, ferme en cette creance; que l'Eglise n'a rien à voir, rien à connoistre sur le temporel de vostre Royaume; et que Jesus Christ le Maistre et Seigneur de tous, a vuidé la question par son commandement: Rendez à César, ce qui est à César, et à Dieu ce qui est à Dieu.'[2]

He claims that ever since popes have taken the right of being elected by the other cardinals, instead of by the French king, as in the time of Charlemagne, they have been extremely unruly;[3] and he mentions with

---

[1] *M.F.*, t. vii, p. 816.
[2] 'De l'exemple . . . du Prince', p. 322.   [3] Ibid., p. 351.

delight Philippe le Bel's action in taking the Pope prisoner, 'luy faisant connoistre que le Roy de France n'estoit pas son subiect'.[1]

This point of view was, however, quite compatible with Catholicism at the time, as was opposition to the monastic life. Montchrestien deplores the solitary life of monks only when inaction makes them useless to the community:[2] 'La vie contemplative à la vérité est la premiere et plus approchante de Dieu; *mais sans l'action elle demeure imparfaite et possible plus préiudiciable qu'utile au bien de Republiques.*'[3]

Man must be useful to the society he lives in; Montchrestien is continually stressing 'l'usage des citoyens',[4] 'l'utilité de nos concitoyens',[5] etc.

It is for the sake of the country and of its economy, rather than for any higher motives, that Montchrestien praises the religious tolerance of the King and his mother; they have given '. . . a vos subiects tant de l'une que de l'autre profession, subiect de faire naistre parmy eux ce beau concert de bonnes volontez, d'où résulte l'harmonie de nostre estat, et la tranquilité de vostre Regne'.

Intolerance causes much bloodshed, and loses many of the country's best craftsmen, who flee to freer countries. On one question, however, Montchrestien is adamant; atheism is, for him, a great danger, and he devotes many pages to condemning it.

The impression one gains of the author in this *Traicté* is that of a man of moderate Catholic beliefs; these beliefs are perhaps stressed from time to time for the sake of the King, but many remarks are innocent of any kind of flattery. The author is a man for whom the material needs of both country and individual are very important, and his religious views appear to be modified wherever they come into conflict with these interests; in other words, his beliefs appear to be fairly lukewarm, and less important than his materialist interests.

The religious arguments are few compared with the mass of other arguments, many from classical sources. He appears to have used the first argument that came to mind to support each economic measure he suggests; the general religious impression is that of a man who has been brought up as a Catholic, and who takes his beliefs very much for granted.

---

[1] 'De l'exemple . . . du Prince', p. 353.

[2] Though this might seem a contradiction to his praise of Sœur Anne de Marquets, note that he praises her above all for her activity in writing poetry.

[3] 'Des Manufactures', p. 26.

[4] Ibid.

[5] Ibid., p. 158.

(c) *1618–1621*

At Montchrestien's wedding, in 1618, one of the witnesses was Protestant, another Catholic. His bride, Suzanne, was of the Protestant family of Thézart, and it has been suggested that she converted him to this form of religion. Certainly he was described by his servant, Pierre Paris, as being '. . . domicilié en la ville de Châtillon-sur-Loire, province de Berry, où il vivait de son bien et revenu, faisant profession de la religion prétendue Réformée . . . '.[1]

This might provide the explanation for Montchrestien's participation in the 1621 Huguenot rising. But participation in such a rebellion, as we have seen, did not necessarily mean that one was a fervent Protestant; many people entered it for purely political reasons, or even for personal gain. The *Mercure* says of Montchrestien that he was not 'tant Huguenot et zelé en sa religion', and, if one considers how lukewarm he seems to have been when a Catholic, this seems quite possible.

The most likely reason for his joining the rebellion is a desire for power, personal glory, and gain. The materialist outlook he displayed throughout his life probably governed his judgement in this case; his whole life shows its influence, with the duels, lawsuits, commercial and maritime ventures all contributing to his success. The crowning achievement was probably his marriage, which brought him much money, and also strengthened his claim to nobility. But by the time of the rebellion, probably owing to the death of his wife, he was once more 'pas des plus aisez des biens de ce monde',[2] and may have been looking for some way to restore his fortunes.

The civil war must have seemed a chance to gain both power and money. His exclamation on leaving Sancerre, 'Quelle fortune ie perds par la meschanceté des traistres de là dedans qui m'ont vendu!',[3] seems to point to this, for it is a purely personal remark, making no reference to the cause he was supposedly following. His acceptance of money to leave the town gives one the same impression.

Though the picture of him painted by the *Mercure* is very black, it may well be true:

Il retourne en Normandie, sa patrie, *et s'imagine . . . de s'y faire Lieutenant de Province* pour l'Assemblée de la Rochelle, *de se faire tout d'or au maniement*

---

[1] *L. H. des I.*, p. 26. Pierre Paris's evidence is uncertain, as Lachèvre points out: his claim to have followed Montchrestien for eighteen years is an extremely unlikely one. But it is quite probable that, since his marriage, Montchrestien had become a Protestant.

[2] *M.F.*, t. vii, pp. 801–2.   [3] Ibid., p. 383.

des deniers Royaux, du revenu des biens des Ecclésiastiques, et des rançons et butins. Il n'estoit pas des plus aisez des biens de ce monde, comme il sera dit cy apres, ny tant Huguenot et zelé en sa Religion, *mais grandement ardent à se vouloir faire riche.*[1]

Many other people behaved in the same way in the civil wars both before and after this time.

So there is very little evidence of Montchrestien's religion at the time he was actually writing his plays; but in the period just after he gave up writing for the theatre, he may have been a Catholic, though his religion does not appear at any time to have been an urgent problem for him. It is thus possible that he was a Catholic at the time of writing the plays. His marriage in 1618 may have converted him to Protestantism; but his participation in the 1621 rebellion might have had purely material ends.

All this merely shows how dangerous and uncertain any attempt to ascribe particular religious attitudes to Montchrestien at any specific time of his life can be.

Montchrestien's life is interesting in itself, not only in its variety and its adventurousness, but also in the picture it gives us of certain little-known aspects of the society of the time. It has little relation to his dramatic works; but this fact itself is of some importance, for it shows Montchrestien to be well in the line of Renaissance tragedy, and to be devoted to artistic and rhetorical expression rather than to the furthering of political or religious ends, which only later receive any extensive treatment in his works, in the treatise on political economy.

Like certain other Renaissance dramatists, Montchrestien gave up the writing of tragedy at an early age. This should not surprise us; for many people in this age the art of poetry was subordinate to the more serious matters of life; something to be practised in one's youth, but to be given up in one's maturity. Youthful as the author of these six tragedies was, they stand none the less as one of the summits of the achievement of Renaissance tragedy.

---

[1] *M.F.*, t. vii, pp. 801–2. My italics.

2. Some Characteristics of French Renaissance Tragedy

᠁᠁᠍᠍

ONTCHRESTIEN'S works stand as the culmination of the
Renaissance drama; and in studying his methods we shall
naturally be led to a consideration of the whole range of
sixteenth-century dramatic theory and practice. It might therefore be
wise to draw attention to certain aspects of this type of tragedy which
differentiate it from that of later centuries.

For too long sixteenth-century tragedy has been regarded as some
kind of forerunner of the tragedy of the classical age, differing from it
only in its imperfect nature.

Though certain voices, and particularly that of Lanson, were raised
to claim the right of this genre to be studied on its own ground, in
relation to its own aims, it is only within the last couple of decades that
critics have come to accept the great gulf that differentiates the tragedy
of the two centuries. Though the plays often have the same subject-
matter, and share an oft-stated debt to the ancients, the basic core of
aim and achievement is far from the same in the two cases.

(a) *Effect rather than Cause*

We do wrong if we look, in these plays, for any detailed discussion
of the reasons for the tragic event. Where later playwrights, and
particularly those of the seventeenth century, were to be concerned
above all with the inner psychology of their characters, and the flaws
in character which brought about their downfall, the Renaissance
tragedian accepted the event as inevitable, and sought to show the
effects of it upon his characters. The resultant lack of dramatic tension
has been condemned by many critics who insist on viewing tragedy
from the modern standpoint, and who are shocked by the protagonists'
lack of 'inner struggle'.

The Renaissance tragedian comes much nearer to the classical conception of tragedy. Whether he does so consciously, or purely as a result of his imitation of classical models,[1] one cannot be sure; but Fate rules Renaissance tragedy as it had ruled the tragedy of the ancients. At times this conception of fate, clashing as it does with the Christian idea of a loving God, must have worried these dramatists (as we can see in the 'Avant-Propos' to Garnier's *Troade*); but no attempt was ever made to modify it, for to do so would be to condemn the classics, and the classics could do no wrong.

Our modern conception of the tragic hero, based as it is on the idea of *hamartia* as a 'tragic flaw' (in character), is entirely at odds with the original Greek conception. For the Greeks *hamartia* was a 'fault', or 'error of judgement', often containing no suggestion of 'right' or 'wrong' in the moral sense. Indeed, very often the tragic hero has no conception of the nature of the act he is committing, nor of the probable consequences; in *Oedipus*, for example, the hero does not realize that he has killed his father and married his mother. His unknowing acts were caused by *ate*, the divine power to blind man's judgement and cause him to make a wrong decision. Even *hamartia* can thus be ruled by fate, and is outside the human being's power.

Fate, *ananke*, rules all. The aim of classical tragedy is to show the behaviour of man when faced by this inevitable fate. However, as D. W. Lucas points out, 'this determined decision did not entirely relieve the man of responsibility. . . . A man's decision might be in accordance with a plan predetermined by the gods but his decision remained his own.'[2]

The fate of the tragic hero may be caused by something which happened long before he was born, e.g. by a family curse; or it may be caused by the gods, through jealousy, or for some inscrutable purpose of their own; his 'error of judgement', forced on him by this fate, may take many forms, from the most innocent-seeming action to the complete disordering of the senses by *eros*, love. But the issue is never in doubt, and we must look to more modern dramatic theory for the concept of dramatic tension.

In imitating Seneca (and to a certain extent the Greeks), Renaissance dramatists took over this conception of fate. In doing so they were

---

[1] The principal model is, of course, Seneca; but though Seneca's composition and style are very different from those of the Greeks, his conception of fate is very similar to theirs.

[2] D. W. Lucas, *The Greek Tragic Poets*, London 1959, p. 67.

divorcing their tragedies from real life, for whereas the ancient audiences believed in, or at least pretended to believe in, the forces which held sway in their tragedies, these forces stood in complete contrast to the Christian beliefs of the sixteenth century. Whatever conception of grace a Christian might have, he could hardly stomach the savage, unreasoning rule of *ananke*. Many tragedians must have copied the originals unthinkingly, ignoring any contradictions between their own thought and that of their models. But in Garnier we find a hint of uncertainty: '. . . Voyant nos ancestres Troyens avoir, *par l'ire du grand Dieu, ou par l'inévitable malignité d'une secrette influence des astres*, souffert jadis toutes extremes calamitez . . .'.[1] Despite this, the conception of fate remains that of the ancients, even in the Biblical tragedies. It is interesting, on this score, to compare the *Saül le furieux* of Jean de la Taille with the *Saül* of Du Ryer, written in the next century. La Taille's Saul, the great man destroyed by fate, has committed an 'error of judgement' by performing what to us would seem a good action. He is punished, Samuel tells him:

> Et le tout pourautant qu'à la divine voix
> Obeï tu n'as point ainsi que tu devois,
> Qu'executé tu n'as sa vengeance dépite
> (Comme ie t'avois dit), contre l'Amalechite.[2]

Thus it is an act of clemency which brings about his downfall, as in the Old Testament account, and in Josephus:

. . . Because thou obeyedest not the voice of the Lord, nor executedst his fierce wrath upon Amalek, therefore hath the Lord done this thing unto thee this day.[3]

. . . Because thou disobeyedst God in the war with the Amalekites, and didst not observe his commandments, even as I foretold to thee when I was alive.[4]

This savage, un-Christian idea does not repel the sixteenth century, because it fits in so well with the classical conception of the tragic fault. Right and wrong, in the Christian sense, are irrelevant; fate destroys a man for an error of judgement.[5] Du Ryer, however, writing in the early seventeenth century, is forced, by his age's moral view of the

---

[1] 'A Monseigneur l'Archevesque de Bourges', Dedication to *La Troade*. My italics.
[2] Jean de la Taille, *Saül le Furieux*, ll. 773–6.
[3] 1 Samuel 28 : 18.
[4] Josephus, *Jewish Antiquities*, vi. 336.
[5] For this reason the view of *Saül le Furieux* as a Protestant tragedy of predestination seems very difficult to uphold.

tragic fault, to change the Biblical story. His Samuel accuses Saul in the
following words:

> Pense à ce peuple saint par tes Lois égorgé
> Pour avoir contre toy l'innocent protegé,
> Pour avoir fait trouver dans l'enclos de sa ville
> Au malheureux David la faveur d'un azile.[1]

The reason he gives here for Saul's tragic fate is an event which
actually took place long after God's initial desertion of Saul in favour
of David.

The Biblical tragedy of the Renaissance cannot be said to have any
religious or moral message,[2] except in the case of those plays which
were created as vehicles for religious polemic, and which usually lost
thereby the characteristics of regular tragedy. The Biblical subjects
were chosen for their suitability for classical fate-tragedy; *Saül*, for
La Taille, is an example of man bearing an undeserved fate; Saul's
family, in the sequel *La Famine ou les Gabéonites*, suffer from the curse
laid upon the dead Saul by an intractable God. God has become *ananke*,
and the children suffer for their father's fault.[3] In the same way,
Montchrestien's *David* and *Aman* are subjects chosen respectively
for examples of man destroyed by *eros* and *hybris*.

The concept of right and wrong does not concern this type of
tragedy, and fate rules it so strongly that the tragic outcome is inevitable. The audience is therefore expected to find its enjoyment in the
contemplation of man in adversity; this point is stressed again and
again by the theoretical writers, who give no thought to the cause of
the tragedy:

Tragoedia, ut refert Diomedes, est heroicae fortunae in adversis compre-
hensio.... Nam reges et principes qui se primum perbeatos et perquam felices
arbitrantur, in fine tragoediarum in extremam miseriam redacti exclamationibus et dedignationibus caelum et terram confundunt, omniaque et caelestia
et terrestria incusant.[4]

. . . Imitatio per actiones illustris fortunae, exitu infelici, oratione
gravi metrica.[5]

---

[1] Du Ryer, *Saül*, ll. 991–4.
[2] *Sententiae* in the religious plays naturally have such religious and moral content
but *sententiae* were regarded above all as ornament. The plots, and the tragic fates, contain
no moral message, in our sense, except that of the fall of the great and the perils of fortune.
[3] Here the subject was obviously chosen for its similarity to Seneca's *Troades*, and
large passages are based on this play.
[4] Jodocus Badius Ascensius, *Praenotamenta*, cap. iv (Lawton, p. 28).
[5] Scaliger, *Poetices libri septem*, lib. i, cap. 6 (Lawton, p. 130).

(b) *Seneca rather than Euripides*

This concern with results rather than causes, with the fate of heroes in adversity rather than the deeds which lead to their downfall, is a legacy from classical literature. Yet specifically Renaissance reasons (to a great extent bound up with Renaissance trends in rhetoric) led to a choice of classical models which might well, to a modern eye, appear unusual.

Imitation of the ancients was the mainstay of Renaissance literary production. The dramatists were no exception to this. They pillaged the ancients for models. But, while for individual speeches or scenes within their plays they often called on a whole variety of authors, dramatic and non-dramatic, the most constant source was Seneca; and the whole shape of their tragedies, and the literary concepts which lay behind this shape, were Senecan rather than Greek, even though, on this Senecan basis, their specifically Renaissance preoccupations grafted distortions of all kinds. Why was it that Seneca, rather than the Greeks, became the main model?

At first sight this seems very odd. For these writers spent all their time praising the Greek dramatists, and comparing each other to Euripides, etc. Why, with occasional exceptions such as the neo-Latin dramatist Buchanan, did they follow such a Senecan pattern in their plays? If they did not actually know Greek, they could have read certain Greek plays in Latin translation; and the use they occasionally make of Greek models for individual scenes within their plays shows that they were not unfamiliar with Attic tragedy.

The answer lies in these authors' basic literary preoccupations, which were nearer to Seneca's than to those of the Greeks; or rather, which could make use of Seneca more easily than of the Greeks. Tragedy, for them, was just one more literary vehicle for the 'illustration' of the French language. Du Bellay's exhortation to the authors of his century, in the *Deffense et illustration de la langue françoyse* (book ii, ch. 4), is very clear on this point: 'Quand aux comedies et tragedies, si les roys et les republiques les vouloient restituer en leur ancienne dignité, qu'ont usurpée les farces et moralitez, je seroy' bien d'opinion que tu t'y employasses, et *si tu le veux faire pour l'ornement de ta langue*, tu sçais où tu en doibs trouver les archetypes.'

The Renaissance tragedian found within Seneca a stylized framework suitable for such ornamentation of the language. Rhetorical elaboration, within stylized forms, is the ultimate aim.

The particular form which this elaboration took is very much influenced by the Renaissance training in rhetoric, which had taken some
unusual and extreme turnings in comparison with classical rhetoric.

(c) *Two Forms of Rhetoric*

The full influence of the rhetorical training of the Renaissance upon
the form and content of the poetry has only recently begun to be
realized. Rhetoric was one of the basic elements of any man's education at school and university; and certain habits of thought, of composition, and of style are directly traceable to this rigid early training.

At the time of the Renaissance, the balance which distinguished
rhetorical training in the time of Cicero had been neglected, and certain
parts of it were concentrated on, to the exclusion of others. This un-
balance accounts for much that is peculiar to Renaissance poetry, and
it would be as well to go into this matter more deeply.

Ciceronian rhetoric had been divided into five parts: (1) *inventio*, or
the discovery of arguments; (2) *dispositio*, or the arrangement of these
arguments; (3) *elocutio*, or style; (4) *memoria*, or memory; (5) *pronun-
tiatio*, or delivery. Apart from these last two parts, which are relevant
only to spoken rhetoric, this scheme can be seen to be concerned with
two separate things, i.e. Thought and its organization (in *inventio* and
dispositio), and Style and elaboration (in *elocutio*).

There were two possible ways of developing this five-part rhetoric:
(*a*) by theoretical study, and (*b*) by imitation. A dichotomy between
these two types of training continued throughout the history of
classical rhetoric, though they rarely combined in individual rhetorical
works.

In the period we are studying there are two important traditions of
rhetorical study. Each of these types, formulary rhetoric (or rhetoric by
example) and stylistic rhetoric, grew up in the Hellenistic period, and
recurred in late classical times, continuing throughout the Middle Ages.
But it appears to be in the Renaissance that their influence became both
overriding, and at times contradictory.

Stylistic rhetoric is based on the theoretical study of the tropes and
figures of the third part of the Ciceronian plan, *elocutio*. In late classical
times style became the element of prime importance, and this concentration on ornament can be seen in many poets of that age, Seneca the
dramatist being a very good example. The Renaissance dramatists' pre-
ference for Seneca shows us to what extent the two periods were in

agreement as to what constituted good style. The principal aim of stylistic rhetoric was to *impress*, or to *please*, both of which aims were essentially deviations from the original aim of rhetoric, from Isocrates onwards, which was to persuade.

Formulary rhetoric, on the other hand, is based firmly on imitation. Though it deals almost entirely with the internal structure of the speech, i.e. with the arguments one was to choose, and the order in which one was to use them, this training was illustrated systematically by models of the various types of speech which might be needed, and within these models there was a very rigid sequence of ideas.[1] The *progymnasmata* (these model exercises) were educational instruments, concerned with reproducing and continuing strict genres; but their aim (based as they were on *inventio* and *dispositio*) was still essentially that of persuasion.

One of the main faults of criticism on this subject up to the present time has been that the critics have been obsessed with one or other of these two streams, and have either ignored or attempted to play down the other. W. S. Howell, for example, dealing with rhetoric in England,[2] denies any importance to formulary rhetoric, because Richard Rainolde's vernacular rhetoric, based on Aphthonius, did not run to a second edition. Because, as we shall see, Ramism was crowding out traditional stylistic rhetoric, Howell presumes that it was crowding out all other rhetoric, formulary included. That this cannot be true is shown by his later statement that there were a great many *Latin* editions of Aphthonius after this date. He has fallen into the common error of presuming that it is necessarily the vernacular which influences people; yet we are dealing here with the schooling of our poets, and with their rhetorical training, which was necessarily linked with the study of Latin.

Until the advent of Ramism, then, there were these two parallel streams of rhetoric developing side by side, and taught at the same time; eventually Ramist rhetoric took the place of the one, but the dichotomy continued. That these two streams, which appear so mutually contradictory, could be taught together, is typical of Renaissance veneration for the ancients, and its acceptance even of what seemed

[1] Two of the main formulary rhetorics to be taught in the schools were those of Aphthonius and Hermogenes, of whom Latin translations existed. The Renaissance edition of Aphthonius, compiled by Lorichius from translations by Agricola and Cataneus, contained many extra model themes, some written by Lorichius himself, others collected from other Renaissance writers.
[2] W. S. Howell, *Logic and Rhetoric in England, 1500–1700*, Princeton 1956.

contradictory. The mingling of the two leads to some inconsistencies, for the aims of the two are on the whole different, i.e. persuasion and delectation.

The inconsistencies which result from this are often large enough to destroy the whole point of the formulary art; for example, the progymnasmatic model, with its strictly economical plan, aiming at convincing the spectator, might suggest the use of *one* illustration to support the argument; the Renaissance dramatist, using the similes as a delightful end in themselves, might use three. The shape of the progymnasmatic argument is continually strained by the addition of figures of speech and thought, added merely for ornamentation and delight. Formulary and stylistic rhetoric can often defeat each other's ends; if they are both used carefully and restrainedly, they may yet blend; if not, one finds something of a hybrid, such as Ronsard's *Hydre desfaict*, or his *Ode à Madame Marguerite*, or the speech of Scipion to Massinisse in Act IV of Montchrestien's *Sophonisbe* (1596).

But before we move on to the effect of rhetoric upon tragedy, we should perhaps attempt to clear up the problem of Ramism.[1] The effect of Ramus's teaching was, of course, immense, not so much for what he said, which was often second-hand, or even second-rate, as for the methods he used and for the implications of those methods. In the field of rhetoric, however, I feel that Talon's *Rhetorica*, the mouthpiece of Ramist rhetoric, has been given something of a false place. It is yet another *stylistic* rhetoric; the tropes and figures are arranged carefully according to Ramist method; but the outlook is essentially the same as that of the stylistic rhetoricians. Much has been made of the fact that Ramus and Talon had reorganized the disciplines of logic and rhetoric by transferring Invention and Disposition from Rhetoric to Logic; but this had already been done, *implicitly*, by all the stylistic rhetoricians right back to Bede, or even further. Howell's distinction that stylistic rhetoricians were 'openly mindful that invention, arrangement, memory, and delivery . . . were also legitimate parts of the full rhetorical discipline' is a false distinction, for stylistic rhetoric was certainly taught as an end in itself in the Renaissance.

No; the main originality of Talon's *Rhetorica* would seem to lie in its treatment of the figures of thought, and in particular of the metaphor. The importance of the senses is stressed far more than it has been before, and we are told that 'Tropus autem nullus est florentior quam

[1] For a study of Ramist logic, and of certain aspects of Ramist rhetoric, I would refer the reader to the work of W. J. Ong, S. J., *Ramus: Method, and the Decay of Dialogue*.

metaphora, nec qui plus luminis afferat orationi: praesertim si ratione sumpta est, et ad sensus ipsos admovetur, maxime oculorum, qui est sensus acerrimus'.[1]

This stress on the senses would seem to have had far more influence on the poetry of the late sixteenth and early seventeenth centuries than any influence of Ramist *logic* which has so far been suggested. This latter has always seemed to me particularly difficult to trace clearly and definitely, if only because the metaphysical poets in England, with their structural and logical use of imagery, are among the least vocally Ramist of people, while Milton *does* have a claim to be Ramist; and also because Maurice Scève was using images in a similar way before the advent of Ramism.

In the sixteenth century, then, there are these two streams of rhetoric, stylistic and formulary, which run side by side, and are taught simultaneously. Much that is peculiar to French sixteenth-century tragedy stems from this teaching.

(d) *Effects of these two Forms of Rhetoric*

The static nature of the tragedy which stemmed from the ancients was more favourable to linguistic expansion and stylistic ornament than that of the seventeenth century was to be. Close depiction of changing human psychology, with everything having relation to the coming tragic event, does not leave much time for elaboration. On the other hand, a concern with a depiction of the emotions aroused by tragedy, simple, unchanging emotions, allows every opportunity for the enjoyment of language.

The two trends in rhetoric which have just been described tended to increase the static nature of this tragedy. Formulary rhetoric, dealing as it did with separate speeches, either of persuasion or of mood, which were separate entities in themselves, created a tendency towards making of drama a string of such 'set pieces', often very loosely strung together. All this we shall see clearly in this study of Montchrestien. Normal dramatic progression, the realism of dramatic scenes, are sacrificed for an almost operatic technique of solo arias, or of stylized and unrealistic discussion. This is in truth a series of elegies; but for all this it must not be taken that it is not drama. Only drama can provide the framework for such a series of set pieces, which in the best authors are often enhanced by their placing in relation one with another. Only

---

[1] Audomari Talaei, *Rhetorica*, cap. 8, 'De Metaphora'.

drama, too, can convincingly display the gamut of emotions which this 'dramatic poetry' provides.

Stylistic rhetoric, which finds its final flowering in Ramist rhetoric (of which Father Walter J. Ong says: 'in its final stage, Ramist rhetoric relies more on ornamentation theory than perhaps any other rhetoric ever has'),[1] nevertheless has its origins back in classical times. The unbalancing of the Ciceronian pattern originated possibly in the confusion between Rhetoric and Poetic which grew up in late classical times, and in the Middle Ages; for, as D. Lemen Clark says, 'the coincidence of rhetoric and poetic is in style. They differ typically in movement or composition; they have a common ground in diction.'[2]

Though by now rhetoric had been taught for centuries from the standpoint of style, the delight in ornament evinced by Renaissance writers tends to put even the writers of Seneca's time in the shade.

What 'style' meant to Renaissance theorists is shown by Puttenham's *Arte of English Poesie* (1589), in which well over half of the volume is devoted to the discussion 'Of Ornament'. Comparing Ornament to the necessary yet becoming clothes worn by great ladies, Puttenham himself presents us with a passage of prose loaded with ornament, and with similes of all kinds:

And as we see in these great Madames of honour, be they for personage or otherwise never so comely and bewtifull, yet if they want their courtly habillements or at leastwise such other apparell as custome and civilitie have ordained to cover their naked bodies, would be halfe ashamed or greatly out of countenaunce to be seen in that sort, and perchance do then thinke themselves more amiable in every mans eye, when they be in their richest attire, suppose of silkes or tyssewes and costly embroideries, then when they go in cloth or in any other plaine and simple apparell. Even so cannot our vulgar Poesie shew it selfe either gallant or gorgious, if any lymme be left naked and bare and not clad in his kindly clothes and coulours, such as may convey them somwhat out of sight, that is from the common course of ordinary speach and capacitie of the vulgar iudgement, and yet being artificially handled must needes geld it much more bewtie and commendation. This ornament we speake of is given to it by figures and figurative speaches, which be the flowers as it were and coulours that a Poet setteth upon his language by arte, as the embroderer doth his stone and perle, or passements of gold upon the stuffe of a Princely garment, or as th'excellent painter bestoweth the rich Orient coulours upon his table of pourtraite . . .[3]

[1] W. J. Ong, op. cit., p. 277.
[2] D. L. Clark, *Rhetoric and Poetry in the Renaissance*, New York 1922, p. 35.
[3] Puttenham, *The Arte of English Poesie*, 1589, pp. 114–15.

The aim of the Renaissance tragedian, as we have seen, was the elaboration (by use of all the devices of stylistic rhetoric) of certain emotions and moods, within the framework of various types of stylized 'set piece'. The monologue, the tirade, the *récit*, the chorus, stichomythia, all had their set, and stylized, rules of construction. Often, as in the case of the *récit*, the hallowed inner shape of the 'set piece' was based upon the practice of Seneca; but in the somewhat freer 'set pieces', the monologues and the tirades, the dramatists, searching for models at all costs, often follow, where possible, the strict plan of a progymnasmatic exercise.

It was the Renaissance desire for imitation, after all, which appears to have caused the eminence both of stylistic and formulary rhetoric. Each, in a way, gave exact formulae to be copied, where Ciceronian rhetoric had often given far more general advice. Rather than puzzle about invention and disposition, people turned to concrete models for all purposes; and, as far as ornament was concerned, *compendia* of various kinds gave all that stylistic rhetoric could desire. (The author might have at his disposal not only his own commonplace books, but also collections of *sententiae* such as Mirandula's *Illustrium Poetarum Flores*, of 'poetical phrases' such as Buchlerus's *Thesaurus Phrasium Poeticarum*, of epithets such as Textor's *Epithetae*, and of apposite stories such as Erasmus's *Parabolae* and *Apophthegmata*. The use of such *compendia* is a typical Renaissance transformation of the nominally theoretical study of the figures of stylistic rhetoric.) Though the writers of the Renaissance had read Cicero and Quintilian, they appear to have used mainly those parts of them which provided this kind of useful information; and the fourth book of the *Rhetorica ad Herennium* appears to have been the most popular.

Renaissance tragedy is essentially a series of stylistic exercises set in stylized forms. This does not condemn it; very often the achievement, within these limits, is very high. The tragedians followed the precept of the Pléiade, that literature should be written for a cultured élite; and the appreciation of their plays depends on a sense of style, and a knowledge of the models, and of the forms, so that any departure from them can be appreciated to the full.

The language of the sixteenth century, in its richness and variety, was eminently suited to this conception of tragedy.

(e) *The Place of Montchrestien*

The external form of Montchrestien's tragedies is in complete accordance with these theories. The stylized forms and the set speeches show a desire to 'conprehendere' the fortunes of heroes in adversity, and to portray the emotions aroused by the tragic event. Within these forms, all is subordinated to stylistic expression. What would be the point of this essentially sixteenth-century form, if the style contained by it were not the ornamental, florid style of the Renaissance?

In one of the appendices to this study, Lebègue's claim that Montchrestien's style is influenced by the reforms of Malherbe is shown to have very little foundation in fact. Montchrestien shows little sign of having been affected by anti-Ciceronianism, either. He remains a Renaissance poet, writing in Renaissance forms, and using Renaissance methods of imitation.

In a genre in which the most important thing is stylistic excellence, and in which every other attribute is directed towards that end, only a poet with an outstanding style can achieve greatness. Many of the sixteenth-century tragedians are abysmal failures for this reason. Only Garnier and Montchrestien (and possibly Jean de la Taille) stand out above the rest of those who wrote in the vernacular. Montchrestien's perfect, limpid, elegiac style, a contrast to the rather more vigorous style of Garnier, reaches an equally high standard, and creates certain masterpieces in the genre.

In most things Montchrestien is a typical Renaissance dramatist. The points in which he is not typical of the dramatists of his time are the very points where certain Renaissance attitudes have been taken to excess in other writers, and have tended to work against the object of the tragic form: e.g. excessive displays of erudition (caused by the desire for an élite audience).

Similarly, he has avoided religious and political polemic of all kinds, which detract from the value of so many other plays of the period.

Stripped of these distractions, his aims stand out even more clearly as those of the sixteenth century. He transfers with great success the rhetorical procedures he had learned at the university into the framework of a classical fate-tragedy.

3. Imitation of Sources

IMITATION of the ancients was one of the main characteristics of Renaissance literature. Writers were convinced, firstly, that they must create in their own language a literature which could stand comparison with any other, and, secondly, that the main way to do so was to imitate the examples that had come down to them of the two most perfect literatures yet created. As Jacques Peletier du Mans explained in his *Art Poëtique*: 'C'est chose toute receue et certaine qu'homme ne sauroit rien ecrire qui lui peut demeurer à honneur, et venir en commandation vers la postérité, sans l'aide et appui des auteurs Grecz et Latins.'

Dr. Grahame Castor quite rightly points out in his book *Pléiade Poetics* that this concept of imitation was matched, in what to modern eyes would seem a contradictory manner, by a stress on invention. Yet there is no contradiction in this, for 'originality' is a concept unknown, in the modern sense, to the sixteenth century, and invention to a great extent consists of the *manner* in which one imitates. All this is examined in great detail by Dr. Castor, and there is no need to go into it here; it is enough, for our purposes, to point to the importance of imitation of Latin and Greek literature (and indeed of Italian and neo-Latin literature, which had shown the way to the French). For the modern age, as opposed to the ancients, whose main art consisted in invention, must be content with taking as its mainstay the imitation of their excellence:

Se compose donq' celuy qui voudra enrichir sa langue, à l'imitation des meilleurs auteurs Grecs et Latins, et à toutes leurs plus grandes vertus, comme à un certain but, dirige la pointe de son stile; car il n'y a point de doute, que la plus grand'part de l'artifice ne soit contenue en l'imitation; et tout ainsi que ce fut le plus louable aux anciens de bien inuenter, aussi est-ce le plus utile de bien imiter, mesmes à ceux, dont la langue n'est encor bien copieuse et riche.[1]

[1] J. du Bellay, *Deffense et illustration de la langue françoyse*, chapter 8, 'D'amplifier la langue Françoise par l'imitation des anciens auteurs Grecz et Romains'.

It is at this point, however, that a complication occurs: the question of differentiating between translation and imitation. On this, as on many other matters, the Renaissance theorists are very vague. Translation is, indeed, seen by some as a major art. But a quick glance at some Renaissance translations will show that on the whole translation was very free, and that the translator put a great deal of himself into the work. On the other hand, many works which made no claims to be so were, in fact, virtual translations, so slavish was the imitation involved. Theories on this subject were, as has been said, vague; they tended to pay lip-service to the twin aims of imitation and invention but to say little about method; and it is only by examination of the works themselves that we can form a true picture of the methods of Renaissance imitation.

One statement of general aim will be of use to us: that provided by Du Bellay in his *Deffence et illustration*, where he depicts the Romans as 'immitant les meilleurs aucteurs Grecz, se transformant en eux, les devorant, et apres les avoir bien digerez, les convertissant en sang et nouriture, se proposant, chacun selon son naturel et l'argument qu'il vouloit elire, le meilleur aucteur, dont ils observoint diligemment toutes les plus rares et exquises vertuz, et icelles comme grephes . . . entoint et apliquoint a leur Langue'.[1]

This can be taken, indeed, as the Renaissance ideal of imitation. It should not be slavish, but the subject of imitation should be transformed *en sang et nouriture*. This means, essentially, that the classical influence should become transformed by the poet's own invention; that, eventually, it should become part of the poet's own cultural background; and that his imitations should thus be a personal expression, rather than the prosaic copying of phrases either from the original authors or from notebooks of alphabetically arranged *Flores*.

Slavish imitation of this latter type did, however, exist throughout the Renaissance. Much of Ronsard's early *Odes* is direct imitation of a model in the ancients. Much of Du Bellay's *Olive* is direct translation of Petrarch and of the Italian Petrarchists. What one must realize is that it is imitation such as this, and the type of learning of which the note-books are so typical, which eventually provide the basis of that general cultural background required for imitation to be *sang et nouriture*. The concentration on facts and details, exemplified by the principles of Erasmus's *De Copia* and the notebook system, and on

---

[1] *Deffense et illustration de la langue françoyse*, chapter 7, 'Comment les Romains ont enrichy leur langue'.

memory, exemplified by the fantastic mnemonic systems of people such as Leporeus,[1] led to a thorough grounding in the classics. From an early age people were taught to organize their knowledge, and to learn things by heart; so that authors could have, within them, the seeds of an imitation which, blended with their own invention, could flower as something new and vital. By the later Renaissance, the cultural background of the authors was no mere veneer; it was a natural part of the educated life of the period:

... Once a student had embarked upon the recommended course, once he had started analysing and memorising, the techniques he employed acquired, like some powerful engine, an impetus of their own and took in everything, irrespective of its interest, so that the whole or nearly the whole of the classical heritage passed into the common stock of European thought.[2]

While all this is true, nevertheless there remains throughout this period a tendency on the part of authors to rely on specific passages from classical authors for imitation in their works. In the major authors, such as Ronsard, Du Bellay, Garnier, the imitation itself becomes far freer and less slavish; sources are juxtaposed, many different sources are used, and the author ranges wide in his variations on the source-theme. In minor authors, or in certain authors once popular, but now less so (such as Desportes), the imitation often remains as slavish as in the first flush of Pléiade creation.

The dramatic art was originally regarded as just another genre with which to 'illustrate' the French language, as we have seen.

In the imitation which Du Bellay advises, the tragedians show as much variety in their methods as the poets. In the beginning this imitation was very uneven. At times, to a modern eye, the tragic authors appear to have imitated too slavishly, and to have ignored Du Bellay's precepts. If, however, one looks at one of the most extreme examples, La Péruse's *Médée*, which has at times been mistaken for a translation rather than an original work, one can see that even here the imitation is not purely slavish, and that the author, while following his sources closely, has also succeeded in using them for his own purposes. To a great extent he follows the technique of *contaminatio*, just as Ronsard and Du Bellay were doing in their poetry; that is to say, he blends different sources, using what he considers to be good from each, and adding certain original contributions of his own. His main source

[1] See R. R. Bolgar, *The Classical Heritage and its Beneficiaries*, Cambridge 1954.
[2] Ibid., p. 301.

is Seneca, but he also uses Euripides to a certain extent. He skilfully blends elements of their dramatic construction, and of their treatment of the story. As for his textual imitation, it varies from direct, slavish copying to passages only loosely connected with the original; and there are certain parts which are entirely unconnected with either of his main sources.

Despite these things, La Péruse's play is far less free in its imitation than the best plays of the century. The plays of Garnier and of Montchrestien show us the finest flowering of this technique.

M. Lebègue claims that Montchrestien was the most free of the sixteenth-century dramatists from the point of view of imitation: '. . . Par sa manière d'imiter et par son style, il appartient aux temps modernes plutôt qu'à la Renaissance.'[1]

The examination of Montchrestien's methods will, however, show this to be false. Montchrestien's whole concept of imitation is essentially that of the Renaissance, and his plays are no less free of it than the plays of Garnier. His methods are completely unlike those of modern dramatic literature from the seventeenth century onwards.[2]

Our study of Montchrestien's methods of imitation can be divided into four main categories, very different one from another: (a) Dramatic construction. (b) The plot. (c) 'Set pieces' (speeches, etc.). (d) Stylistic details, images, etc. In each of these categories he is derivative in various ways; and in his use of these various categories of imitation, one can see a reflection of his dramatic aims.

(a) *Dramatic Construction*

Like almost all the tragedians of the Renaissance, Montchrestien used as the basis of his dramatic construction the five-act plan of Seneca; and in most of the details of construction the Senecan influence is clear. This, however, is not the point in question here. What we are examining is Montchrestien's use of specific sources for specific plays.

Now M. Lebègue may well have been misled in his view of Montchrestien by the fact that none of this author's plays are taken from Greek or Latin tragedies (in contrast with, for example, Garnier); though even this fact might only have meant that dramatic *construction* had not been imitated. Seneca, then, is not a *specific* influence in the sense agreed above. Nevertheless, there are specific dramatic models

---

[1] *La Tragédie française de la Renaissance*, Brussels 1944. This statement is not developed at all.

[2] Montchrestien's style will be studied later in this volume.

for two of Montchrestien's plays. The influence of both has, on occasion, been denied; but all the evidence clearly points to a close connection between them and Montchrestien's plays.

These two plays are *La Cartaginoise*, based on Trissino's *Sofonisba*, and *Aman*, based on Roillet's neo-Latin play of the same name. Montchrestien does not seem averse to taking somebody else's dramatic lay-out already made, if he considers it good (and it is significant that he takes Roillet's rather than Rivaudeau's *Aman* as his model). On the other hand, he does change it when he considers he can improve it.

In his preface to the 1596 *Sophonisbe*, Montchrestien denies previous knowledge of Sainct-Gelays's French version of Trissino's play. However, as Fries has shown, he must definitely have known the Italian play. One or two details point to the fact that he has used the version of Trissino rather than that of Saint-Gelays.[1]

The layout of the scenes shows that Montchrestien, on this matter at least, is following Trissino closely:

ACT	*Montchrestien*	*Trissino*
I	Sophonisbe–Nourrice	= Soph.–Herminia
I	Sophonisbe–Messager	= Soph.–Messo
II	Mass.–Sophonisbe	= Mass.–Soph.
III	Lelie–Mass.	= Mass.–Lelio
III	Mass.–Soph.–Nourrice	= No equivalent
IV	Scipion–Siphax	= Scipione–Syphax–Catone
IV	Scipion–Mass.	= Scipione–Mass.

Act v is the only point at which Montchrestien's plan differs from Trissino's. In Montchrestien, there is a long monologue from Massinisse; and then Sophonisbe accepts the poison from Hiempsal, on the stage. In Trissino, Massinisse arrives on the stage to save Sophonisbe, but too late.

Seiver says of the *Aman*s of Montchrestien and Roillet that 'the similarity of the original material may account for whatever parallels exist between the two plays'.[2] Now, if one considers the extraordinary diversity of all the neo-Latin, German, and French plays on this subject, all of which take the Bible as their starting-point, one finds a striking similarity of composition between the plays of Roillet and Montchrestien, which singles them out from the rest; for, of all the

[1] See L. Fries, *Montchrestien's Sophonisbe, Paralleldruck der drei davon erschienenen Bearbeitungen*, Marburg 1889, pp. 23–30.
[2] Introduction to his critical edition of *Aman*, p. 33.

possible scenes which could have been chosen for depiction, these two plays, in opposition to all the others on the subject, tend to choose the same ones.

As Schwartz has pointed out,[1] Roillet's *Aman* is extraordinary among the German and neo-Latin plays on this subject for its compactness, and for the choice that has been made of salient facts and scenes. The trend towards coherent dramatic construction, which started in the play of the German neo-Latin author Naogeorgus (1543), before which the authors had been content to follow the Bible story scene by scene without thought of planning, here reaches its climax.

In France, Roillet's play (1556) was the first modern one on the subject, but here, too, it contrasts with the apparent shapelessness of the treatment of the theme in the *Mystère du Viel Testament*.

Roillet's plan stresses the importance of Aman himself, as does that of Montchrestien, by bringing him on at the very beginning. Both of them leave out the story of Vasthi, and only mention the eunuch's plot in connection with Mordecai's reward. Other playwrights in this century either condense the plot even more (Rivaudeau), or revert to the extended treatment of the Mystère (Matthieu).

The similarity of the layout of Roillet and Montchrestien can easily be seen:

ACT	Roillet		ACT	Montchrestien
I	Aman, Senex	=	I	Aman, Cirus
I	Assuerus, Aman	=	II	Assuérus, Aman
II	Mardocheus (mon.)	=	III	Mardochée (mon.)
II	Back and fore between Esther and Mard., with Athach as go-between	=	III	Same, with Athac and maidservants as go-betweens
II end	Prayer of Mard. and Chorus	=	III end	Mard.'s prayer
III opening	Hester's prayer	=	IV opening	Esther's prayer

From here onwards there is less similarity, for Montchrestien shows us much that Roillet only gives us in *récit* (Esther–Assuérus scene, Assuérus–Aman scene). But Act v of both plays finishes with Esther's banquet.

Montchrestien's use of the plays of Trissino and Roillet as models is, however, almost entirely confined to their plan. Within this framework much is entirely different; for the content he usually returns to the

---

[1] In *Esther im deutschen und neulateinischen Drama des Reformationszeitalters*, Leipzig 1894.

original historians or poets (i.e. Livy, Petrarch, the Bible); and the scenes themselves, while being between the same people as in the model, are often of completely different import.

Thus Trissino's first scene, between Sophonisba and Herminia, is a full exposition of everything that has preceded the play: Montchrestien, who has no need of an exposition, devotes this act to a stock scene, with the nurse trying to dissuade Sophonisbe from her grief. Similarly, in Roillet's opening scene Aman's confidant moralizes, and disagrees with him, while in Montchrestien the confidant praises Aman, and agrees with him.

Montchrestien, then, has taken the pattern of a previous play, but has filled it out with different material. Why then, did he choose the plans in question?

Probably because they offered an impressive array of *scènes à faire* and of opportunities for 'set pieces'. Montchrestien's concern is not primarily dramatic impact, but expansion of rhetorical set speeches, arguments, and *lieux communs*. Thus Trissino's plan offered him (*a*) A scene between the main character and her confidante: this he prefers to fill with a set scene of grief and of dissuasion (there are 135 marked *sententiae* in the 1604 edition) than with a recital of facts. (*b*) A messenger scene, a *récit*. (*c*) The meeting between the two lovers, a *scène à faire*, and also an opportunity to imitate the set speeches of Livy and Petrarch. (*d*) A scene of moralizing by Lélie (even though he offers to help). (*e*) The *scène à faire* between Scipion and Siphax, also to be found in Livy and Petrarch, a contrast of present and former glory, and the reversibility of fortune. (*f*) The scene between Scipion and Massinisse. Where Montchrestien changes the plan, it is either to add another valuable scene (the last meeting between Massinisse and Sophonisbe, Act III, end) or a new speech (Mass.'s monologue, taken from Petrarch), or to give us something on the stage which in Trissino we only heard in a *récit* (Sophonisbe's acceptance of the poison).

Roillet's plan offered him (*a*) A prideful tirade. (*b*) A conversation between tyrant and confidant. (*c*) A king's tirade (cf. Garnier's Nabuchodonosor). (*d*) Prayers of Mardochée and Esther (set pieces). Montchrestien's main changes consist in giving us scenes instead of *récits*.

Thus, though Montchrestien approves of Roillet's concision and compression of the story of Esther, he does not go to the extreme of Rivaudeau, whose play, taking place within the exact time of the stage representation, consists almost entirely of *récits*. If a scene can be performed on the stage, Montchrestien allows it to be so; he reserves the *récit* for battles or for deaths. It is significant that his main departure from his models, in the matter of dramatic construction, is the addition of scenes instead of *récit*s.

Montchrestien's dramatic models, Trissino and Roillet, were chosen for the opportunities which their schemes offered for the development of rhetorical devices; from time to time, in the Renaissance tradition of imitation, Montchrestien adds further scenes which provide similar 'set pieces'.

(b) *The Plot: 'Historical' Sources*

The term 'historical' will be used at this point for all sources which have reference to the plots of the plays. Indeed, at times it is as difficult in this context to differentiate between poetry and history, as it has been to divide translation from imitation. For historians, whether of classical times or of the sixteenth century, had to a certain extent been free to invent. Provided they gave the main lines of the truth, they could compose speeches for the main characters, and in other ways tidy up the story. As late as the end of the seventeenth century this was still true, as Dr. Vivienne Mylne has pointed out:

An elegant style, a dignified handling of events, a talent for drafting impressive speeches for great occasions, all these were requirements at least as important for most historians as the ability to sift the true from the legendary. . . . Respectable and respected seventeenth-century historians considered that they had the right, and sometimes even a duty, to supplement the known facts with details of 'what must have been'. If the results of a conversation between two kings are known, one can reconstruct the conversation; if the rebellious citizens are calmed by a harangue from a bishop, the gist of his speech can be deduced.[1]

The historians and the poets, whose plots the sixteenth-century dramatists followed, were of two kinds: (1) Men in whose works rhetorical 'set pieces' of this kind were available: historians such as Livy, Plutarch, or Pierre Matthieu, poets such as Petrarch; (2) Men whose works, without containing such 'set pieces' nevertheless provided a perfect framework for rhetorical developments. We shall later

[1] *The Eighteenth-Century French Novel*, Manchester University Press 1965.

be seeing the influence of the 'set pieces' themselves; what interests us here is the use made of basic story-line as a framework.

In Montchrestien we find a clear example of a historian of the second type being closely followed. A study of Dares the Phrygian's *Histoire veritable de la guerre des Grecs et des Troyens*[1] shows beyond doubt that Montchrestien used it as the main basis for his play *Hector*. Not only this, but one can immediately see the factors which Montchrestien must have looked for, and which must have arrested his attention when reading this book. The relevant passage occurs, in Charles de Bourgueville's translation, on pages 44, 45, and 46. I use this translation, printed at Caen in 1572, because it is the most probable one for Montchrestien to have used.

Ainsi que la trefue fut faillie, et que le temps du combat fut reuenue, Andromache femme d'Hector eut auertissement par vision, apprehension, ou reuelation en dormant, qu'Hector se deuoit et feroit beaucoup de se desister d'aller en bataille ce iour là . . .

The dream, or vision, was one of the mainstays of Renaissance tragedy, as was the advice of the confidant to put no trust in dreams; Montchrestien uses both in Act II.

. . . Mais comme elle luy eut raconté sa peur, et telle vision, il estima cela comme une crainte imaginée, et parolles inutiles de femme.

This is again a typical scene, the husband ignoring the wife's advice to stay in safety (cf. Grévin's *César*). Andromache implores Hector to stay with her at the end of Act I.

Andromache ne se contentant, toute contristée, enuoye vers Priam : à fin que par deffense, ou priere il l'empechast de combatre ce iour seulement. . . . Elle toute esplorée court au Palais vers le Roy, luy reciter ce que elle auoit veu par vision en songe : et que neantmoins les gracieuses prieres qu'elle avoit faites à Hector, de ne aller pour ce iour a la bataille, il s'estoit disposé et promptement fait armer sans crainte : à fin de s'y trouuer, voire plus hastiuement que de coustume.[2] Et deslors se ietta auec son petit fils Astianax aux pieds de Priam : à fin qu'il eust à faire rappeller Hector de son entreprise.

Here we have another scene of pleading, of argument, of persuasion (middle of Act II), containing a 'set piece', the *récit* of the dream.

---

[1] Until now the only suggested sources have been Homer, and Jacques Millet's *mystère La Destruction de Troie*. However, Homer appears merely to have been the model for a couple of 'set pieces' (Hector and his child and Andromache's scene with Hector), and M. Lebègue has shown the unlikelihood of Millet being a source.

[2] Even a small detail like this is transferred to the play. Andromache says: 'Jamais il n'eut le cœur si bruslant du combat' and 'Mais telle promptitude a bon droit m'est suspecte.'

. . . Priam le retient, et commande à tous autres d'aller à la bataille . . .

This presents the playwright with the opportunity for a scene of argument between Priam and Hector (end of Act II).

The short scene between Hector and Antenor at the beginning of Act III is an addition, probably to set Hector's love of honour even more before our minds. Antenor is then sent off to see what is going on in the battle; Hector and the chorus fill in with another dialogue, and then a messenger comes on with news of the battle.

Mais comme Agamemnon, Achille, Diomede, et Aiax de Locre s'apperçoivent qu'Hector n'y estoit, ils combatent fort asprement, et tuent plusieurs Capitaines Troyens. Hector ayant entendu par un bruit et murmure populaire, que les Troyens estoyent par trop harassez, mal-menez, et pressez, il court hastiuement à la meslée . . .

The 'bruit et murmure populaire' is converted into a long messenger speech, at the end of which Hector does indeed run off. The messenger asks:

Où court si tost Hector transporté de colère?

after which the chorus is left to comment on the situation.

The rest of the play still takes place within Troy, so that news of the battle has to be received in two further messenger speeches. The description of the battle seems to follow Dares rather than Homer, for Achilles is injured in the thigh, and there is no question of Hector fleeing.

Apart from two *récits*, these two acts are filled with the forebodings, and then the lamentations, of Priam, Hecube, and Andromache, all of which are implicit in the passage of Dares which we have seen. Dares' description of Hector's death ends with the words: 'Toute la nuict les Troyens pleurent et lamentent la mort d'Hector.'

If these three pages of Dares were not enough to prove Montchrestien's use of his text, one could always point to the conversation between Cassandre and the Chorus in Act I,[1] where reference is made to Hercules's razing of Troy, and the kidnapping of Hesione by the Greeks, details which occur *only* in Dares the Phrygian, in an attempt to justify the position of the Trojans. Also, there is no mention of the gods as characters (another characteristic of Dares).

Dares, though now known to be a forgery, was believed at the time to be true, truer even than Homer, who was not an actual eye-witness

[1] *P. de J.*, pp. 6–7.

of the Wars. He was still to be used, in the next century, as a model for Hardy and Benserade. (See the prefaces to their plays on the *Mort d'Achille*.)

It is clear that Montchrestien has kept fairly close to the text of Dares, which, however, by its very concision, has given him a great amount of freedom. The original text abounds in *scènes à faire*, in opportunities for *récits*, arguments, and 'set pieces'. To these Montchrestien has added two 'set pieces' almost entirely unconnected with the theme of the play, i.e. the *fureurs* of Cassandra, at the beginning of Act I, and the lamentations of Helen, at the end of Act III. These, while not having a direct connection with Hector's fate, are nevertheless 'set pieces' inspired by the setting in which Hector's drama is played out. They both have a foundation in original sources; and Montchrestien obviously considered a play which takes place during the siege of Troy to be incomplete if it did not take in two such obvious opportunities for rhetorical elaboration.

He takes a similar attitude in relation to another of his plays, which is based on Plutarch. The plot of *Les Lacènes* is based on Plutarch's *Agis and Cleomenes*, chapters lxix–lxxiii. That he has chosen it for the opportunities for scenes of lamentation, stoic resignation, etc., is obvious. Certain of the *récits* are closely based on originals in Plutarch. And in his preoccupation with using all possible scenes provided by the author, Montchrestien even uses one which has no place in the play at all, as it takes place long before the action, which Montchrestien has fitted into twenty-four hours. This is the scene between Cleomenes and Thericion. In his determination to fit the scene in, Montchrestien brings on the ghost of Thericion at the beginning to describe it to us. In the rest of the play much is as freely based on the original text as is *Hector* (i.e. there are opportunities for scenes and 'set pieces' in the original, but the models for these 'set pieces' are often taken from other sources); though the *récits* are very close to Plutarch. Miss G. E. Calkins has dealt thoroughly with the sources of *Les Lacènes* and there is little need to give any detailed account here.

Of *L'Escossoise* the sources are far less certainly known, perhaps because the events were so recent that the author may even have relied, for some of his facts, on hearsay. That he did, however, make extensive use of a contemporary historian has been shown by Miss Frances Yates's discovery of Pierre Matthieu's *Histoire des derniers troubles* as a source.[1] Matthieu was a historian of the type described earlier; he made

---

[1] Frances A. Yates, art. cit.

up speeches and scenes of argument for every occasion, and his book is a treasure-trove of rhetorical devices of every kind, including a ten-page *comparatio* between Caesar and the Duc de Guise. He was the perfect model for a Renaissance tragedian; in fact, as a tragedian himself, he drew heavily on the speeches in his *Histoire des derniers troubles* for his own play *La Guisiade*. In *L'Escossoise* his most obvious influence, as far as set pieces are concerned, is on the discussion between Elizabeth and her Counsellor in Act I. As Miss Yates admits, this was 'Montchrestien's chief, but not quite his only source'.[1] Other contemporary sources, and historians, were probably used (though Lanson's discussion of possible sources[2] is inconclusive). The facts, taken from the diverse sources, are tailored to sixteenth-century elegiac and tragic requirements.

There are various complications with relation to the plays *La Cartaginoise* (*Sophonisbe*) and *Aman*. As we have seen, both these plays are based, for their dramatic structure, on other plays; but within this structure the author has not necessarily followed the ideas expressed in the original play. What he has done, in fact, is return to the original 'historical' sources. His 'set pieces' on the whole conform more to their originals in the historians than to what the other dramatists may have made of them; and the historical facts also conform more to the historians than to the dramatists. These dramatists, Trissino and Roillet, were both Renaissance tragedians, and had used their historians in a similar manner to Montchrestien; but an examination of the texts makes it obvious that Montchrestien had referred back to the original sources.

This is especially obvious in *Sophonisbe*, where Montchrestien has clearly used Petrarch as an added source to Livy, and has not used Appian; Trissino's main sources are Livy and Appian. In the 1596 version of *Sophonisbe*, the influence of Petrarch's Latin epic *Africa* is particularly to be found within the 'set pieces'. This epic was, of course, itself closely based on Livy, and the 'set pieces' within it were often elaborations on Livy's originals. But whereas a critic such as Andrae, mentioning *Africa* as one of Montchrestien's sources, clearly has no idea of how far-reaching this influence was (for he gives us only one or two examples) a close examination of the 1596 text of *Sophonisbe* will show us that in most cases Petrarch's text was used rather than Livy's.[3]

---

[1] Art. cit.
[2] G. Lanson, 'Les Sources historiques de La Reine d'Escosse', *Revue Universitaire* (1905).
[3] See lines 639–42, 713–18, 721–4, 775–6, 801–7, 843–6, 865–8, 913–30, 1610–17, 1736–40, 1858–63, 1867–71, 1878–9, 1894–1911, 1916–25, 1934–6, 1968–90, 1996–2011, 2168–71.

Livy, however, is also used as a model. And he, too, is used as a source for 'set pieces', rather than the dramatic source. For example, let us take Sophonisbe's request. Livy, xxx. 12. 13, gives us the following:

Precor quaesoque, per majestatem regiam in qua paulo ante nos quoque fuimus, per gentis Numidarum nomen, quod tibi cum Syphace commune fuit, per hujusque regiae deos, qui te melioribus ominibus accipiant quam Syphacem hinc miserunt, / hanc veniam supplici des, ut ipse, quodcumque fert animus, de captiva tua statuas, neque me in cujusquam Romani superbum et crudele arbitrium venire sinas.

Trissino reverses this, placing the first half (the address) after the second (the request itself):

> I chieggio a uoi quest' una gratia sola.
> La qual'e; che ui piaccia per uoi stesso
> Determinare a la persona mia
> Qualunque stato, al uoler uostro aggrada;
> Pur che non mi lasciatur ir ne le mani,
> E ne la seruitù d'alcun Romano
> Da lei Signor potete liberarmi
> Voi solo al mondo; & io di cio ui priego
> Per la Regale, e gloriosa altezza,
> Ne la qual poco auanti anco noi fummo,
> E per i Dei di questi luoghi, i quali
> Riceuan entro uoi con miglior sorte,
> Di quella, che hebbe a l'uscir fuor Syphace . . .

Montchrestien, however, reverts to Livy's order:

> Grand Roy, ie te suppli' par la splendeur Royalle,
> Qui nous fut auec toy n'a pas long tens égalle,
> Par le nom de Numide, et par ton sceptre encore . . . etc.
> . . . Qu'il te plaise, benin user de ta clemence
> Enuers moy, que le Sort reduit en ta puissance . . . etc.[1]

The request is slightly differently phrased from that of Livy, but the order of the Latin is respected.

Montchrestien's use of Petrarch, whose style is so much more elaborate than that of Livy, and in whose work Livy's speeches are expanded far beyond their original length, is a clear sign of his particular concern with linguistic and rhetorical elaboration. Trissino's play

---

[1] *Sophonisbe*, A 703–5, 711–12.

had, above all, been simple and direct; his concerns had been more dramatic than Montchrestien's, and he had been careful to attempt *vraisemblance* in the plot, and coherence in his characters. Montchrestien, having used Trissino's convenient dramatic structure, ignores the rest, and relies entirely on his 'poetic' and 'historic' sources for the internal, linguistic structure of the play. This leads to a very different emphasis.

Montchrestien's failure to use Appian as a source,[1] for example, means that there is no hint that Massinisse and Sophonisbe were formerly betrothed. Trissino does use this fact, as do all other French authors of plays on this subject. This engagement might have helped to explain much that seems *invraisemblable* in Montchrestien's plot, particularly the first scene between Massinisse and Sophonisbe.

This scene, instead of giving us the calm, reasonable discourse, full of *sententiae*, which we find in Trissino, returns to the passionate scene of love at first sight described by Livy and Petrarch. Whereas Trissino's protagonists (even though they are former fiancés) behave coldly, in a traditional victor–vanquished relationship, dwelling on the values of generosity, gratitude, etc., and never once mentioning love, the Massinisse of Montchrestien behaves in an entirely irrational, *invraisemblable* way, as does that of Livy, 'ut est genus Numidarum in Venerem praeceps'.[2] While Trissino's Masinissa confines himself to such statements as:

> Altro merto non uo, pero che'l bene
> Solo si deue far, perch'egli è bene;
> Il quale è'l fin di tutte l'opre humane.

Montchrestien's hero already refers to Sophonisbe as:

> Mon tout, mon petit cœur, la moitié de mon ame,

and in the 1604 version cries out immediately after Sophonisbe's speech of supplication; 'Beauté Reine des cœurs . . .', etc., saying, with Petrarch, that he will make her his wife.

For the characters, as well, Montchrestien returns to Livy and Petrarch. That is to say, he copies their text, and the moods of their characters, without worrying about characterization. Thus Massinisse

---

[1] Though there is one passage in the play which *might* seem to point to a knowledge of Appian, i.e. the point where Syphax blames Sophonisbe for his fate, this is no sure pointer, and critics such as Fries have discounted it.

[2] Livy, xxx. 12. 18.

loses much of the nobility with which Trissino credits him; he helps Sophonisbe because of his love, and not from higher motives, and this love seems to disappear as quickly as it came. He gives in straight away to Scipio, and only wishes to know how to keep his oath. Trissino's hero had acted originally from compassion, marries Sophonisba to protect her, then energetically opposes the will of Rome, both to Lelio and Scipione; he even makes an attempt to carry off Sophonisba. Similarly, Montchrestien's Sophonisbe has become once more as energetic, and patriotic, as the heroine of Livy and Petrarch, losing much of the tenderness and piety given to her by Trissino.

Among other things introduced by Trissino, but left out again by Montchrestien, we find the role of Herminia, that of Catone, Massinissa's plan to save Sophonisba, and the fact that Sophonisba and Siphax had a son.[1]

Aman is a similar case. It is based, for its construction, on the play by Roillet. For the actual story, however, and for the basis of his 'set pieces', Montchrestien has gone back to the original source which Roillet also had used, the Bible.[2] Also, as in other plays, he has, of course, gone to various other sources for his 'set pieces' as well. Montchrestien's return to the Bible is not only shown by textual details; it is also clear from the elements of the story which are contained in this play, and not in Roillet's: the Jews' vengeance against their enemies, Mordecai's elevation to Aman's position, and the scene between Aman and Sarès.

Montchrestien's method, then, in these five plays, has been as follows: in pursuing his aim of creating a play consisting of a certain number of 'set pieces' for rhetorical expansion (monologues, tirades, *récits*, arguments, etc.), he has, where he has found a dramatic layout ready-made which creates the opportunity for such pieces, imitated it closely. His historical sources have been chosen for the same reason. Some of them, indeed, have been chosen because they contain actual examples of such 'set pieces', which create the opportunity for close textual imitation. This being so, in the two plays for which he has both dramatic and historical sources he tends, as far as content is concerned, to follow the latter.

In the plays based purely on historical sources, *Hector*, *Les Lacènes*,

---

[1] In Montchrestien's play there are occasional lines obviously based on Trissino (see Fries), but these are rare.

[2] Seidmann rightly points out the doubtful nature of the claim that the Targoum Cheni had been used.

and *L'Escossoise*, on the other hand, these sources are modified to a certain extent in order to fit the strict form of Renaissance tragedy.

This is where the play *David* stands out from all the rest. Like the others, it is true to its sources. But no attempt has been made to change the facts around to suit dramatic requirements. The play is formless, the action is not bound by unity of time, the repentance of David is not prepared for in any way.

The source is 2 Samuel 11 and 12 : 1–14. Montchrestien's Act I gives us Chapter 11 : 2–6. David describes his first sight of Bethsabée, Nadab brings the news of Bethsabée's pregnancy ('And the woman conceived; and she sent unto David, and said, I am with child'). David sends for Urie. Act II gives us Chapter 11 : 7–12, with David trying to persuade Urie to go and sleep with his wife. In Act III, we find Chapter 11 : 13–15; David describes how he has even tried to make Urie drunk; he gives Urie the fatal letter (before this, Montchrestien adds *stichomythia* between Nadab and David). In Act IV, a messenger brings a description of Urie's death, based on Chapter 11 : 16–25, with the reactions of David being the same as those foreseen by Joab in the Bible. At the beginning of Act V, the lamentations of Bethsabée conform with Chapter 11 : 26. David immediately makes a speech asking her to be his wife (which presumably she accepts); this must be presumed to be some time after Urie's death, for he says: 'Ton dueil, chere Maistresse, a trop longtemps duré.' (The Bible says, Chapter 11 : 27: 'And when the mourning was past . . .'.) The rest of Act V is based on the scene with Nathan, Chapter 12 : 1–14, which contains the parable and also the curse, two fine opportunities for 'set pieces'.

It can be seen that the shapelessness of this play is due to too close a following of its source. As with all the other sources for the other plays, the Bible has here been used for the opportunities and examples it offers for 'set pieces', but, in contrast to the other plays, there is here no shape or dramatic structure in the sixteenth-century classical sense. The theme is treated as it might have been in a mystery (though of course more succinctly), or in one of the irregular tragedies of the time. It is a strange exception to Montchrestien's classical regularity.

(c) *Imitation of 'Set Pieces'*

Montchrestien's plays contain many 'set pieces' for which the models are to be found in his 'historical' sources. For example, there are imitations of long speeches from Livy and Petrarch in *Sophonisbe*, of dramatic scenes and dialogue from the book of Esther in *Aman*, of prayers from the Apocrypha in the same play, of *récits* from Plutarch in *Les Lacènes*, of scenes of argument from Matthieu in *L'Escossoise*, and so on.

There are also 'set pieces' in these plays which closely follow other sources. Wherever the author feels that they will fit in with his subject, he incorporates these diverse influences into his text. Just as Garnier had made use of Horace's Odes for his choruses, so Montchrestien, in *David*, bases one chorus on Du Bartas; and there are speeches in Act I of *Hector* based on Homer, translations of the Psalms in *David* and *Aman*, etc.

Added to this there are, of course, in Montchrestien's plays many stock kinds of 'set piece' (dream *récits*, tyrant speeches, etc.) which are in the mainstream of certain traditions, and use various stock turns of phrase, images, and even dispositions of ideas. In such traditions it is, of course, difficult if not impossible to trace one source rather than another. The interest, as with the speeches based on strict rhetorical model exercises, lies in the variations on a stock theme—variations of disposition, variations of imagery, variations of phrase. All this will be discussed in a later chapter. We shall be dealing, here, with the author's imitation of definite models, whether from his historical source or from outside.

The procedure followed by Montchrestien is, on the whole, typical of Renaissance tragedians. He tends to leave the plan of the speech, or of the discussion, or (in the case of choruses) of the poem, alone. That is to say, he follows his model fairly closely as far as the invention and disposition of the 'set piece' are concerned. Occasionally one part of the plan is misplaced, or left out; even more occasionally, additions are made to the plan. But, basically, that part of the composition which depends on the first two parts of Ciceronian rhetoric is left alone.

It is when we come to the third part, *elocutio*, or style, that we see the main preoccupations of the author. Just as both dramatic and historical sources have been used mainly as frameworks on which to hang 'set pieces' of various kinds, so the 'set pieces' are used as frameworks for stylistic elaboration. The 'freedom' of the imitator lies essentially in his variations on the source's theme, and in his linguistic elaborations of various kinds. As has already been said in a previous chapter, such elaboration could at times be excessive; and often it could mar the framework of an argument which, clear in the original source, unchanged in its new position, nevertheless could get lost beneath a welter of words. Certainly this type of elaboration makes the static plays of the Renaissance even more undramatic than they might otherwise have been.

In this manner of imitation Montchrestien is no 'freer' than any other dramatists of the sixteenth century, despite M. Lebègue's statement. Like Garnier and La Taille, he never goes to quite the unreal lengths of over-elaboration practised by some of the minor tragedians. His elaborations are at times lengthy for modern taste; but between the three editions of *Sophonisbe*¹ several of the most extreme examples of this are severely cut down. His aim has been the *illustration* of language, which he achieves in calm, balanced verse which weaves elaborations around his source.

That he is neither more nor less free in his imitation than his contemporaries is shown by a comparison of various passages of his *Aman* with the equivalent passages in Matthieu's play of the same name, published in 1589. The two authors have, in fact, chosen different passages to expand, so at times the one elaborates more on the original text, at times the other; and at times both are quite clear and simple in their following of it.

For example, there is their rendering of Chapter 13, verse 10:² 'Tu fecisti caelum et terram, et quidquid caeli ambitu continetur' is rendered by Matthieu as:

> Tu as formé du ciel ceste voute dorée,
> Tu as enuironné par la mer azurée
> De la terre les murs, ce que tu veux se traite,
> Ton œuure est admirable, et ta grandeur parfaite.
>
> (*Aman*, Act III)

Matthieu has thus expanded the text to a certain extent; but Montchrestien seizes the opportunity to expatiate on 'quidquid caeli ambitu continetur', and we get the following:

> Aussi fut-ce pas toy qui creas Ciel et Terre?
> Cela que d'admirable et l'un et l'autre enserre,
> Se vante, ô tout-puissant, l'ouurage de tes doits:
> Les Animaux des champs, et les Feres des bois,

¹ See Appendix I.
² It is most likely that Montchrestien used a French text, but as Matthieu almost certainly used the Latin version of Esther's prayer and as the Vulgate is probably more accessible to the reader than a French Bible containing the Apocrypha, I quote the Latin source.

> Du grand vague de l'air les bandes vagabondes;
> Les poissons escailleux qui nagent par les ondes;
> Bref tout ce qui fut onq et doit estre d'humains,
> Prist et prendra, Seigneur, son estre de tes mains.

Similarly, verse 12: 'Cuncta nosti, et scis quia non pro superbia, et contumelia, et aliqua gloriae cupiditate, fecerim hoc, ut non adorarem Aman superbissimum', which in Matthieu becomes:

> Tu perses de tes rais de mon cœur la verriere,
> Tu sçais si par orgueil ou arrogance fiere,
> Ou pour l'ambition, qui donne à tout mal tige,
> I'ay mesprisé d'Aman d'adorer le vestige.

is greatly expanded in Montchrestien's text:

> Tu connois clairement les plus obscures choses;
> Nos pensers à tes yeux ne sont point lettres closes;
> Leurs rays percent nos cœurs, ainsi que le Soleil
> Peut trauerser le verre exposé à son œil.
> Si donques ie n'ay point adoré ce superbe,
> Qui nous foule à ses pieds comme une puante herbe;
> Et si pour éviter son dépiteux couroux,
> Ie n'ay voulu fléchir deuant luy mes genoux;
> Tu sçais que ce n'est pas par mon outrecuidance.
> Tu veux qu'aux Magistrats on porte reuerence:
> Aussi ne suis-ie tant de moy-mesme abuzé
> Que pour me priser trop ie l'aye mesprisé.

(A 719–30)

These two examples show perfectly Montchrestien's method in such a passage, a static 'set piece' of prayer. He takes the text as a starting-point, and on it he hangs similes, images, phrases. It becomes a kind of aria rather than a monologue. Thus, in the first passage, he uses the short remark 'Quidquid caeli ambitu continetur' to make a list of birds, beasts, and fishes. In the second, he introduces the images of the sun traversing glass, and of the proud man treading them down 'comme une puante herbe'. He also introduces the antithesis in the last line, and in line 728 we find a semi-*sententia*, which by 1604 has become a definite one, marked with inverted commas:

> Aux sacrez Magistrats on doit la reuerence.

The whole prayer is greatly lengthened; beside it the text of Matthieu seems almost succint, yet he also is embroidering the original text, introducing images, etc.

Entirely the opposite situation is found if we compare the way in which these two authors deal with the scene between Assuérus and Aman, in Act v. Here it is Montchrestien who is the more simple, Matthieu the more ornate.

In Montchrestien's play the king's question is as simple as that in the Bible:

> Dy moy, mon pere Aman, qu'est il besoin de faire
> Pour honorer quelqu'un par dessus l'ordinaire?[1]

Matthieu's king is meanwhile lost in compliments:

> Aman tu entens bien,
> Combien ie fais voisin de mon ombre ton bien.
> Tu sçais que ie t'estime estre le seul organe
> De tout ce que ie fais de l'Inde iusqu'au Tane,
> Dis moy donc qu'il faut faire à celuy que le Roy
> Desire d'honnorer?[2]

Aman's description of the honours to be given is, in Montchrestien, almost shorter than the text in the Bible, and follows it very closely. The author allows himself one bit of ornament, the line: 'Ce cheual escumant alentour de son frein',[3] which is probably used more as an aid to the transference of the text into verse, than as ornament *qua* ornament. In Matthieu the impact of this speech is lost in a mass of ornament (I italicize the parts actually based on the Biblical text):

> *Un Roy qui entreprent et de grace et d'accueil*
> *Quelqu'un fauoriser* d'un louable receuil,
> Enuoyant sur son chef mille rais de son ame
> Plus odorants à tous que le musc ou le bame
> Des mols Arabiens, *il luy doit presenter*
> *La coronne Royale, et sur son chef l'enter,*
> Ainsi qu'elle apparoit sur sa blonde perrucque,
> Qui luit comme un flambeau depuis Perse au Moluque
> Puis ensceptrant ses mains, il faut que ses habits
> Soyent couuers de saphirs, de perles, de rubis,
> Et des fleurs que l'on voit, quan l'aurore est déclose
> Et des lingots dorez que le grand Phase arrose:
> *Lors monté* valeureux *sur un cheual guerrier*
> Du Roy le seul Phenix coronné de Laurier,
> Arbre diuinement qu'au grand Phebus on vouë
> Lors que sur Helicon du Lut d'iuoire il iouë,

---

[1] *Aman*, A 1483-4.   [2] Matthieu, *Aman*, Act IV.   [3] *Aman*, A 1494.

Ainsi fauorizé d'un si superbe arroy
Son escuier sera un Prince qui du Roy
Receura plus d'honneur criant par toutes places
Les faueurs qu'il reçoit de ses royales graces.[1]

The climax of the scene, which in Montchrestien is short and striking
(and in Du Ryer and Racine will be delayed, and thus will create more
suspense), is almost unnoticed in Matthieu. Montchrestien's king
delivers his message in five lines:

> Fay tout ce que tu dis et sans plus differer
> Au vieillard Mardochée qui se tient à ma porte,
> Afin de luy montrer l'amour que ie luy porte,
> Suis donques ton Conseil et mon vouloir parfait
> Si bien qu'a ton discours se rapporte l'effet.

He then goes out, so that we immediately get the chance to hear the
effect of this blow upon Aman. Matthieu's king, however, cannot resist
the opportunity for a tirade. He makes a long speech, in which he
repeats all the instructions that Aman has suggested, and then, until the
end of the scene, gives us a general discourse on the liberality of kings;
Aman has no chance to say a word, until the next scene in which he
appears, with his wife.

Montchrestien, then, is neither more nor less free than Matthieu in his
textual imitation. He uses the original text as a basis on which to elaborate; and if we sometimes find ourselves far from the original text in
the 1604 edition, this is merely because, in the multiple changes of
ornament which he affects between the 1596, 1601, and 1604 editions,
he has no longer been referring back to the original source as his basis
for imitation, but to his own 1596 or 1601 edition. This can clearly be
seen in the case of Massinisse's monologue in Act v of *Sophonisbe*; in
the 1596 version much of this is very close to Petrarch's original text;
by 1604, however, only lines C 1470–9[2] remind us clearly of his
original source.

(d) *Stylistic Details*

Here, as with the stock forms of 'set piece', it is almost impossible
to tie down individual sources. It is enough to say that Montchrestien
was writing in a series of traditions, each of which had its own stock

---

[1] Matthieu, *Aman*, Act iv.   [2] Fries edition.

imagery; and that the other aspects of his literary creation (sentence-form, metre, etc.) were equally bound by rhetorical or poetical proced-ures. The excellence of his dramatic poetry in no way depends on the originality of each image, just as the lyric poetry of a Ronsard or a Du Bellay does not gain its strength from the unusual in this sense. The means by which each poet in the sixteenth century gains his evocative power, his 'originality', is the use he makes of various traditional systems of imagery. All this we shall see in the chapter on Montchrestien's style.

What must be stressed is that the old game of 'source-hunting', by which scholars have so often traced the influence of one poet on another by means of certain common images, is meaningless in the sixteenth-century context. For if these images are common to these two men, they may well be common to many others as well. There was a common stock of imagery in this century, not merely in the collec-tions of *Epithetae* which are the equivalent, for images, of the col-lections of sententious *Flores*, but also, more spontaneously, in the common reading of many poets, and of certain poets in particular, by all men of learning. The poet, a man of erudition, would have read most of the important Greek and Latin literature; he would have read, too, Petrarch, Ariosto, and the Italians. The neo-Latin poetry of his own age would not have been neglected, and, by the time of Montchrestien, the works of the masters of the Pléiade themselves would be an import-ant part of this general cultural reading.

Small wonder, then, that the range of imagery was so wide, and that it yet remained within such narrow traditions. Small wonder that it is well-nigh impossible to trace an individual source for an image; for much of the imagery which is used by poets of the time must in fact flow from a subconscious stream of literary memory—truly converted *en sang et nouriture*. And the interest and excitement of the reader may well be caused by the unexpected way in which an image is used which also has vague memories for him. How much more so this must have been in the sixteenth century, when the audience's reading had prob-ably been as wide as the poet's!

In his methods of imitation, therefore, Montchrestien attaches him-self firmly to the traditions of sixteenth-century tragedy. He uses dramatic and historical sources as a means of providing a framework on which to place 'set pieces' for rhetorical elaboration; when he imitates a specific 'set piece', he closely follows its layout, using it in its turn as a framework for his own stylistic filling-out of the subject, just as he uses rhetorical exercises and other stock speech-patterns for the same purpose. And then, in the vast overflowing of linguistic enthusiasm involved in this stylistic elaboration, he pours out many traditional images which may or may not have been copied from specific sources, but which, while remaining part of the cultural heritage of the century, gain their originality from the way in which he uses them.

4. The Absence of Modern Dramatic Concerns

~~~~~~~~~~~~~~~~~~

T
HOUGH Montchrestien's plays were written for stage performance, the fact remains that their subjects were chosen more for
the opportunities they provide for the rhetorical elaboration
of 'set pieces' than for any dramatic purpose in the modern sense.
Classical techniques of exposition, dramatic *scènes à faire*, all are subordinated to stylistic purposes, and lose sight of their original aims, as
they do in the other writings of the century; similarly, because of the
traditions of Renaissance rhetoric, characterization of any coherent
kind is ignored, and the author's aim is a series of static depictions of
mood.

(a) *Exposition*

Classical models provide us with five main methods of exposition.
Of these five, however, one was used by Aeschylus alone, and was not
imitated by the tragedians of the Renaissance. This is the use of the
chorus by itself, which we find in *The Suppliant Maidens*, *The Persians*,
and *Agamemnon*. The other four methods were extensively followed by
sixteenth-century dramatists. They are:

(i) A monologue by somebody outside the action of the play, who
does not reappear. This person is usually supernatural, i.e. a god or
ghost. This type of exposition was popular with Euripides and Seneca,
but was not used by Aeschylus or Sophocles. The sixteenth century
used it a great deal, though the dramatists preferred to use ghosts rather
than gods. We find a ghost introducing Jodelle's *Cléopâtre*, Garnier's
Hippolyte, Matthieu's *Clytemnestre*, Claude Billard's *Polyxène* and
Alboin, and many other plays. Furies were popular; Garnier's *Mégère*,
which introduces *Porcie*, was the model for many others, including
that which opens Fonteny's *Cléophon*, and the *Tysiphone* which
introduces Billard's *Mérovée*. The advent of the Christian era had also
extended the scope for supernatural beings; we even find angels (in

Buchanan's *Jephthes* and P.M.'s *La Rocheloise*), and Satan (in Claude Billard's *Mort d'Henri IV*).

(ii) A monologue by one of the characters in the play. This procedure, too, was very popular with both Euripides and Seneca—in fact, most of their plays are prefaced by one or other of these first two varieties of exposition. This type is used a great deal by Renaissance dramatists; we find examples in Garnier's *Marc-Antoine* and Rivaudeau's *Aman*.

(iii) A dialogue, either between two of the protagonists, or between one of the main characters and a confidant. This is, above all, Sophocles's technique; six of the seven plays of his which have come down to us practise it (though in *Oedipus at Colonus* it contains no real exposition, as this is the second play of the trilogy). It is rarer in Euripides and Seneca, however (there is one example in each); in the tragedy of the Renaissance it is fairly common, though the dialogues usually start with a short monologue by the main character (as in Montchrestien). Examples are: Roillet's *Aman*, Mellin de Sainct-Gelays's *Sophonisbe*, Grévin's *César*, and many others.

(iv) A scene containing one of the protagonists and the chorus. This is an extremely rare form of exposition in classical tragedy, though we find an example of it in the *Rhesus* of Euripides, where Hector and the Chorus discourse on the situation as the play opens. There are occasional examples in Renaissance tragedy, one of them being the opening scene of Montchrestien's *Hector*.

The action of a Renaissance tragedy is so restricted by the Unity of Time that a full exposition would seem essential to an understanding of the plot; the tragedy starts *in medias res*, and it is necessary for the audience to know what has gone before. However, though such an exposition is usually given in the first tragedies of the French Renaissance, there gradually appears an indifference to this aspect of dramatic technique, which can only be explained by the fact that the authors, relying on the erudition of their audience, *presumed them to know the story already*. Following the example already set by Seneca, they use the old techniques of exposition *for a rhetorical purpose*, rather than for the purpose of conveying information. The original aim is forgotten, and we find long monologues which inform us of nothing, or which, if they do inform us of anything, do so in such an unintelligible way that one needs a previous knowledge of the story in order to understand what is being discussed. (One of the main rhetorical devices which tends to cause obscurity is, of course, the use of periphrasis.)

Thus the *Prophète* at the beginning of Garnier's *Juifves* tells us nothing except that the Jews are suffering a disaster which they have deserved; and the ghost of Thyestes, in Matthieu's *Clytemnestre*, though he tells us the story of Atreus and Thyestes, does so in such an obscure manner that anyone who does not already know the story would find it extremely difficult to understand.

Montchrestien follows this last tendency, relying on the knowledge of his audience. He makes use of all four types of exposition-scene which have been mentioned; but they are used purely for rhetorical ends. A comparison with true scenes of exposition will show how completely different Montchrestien's aims are. From time to time he does give us information, but only when this forms part of his other aims.

Let us look at each play in detail:

Sophonisbe. This play is on the same subject as Trissino's *Sofonisba* (1526). The shape of the play, act by act, is obviously based on Trissino. But within this shape, much differs, and especially the first act; here it is that we see the difference of Montchrestien's preoccupations.

The main aim, for Trissino, as for his free translators Mellin de Saint-Gelais (1559) and Mermet (1584), is to give us all the information possible. Not only does he tell us all that is necessary for an understanding of the play, but he also treats us to a long digression on the history of Carthage. This digression is included in Mermet's translation, but cut out by Saint-Gelais as an unnecessary *longueur*. The information, in all three cases, is related to Herminia, *who knows it already*. Nor is any new interpretation of the facts given here. (Thus, in Mermet's translation, we find the words: 'Or ie ne laisseray de te redire tout / Ce que desia tu sçais, de l'un a l'autre bout.')

The information is related by Trissino mostly in one very long monologue. Saint-Gelais, attempting to break this up to make it more acceptable on the stage, at the same time succeeds in making the scene even more *invraisemblable*; he puts half the story into Herminie's mouth, so that it is even more obvious that both the characters already know the story they are telling. Their speeches commence with phrases such as the following:

Sophonisbe: Et vous souvient bien . . .
Herminie: Il me souvient . . .
Sophonisbe: Il est ainsy . . .
Herminie: Et ce fut, ma dame, lors que . . .

But obviously, for these three authors, Trissino, Mermet, and Saint-Gelais, the exposition was of such importance that *vraisemblance* could go by the board.

Montchrestien, however, regards this first act as an opportunity for a 'set piece', or rather a series of 'set pieces': the lamentations of the queen, *lieux communs*, consolations of the nurse, description of a dream, discussion on dreams, etc. The way in which exposition is ignored shows his confidence in the erudition of his audience, their knowledge of Livy or of Petrarch; and the few references in this scene to events reinforce this impression, for they are off-hand references, with no attempt at explanation (1604 edition):

> Tu l'esprouues, Siphax. Car lors que tu pensois
> A ton orgueilleux sceptre assuiettir les Rois,
> Voici que la fortune infidele et soudaine
> Te rend captif aux fers de cette gent Romaine . . .

> Siphax iadis l'obiet des pensers de mon ame,
> Le suiet maintenant qui sans cesse l'entame;
> Helas où pensois-tu? . . .

> Mais trop innocemment à toy-mesme inhumain,
> Par mon nouueau conseil tu fis planche au Romain
> Qui l'Afrique a couuert d'enseignes Hesperides,
> Pour venir t'arracher le sceptre des Numides . . .[1]

> Madame, pensez-vous que l'Empereur Latin,
> Pour vaincre la Libye ait vaincu son Destin . . .[2]

There is no mention of Massinisse. The scene thus consists (in the 1604 edition) of (*a*) Sophonisbe's first monologue, of 104 lines (60 of which are marked *sententiae*); (*b*) The nurse's exhortation, 50 lines (16 *sententiae*), to be constant in misfortune; (*c*) Discussion of grief, 96 lines (59 *sententiae*); (*d*) Discussion on dreams, 20 lines (12 *sententiae*); (*e*) *Récit*, the dream, 62 lines. All these episodes are variations on stock themes. After this, we have the scene with the messenger, where the action of the play begins. He gives a long *récit* of the fall of Cirthe, and the entry of Massinisse.

Les Lacènes. At the beginning of *Les Lacènes* we hear *l'Ombre de Thericion*, who gives us a very confused account of the events up till now, so confused that we are completely lost unless we know our Plutarch well. The reason for this seems to be that Montchrestien,

---

[1] *P. de J.*, p. 117.   [2] *P. de J.*, p. 120.

attracted by the only set speech in Plutarch's text[1] which has even a
vague connection with the story of his play, has decided to put it in,
even though it takes place long before the action of the play. The ghost
is merely introduced to tell us what he once said to Cleomenes. Montchrestien again has no desire to give us any information, and thus
transcribes and paraphrases the speech without thought of clarifying
the facts. We are expected to know the story, to know who Thericion
is, that Antigonus was king of the Macedonians, and that he defeated
Cleomenes and the Spartans. All we are told of this is to be found in
the passage A 27–33, 38:

> Ou si ta qualité permet de recourir,
> A ceux qui maintenant te pourroient secourir,
> Et d'aller courtizer les mignons d'Alexandre;
> Encores vaut-il mieux librement s'aller rendre
> Au vainqueur Antigone, homme plein de valeur,
> Que d'un autre seruage accroistre ton malheur:
> Ce Prince aussi courtois après une victoire . . .
> . . . Te fera traitement sortable à ton merite.

Plutarch is here more comprehensible, when he refers to the 'succes-
seurs de Philippe et d'Alexandre', rather than the 'mignons d'Alexandre', for these events take place generations after Alexander's death.
No other explanation is given. In the 1604 text we hear of the 'mol
Ptolomée' to whom Cleomenes is having recourse. We are not told
why 'Ta mère est en Egipte'. (She had been sent there previously as a
hostage.) If unprepared, we are surprised by the line 'Va donc et les
anime à rompre leur seruage', for no explanation is given of where
Cleomenes and his followers are, or why they are enslaved. In Plutarch
all the facts are explained by the rest of the story around this speech;
in Montchrestien it stands alone, and the facts need explanation. In the
next scene, between Cléomène and Panthée, no further exposition is
given, though in the 1601 text there is a cryptic allusion:

> Nous pourrons à la fin mettre au sein de la mer
> La flotte qu'on promet à ton secours armer,

which becomes a little more clear in 1604:

> Attendant que l'on voye embarquer sur la mer
> La flotte, que pour vous l'Egipte veut armer.

---

[1] *Agis et Cléomène*, lxiii.

But as no explanation has been given of the equivocal position in which Cléomène stands in relation to Egypt, it would seem strange that this country should keep him prisoner, and at the same time promise to aid him with a fleet. The description of their plan of escape, which we find later, is another long passage copied from Plutarch. In Act v, Stratonice gives a description of the events in her love affair with Panthée. This is in no way part of the exposition, however. It has no bearing on the play, but is rather an added pathetic effect in the lamentations.

Aman. This play possesses an exposition. But we learn the information in it because it falls in with other plans of the author's. Montchrestien has realized, with Roillet (1556), that Aman is the tragic figure of the play. He therefore brings him on straight away, unlike Rivaudeau (1566) and Matthieu (1589), who start with a monologue by Mardochée, thus centring the attention on the sufferings of the Jews. However, where Roillet's Aman had exhaled his fury against Mardochée in the first 22 lines, Montchrestien's digresses on his own greatness (another *lieu commun*, and one of the favourite types of 'set piece' for Renaissance dramatists; there is a similar speech from Assuérus in the next act). In the course of this speech we learn that Aman is the king's right-hand man, and that nobody is greater than he. The flattery of his confidant, Cirus, raises him to even greater heights. The pride of the character has been fully shown; we have heard of the edict for all to bow before him; and now Montchrestien shows us his anger against the one man who refuses to bow to him, Mardochée, an anger so great that he wishes to destroy the whole nation of the Jews.

The whole act has thus been devoted to showing us the vanity of Aman. The confidant, instead of arguing with him, as does Roillet's 'Senex', makes him even more vainglorious, and the decision to destroy the Jews follows naturally. The sub-title of the play, *Aman ou la Vanité*, has already indicated what is to be Montchrestien's main theme in the play. The information (Aman's status, Mardochée's disobedience, his nationality) is thus given to us unintentionally. We are *not* told of Mardochée's relationship to Esther, nor the name of the king, nor what country we are in.

David. David's opening monologue describes his first view of Bethsabée, and his love for her. But this has been introduced for no other reason than to give (*a*) the picture of a man in love, (*b*) a description of a beautiful woman. No information is given to us other than that which falls in with these two designs, except a digression upon David's former exploits, to show us the change that has been wrought in him. The monologue can be divided thus: (*a*) Description of the effects of love on him; (*b*) His former exploits, and how he is changed; (*c*) A description of Bethsabée as he saw her in her bath (much longer in 1601 than in 1604); (*d*) How he fell in love with her; (*e*) The fact that he will give up everything for her. The only actual information given by this scene, nevertheless, is that he fell in love with her; no mention is made of any actual relationship. (The line 'Lors ie deuins Amant de cette belle Amante', in the 1604 edition, merely means that he fell in love with her, as we can see from the 1601 version of the same line: 'Las ie deuins Amant sans qu'elle fust Amante!'). We are thus surprised when, at the end of his speech, David refers to her as 'mon cœur', and then says:

> C'est sans doute Nadab, il a veu ma maistresse,
> Ie vay parler à luy . . .

and we are even more surprised when one of Nadab's first statements is:

> Elle est grosse sans doute, et ce poinct la tourmente.

No indication had been given of the long interval of time since David's first meeting with her.

An even more extraordinary thing is that we are not informed that she is married, until late in the scene:

> Las, voy ce ventre enflé de son germe Royal
> Ià prest de m'accuser à mon espoux loyal.

and it is later still that we hear her husband's name:

> Mande moy seulement ton corrival Urie.

The casual way in which these two facts are given, shows Montchrestien's lack of interest in exposition. We are not informed, either, who Urie is, though at the beginning of Act II we realize from his words that he is a soldier. The first act of this play, then, gives us most of the information we need, but almost by chance, and much of it long after we should have known it, and in such a way that it looks as though it was presumed that we knew it already.

La Reine d'Escosse. This play possesses a detailed exposition, with regard not so much to facts, as to their causes. Why is there this exception to Montchrestien's normal practice?

The most obvious reason, when taken in conjunction with what we have seen in the other plays, is that Montchrestien is imitating a 'set piece' of discussion and argument (between a Frenchman and an

Englishman), taken from Pierre Matthieu. Another reason could be to explain and justify the historical position to an audience which was bound to know the salient facts of the situation, but was less likely to know all the causes and stresses of it. Particularly Acts I and II might be designed to justify the attitude of Elizabeth; for in France most sympathies were naturally on the side of Mary, and Montchrestien may have felt it necessary to redress the balance a little. Thus we learn of Elizabeth's fear of Spain, and of civil strife; of her kind treatment of Mary, and Mary's ingratitude; and of the danger to the kingdom inherent in Mary's presence (we are given Mary's point of view in a later act, just as winningly presented). This favourable view of Elizabeth is, however, to be found in the source, Matthieu.

The only thing not mentioned is Mary's name; but she is described as 'mere d'un Roy, / L'espouse de deux Roys, et Reine comme moy'.

Most of the rest of the scene is a discussion of the traditional type upon the respective virtues of severity and clemency, with, however, various concrete references to the actual situation.

In the case of this play, then, the audience would have known the situation beforehand, mainly from one point of view. The author, by a fairly thorough exposition of motives, redresses the balance a little. But his main object, as in other plays, has been to produce a 'set piece', this time of argument, based on a specific model.

Hector. The scene between Cassandra and the Chorus, which opens this play, is merely an excuse for the poet to imitate her prophetic ravings, much of which are incomprehensible in relation to the plot. Her prediction of the fall of Troy has no connection with the plot of the play at all, except in so far as it helps to create an atmosphere of doom. Cassandra's speech has been introduced merely as a stock 'set piece', for which the connection of the play with the Trojan wars gives an opportunity. One fact we do, however, gain from this opening scene: the importance of Hector to the Trojans. The chorus say to Cassandra's predictions:

> Qu'en faut-il redouter? la main d'Hector nous garde.

Cassandra says:

> En fin meurt au combat qui par trop se hazarde,

to which they reply:

> Nul des chefs Argiens ne l'égale en valeur.

This is a preparation for the appearance of Hector, and establishes his importance.

Montchrestien's reliance on the audience's knowledge not only of the story of the play, but of the events of Greek and Trojan history, is shown by the following passage in which Cassandra and the Chorus refer obscurely to (*a*) Hercules' sack of Troy; (*b*) the causes for it (i.e. Laomedon's insult to Jason); (*c*) the cause of the present war of Troy (i.e. the rape of Helen); (*d*) a comparison between Paris carrying off Helen, and Thelamon carrying off Hesione (these events are all described by Dares the Phrygian):

Chœur: Encor il souuient bien aux Troyens outragez,
   Que du Tyran Hercule ils furent saccagez.
Cassandre: Ilion fut razé, grande et honteuse perte:
   Mais ce fut un malheur; la guerre estoit ouverte.
Chœur: Et pourquoy ceste guerre! il estoit grand besoin,
   Qu'un voleur vagabond l'apportast de si loin.
Cassandre: La faute est toute à nous, à nous aussi le blasme.
Chœur: Ores elle est aux Grecs armez pour une Dame.
Cassandre: Accusez en plustost vostre concitoyen.
Chœur: Que souffre le Gregeois qu'il n'ait fait au Troyen?
   Ce qui nous sera faute est pour luy priuilege?
Cassandre: Il ne commist iamais ni rapt ni sacrilege.
Chœur: Que l'une soit pour l'autre, ainsi le veut raison.
Cassandre: L'une fut prise en guerre, et l'autre en trahison.
Chœur: L'une vint de son gré, l'autre alla par contrainte.
Cassandre: Par l'une on viola l'hospitalité saincte.
Chœur: Et par l'autre on força tout droit d'honnesteté.
Cassandre: La victoire est ainsi pleine de liberté.
Chœur: Des butins de la guerre on excepte les femmes.
Cassandre: Les femmes du vulgaire et non pas les grand's Dames . . .

Montchrestien has, in his first acts, practised the various techniques for exposition used by the classical authors. Within these techniques, however, he has not produced exposition in the accepted sense of the term. He has used them, instead, for a series of 'set pieces'; what information is provided for the audience tends to appear only accidentally.

(b) *Lack of Dramatic Tension*

Dramatic tension in the modern sense was not the aim of Seneca; nor was it the aim of his imitators, the Renaissance dramatists. Their aim was the depiction of the effects of the tragic event, rather than its causes. Often the tragic event has already happened; usually it is fore-seen from the very beginning of the play.

Where a supernatural being is entrusted with the exposition-scene, he often foretells the outcome of the tragedy; an inexorable fate hangs over the characters. Thyestes, in Seneca's *Agamemnon*, foretells the tragic outcome of the play:

> Rex ille regum, ductor Agamemnon ducum,
> Cuius secutae mille vexillum rates
> Iliaca velis maria texerunt suis,
> Post decima Phoebi lustra devicto Ilio
> Adest—daturus coniugi iugulum suae.
> Iam iam natabit sanguine alterno domus:
> Enses secures tela, divisum gravi
> Ictu bipennis regium video caput.[1]

Similarly, in Euripides' *Hippolytus*, Aphrodite had foretold the manner of Hippolytus' death:

> Theseus shall know this thing; all bared shall be;
> And him that is my foe his sire shall slay
> By curses, whose fulfilment the Sea-king
> Poseidon gave to Theseus in this boon—
> To ask three things of him, nor pray in vain.
> And she shall die—O yea, her name unstained,
> Yet Phaedra dies.[2]

On the two occasions where supernatural beings appear in the tragedies of Montchrestien, they, too, predict the tragic outcome of the plays in which they figure. The ghost of Thericion, in *Les Lacènes*, foretells Cléomène's death:

> Ton terme vient bien tost, tu vas couper la trame
> De ses iours malheureux, et blasphemer le sort
> Qui ne voulut coupler ta desroute à ta mort.[3]

In *La Cartaginoise* the 'Furie' who appears at the beginning of Act III informs us that the happy love of Massinisse and Sophonisbe, which we have just seen, will not last; she foretells Sophonisbe's death:

> Du vainqueur glorieux i'abatray le courage;
> La Femme i'occiray par les mains de l'espoux,

---

[1] Seneca, *Agamemnon*, 39–46.
[2] Euripides, *Hippolytus* (Loeb translation), 42–8.
[3] *Les Lacènes*, Act I.

> Et l'Espoux meurtrira sa poitrine de coups
> Si fort desesperé qu'il luy prendra envie,
> De perdre avec sa femme et l'honneur et la vie.[1]

The outcome of these and the other plays, then, is never in doubt. Even so, dramatic tension might still in a sense be possible; and the occurrence of various *péripéties*, or sudden turning-points in the plot, might well seem to point to such a dramatic intention. Once again, however, the main intention is linguistic and rhetorical, the static portrayal of various moods.

The occasional *péripéties* which we find in these plays are not introduced for the sake of dramatic tension; this can be seen by the fact that the *péripétie* is often really a *quiproquo*, where only the characters are misled, and the audience realizes exactly what is happening.

For example, in *Les Lacènes* there is a false *péripétie*, where Cratesiclea and her women believe news which we know to be false. In Plutarch's life of *Agis and Cleomenes*, Cleomenes and Panteus agree to trick their guards by pretending that Ptolemy has agreed to let them free. No mention is made, however, of this false news having reached the women. Montchrestien's device in *Les Lacènes*, whereby the news does reach them, is therefore an original addition to his model. But it cannot have been added for the sake of dramatic tension, because we, the audience, know the news to be untrue. Why, then, has it been added? Surely, in order to depict the women in another mood. Montchrestien's technique of rhetorical elaboration of a mood is here given another opportunity; he can show Cratesiclea in joy as well as in despair. He can vary the tone of his dramatic verse. The whole *quiproquo* appears to have been designed to this end.

Another false *péripétie* is to be found in Act v of *Aman*. We, the audience, already know that Assuérus is intending to reward Mardochée:

> A qui donc dois-ie plus qu'à ce bon Mardochée . . .
> . . . Mais voy-ie pas Aman, ie veux par son conseil
> Decerner à ce Iuif un honneur nompareil.[2]

So it is only Aman who is deceived by the words:

> Di moy, mon cher ami, qu'est-il besoin de faire,
> Pour honorer quelqu'un par dessus l'ordinaire?

---

[1] *La Cartaginoise*, Act III; 1601 edition, p. 86.
[2] *Aman*, Act v; *P. de J.*, p. 270.

It is Aman's pride which deceives him, for he imagines that the question refers to him. This we gather from his first aside:

> Quelque triomphe neuf m'est encore apresté
> Et si l'on veut qu'il soit à mon chois raporté.[1]

His sudden fall is great, when, after suggesting extreme honours for such a man he hears the king say:

> Usez en donc de mesme et sans plus differer
> Au vieillard Mardochée . . .[2]

This scene is dramatic,[3] but the audience already know what the king is going to say.

The one true example of a *péripétie* in Montchrestien, which has been compared to Corneille's *Horace*, is to be found in *Hector*. Here Montchrestien misleads both the protagonists and the audience by the *récit* in Act IV, just as Corneille was to do in his play. All appears to have gone well, and Hector appears to have driven Achilles to flight; but in Act V another messenger appears, and we hear of Hector's death.

Is this *péripétie* introduced to increase dramatic tension, as those who compare it with *Horace* would suggest? From what we have seen in the case of the false *péripéties*, this would seem unlikely. Once again, it was probably introduced in order to give the author an opportunity to depict characters both in joy and in sorrow. Corneille's dramatic effect was of a different nature, and those who compare the two authors are being misled by seventeenth-century standards.

On the whole, then, dramatic tension is not one of Montchrestien's concerns. The whole of his dramatic technique is directed towards a depiction of the effects, rather than the causes, of the tragic event. And where, occasionally, there are mistaken glimpses of a happier outcome of the action, these are produced not so much for dramatic effect as in order to provide a change of tone amidst the 'set pieces'. Just as Garnier, in the last act of *Hippolyte*, inserts a chorus to change the tone, or, in *Les Juifves*, varies the tone with the premature rejoicings of the Hebrew women, so Montchrestien, within his plays, attempts to achieve a balance of moods. The plays are not just a series of 'set pieces'; each play, in itself, is a kind of mammoth 'set piece' in which diverse elements must balance.

---

[1] *P. de J.*, pp. 270–1. [2] Ibid.

[3] Two of the seventeenth-century versions of this scene are rather more dramatic, in that Du Ryer and Racine delay a little longer before revealing all to Aman.

(c) *Scènes à faire*

In the normal sense, the phrase *'scène à faire'* would be understood as meaning an opportunity for a dramatic situation or confrontation. In relation to Renaissance tragedy, however, it would be wiser to think of it as the opportunity for the production of contrasting, or even complementary, tirades; or as the opportunity for a series of stichomythic exchanges.

The unconcern for dramatic effect felt by most Renaissance dramatists is shown by the way in which obvious dramatic opportunities are missed. For example, in Garnier's *Marc-Antoine* the lovers never meet, and in Montchrestien's *Reine d'Escosse* the rival queens never have a chance to speak to each other personally. The potentialities of such a scene can be seen in Schiller's play on the same subject, *Maria Stuart*.

Montchrestien does, however, usually make use of the opportunities for *scènes à faire* which are offered to him by his sources; opportunities which were often neglected by those of his contemporaries who wrote on the same subjects. He gives us many of those scenes from the *Book of Esther* which his predecessor, Rivaudeau, had cut out, and in the play *Sophonisbe* he depicts the first meeting between Massinisse and Sophonisbe (a scene which was neglected by Montreux in his play, but possibly because he was using neither Livy nor Petrarch as his source).

But as has been said, the idea of a *scène à faire* is not necessarily dramatic. The confrontation of two characters may be merely an excuse for a series of static tirades; for rhetorical elaboration of dialogue, rather than for dramatic impact.

This is particularly the case in the Massinisse–Sophonisbe scene that has just been mentioned. In Mairet's play, to be published in 1634, this scene is extremely effective dramatically; here, in Montchrestien, it is merely an excuse for a series of tirades based on Petrarch, which express the hero's change of mood suddenly, and with very little subtlety. What matters to Montchrestien is the expression of the different moods, and not the change between them. He gives a similar treatment to the Scipion–Siphax scene, and to that between Massinisse and Scipion.

Scènes à faire to be found in the other plays include the Assuérus-Esther scene in Act IV of *Aman*, and the David–Urie scene in Act II of *David*. But again, the intention is not primarily dramatic.

(d) *Mood rather than Character*

The conception of tragedy as the *conprehensio* of the fortunes of heroes in adversity naturally allows the Renaissance dramatist far more scope for expansion and stylistic ornament than was to be permitted to his seventeenth-century counterpart. Racine seems to concentrate upon an acute depiction of psychological nuances; every line in his tragedies means something in relation to the tragic event which is to come; he has no time for elaboration. But the Renaissance tragedian, with the tragic event already explained, is concerned with a depiction of the emotions aroused by it; simple emotions, with none of the subtle changes of mood, none of the 'inner struggles' so typical of seventeenth-century tragedy. Montchrestien, like the others, is concerned above all with the rhetorical elaboration, within stylized forms, of simple, straightforward emotions—love, hatred, sorrow, resignation, etc.

As I have said, there are none of the subtle changes of mood within speeches which are to be found in later tragedy; but there *are* sudden changes of mood, violent, unexplained, in the characters during the plays; sometimes these changes may happen within the course of a single scene. In the past, much has been said about the faulty technique of the authors who produced such *invraisemblance*; should we not, instead of blaming their insufficiency, look to see whether they did not have some aim other than *vraisemblance*?

Let us take, as an example, the scene in Act II of Montchrestien's *La Cartaginoise*, where Massinisse falls suddenly in love with Sophonisbe at first sight during the course of the scene. No attempt is made by Montchrestien to depict the growth of this love, to give us any hint that it is about to blossom forth. Massinisse appears at the beginning of the scene, and gives thanks to the gods for his victory; Sophonisbe then appears, and greets him. Massinisse grants her request to speak to him, in a style that is reminiscent of Trissino's Masinissa; he is courteous, sententious, and cold:

> Vous pouvez librement, ma belle et douce dame,
> Déployer devant moy les desirs de vostre ame:
> Un Prince vertueux doit en toute saison
> Regler ses actions au compas de raison:
> Car qui lasche son cœur aux transports de son ire
> Est vassal de soy-mesme et Roy ne se peut dire.
> Ce doux vent qu'auiourd'huy le sort nous a soufflé
> Ne m'a point le courage outre mesure enflé,

> En ce poinct, Sophonisbe, au Soleil ie ressemble
> Que tant plus ie m'esleue et plus petit ie semble.[1]

Sophonisbe now proceeds with her speech of supplication. What is our surprise when, as she finishes it, Massinisse breaks out with an impassioned avowal of love!:

> Beauté Reine des cœurs dont les douces contraintes
> Rendent dedans les fers nos libertés estraintes,
> Dont les beaux mouvemens mariez à la voix
> Adouciroient le cœur des fiers hostes des bois,
> Sus arrachez ce dueil qui ternit vostre face,
> Et comme un noir nuage en obscurcit la grace;
> Rallumez les doux rais de ces deux clairs Soleils
> Qui produisent en moy des effets nompareils . . .[2]

He addresses Sophonisbe as 'ma mortelle Déesse', and says to her:

> Si i'ay tant mérité, soyez donques ma femme.

How can one explain this abrupt change of mood, and the lack of preparation for it? It can best be explained by the author's training in the rhetorical exercises, and particularly in that of *prosopopœia* (which was not peculiar to formulary rhetoric, but which found there its most stylized expression). It can also be explained by that close imitation of models which we have seen to be one of the characteristics of Renaissance creation.

Prosopopœia, or impersonation, was an exercise in the portrayal of mood. The student had to put himself completely inside a character, and imagine what he or she might have said under given circumstances; in other words, the student had to *become someone else* for the duration of the exercise.

These exercises were related to one moment of time, and to one mood. The titles of the examples in Lorichius's edition of Aphthonius's *Progymnasmata* show us this quite clearly:

Quartum exemplum, continens qualia verba dixerit Hecuba post excidium Trojanum.

Quintum exemplum, continens quae verba taurorum cornibus alliganda protulerit Antiope.

Sextum exemplum, continens quae verba Andromache captiva patrio solo everso, et marito occiso, potuisset dicere.

Septimum exemplum: quae dixerit Andromache, interfecto Hectore, etc.

---

[1] *La Cartaginoise*, Act II; *P. de J.*, p. 128.   [2] *P. de J.*, p. 131.

Each example, then, was a speech complete in itself. It was the expression of one mood, with no attempt at progression from mood to mood. The roundedness and stylization of the examples themselves in Aphthonius made them perfect models for imitation.

When it is used as the basis of a speech in literature, the *prosopopœia* retains these characteristics. In Livy and in Plutarch, the set speeches are compositions in mood, composed by the author, and historical only in so far as they attempt to recreate what the historical character *might* have said. Petrarch, in his *Africa*, copies and elaborates the speeches to be found in Livy. Montchrestien, in his *La Cartaginoise*, bases himself on these two writers, and proceeds to elaborate these speeches still further.

The sudden changes of mood to be found in Montchrestien are, then, typical of the outlook engendered by this rhetorical exercise. Each speech is complete in itself as an example of *prosopopœia*; in each a mood is depicted to the full; but the links between these moods are seen as unimportant.

The author is not interested in exploring the depths of psychological motivation; but this does not mean that his depiction of character is negligible. Within each static speech he attempts to portray a character under the stress of a particular mood; and in his differentiation between these characters and moods he is extraordinarily successful.

Scholl is wrong when he claims that every character speaks as the author:

Es sprechen nicht die auftretenden Personen, sondern der Dichter selbst redet zum Publikum. . . . Die Königin und ihre Dienerin oder der Henker, der tapfere Hektor und der einfache Bote —, sie alle bedienen sich mehr oder weniger derselben Ausdrucksweise. Dabei macht es auch keinen Unterschied, aus welchem Gebiete der Stoff zur Tragödie genommen ist . . .[1]

This is true only in so far as Montchrestien very rarely descends from the *style noble* which was considered suitable for tragedy. Apart from this, his characters speak very differently from one another. For Montchrestien, true to the needs of *prosopopœia*, has placed himself inside each character, in the position in which he finds himself. The ideas are different in each character, and the style naturally follows. Milton's words upon Aeschylus could apply to Montchrestien: 'We must not regard the poet's words as his own, but consider who it is that speaks in the play, and what that person says.'[2]

---

[1] Scholl, *Die Vergleiche in Montchrestiens Tragödien*, p. 66.
[2] Milton; Columbia edition, vii. 307. Quoted by Lemen Clark, *John Milton at St. Paul's School*, New York, 1948, p. 244.

The style of Renaissance authors often varies from character to character, and from mood to mood within the characters, for each situation might demand a different type of imagery. Thus the impassioned lover's speech will be full of Petrarchan imagery, the disillusioned lover's will use a completely different style (Garnier's Marc-Antoine wavers between the two). The Biblical prophets will use forceful, direct imagery, culled from the Bible, and Stoic martyrs will speak in different terms from Christian ones. As Miss Tuve says, when speaking about lyric poetry: 'Writers in this era do not talk about a style suitable to poetry; they talk about many poetic styles suitable to many poetic subjects.'[1]

Thus in Montchrestien, Nathan, berating David for his crime, speaks with the voice of a Biblical prophet:

> Transgresseur orgueilleux de la celeste loy . . .[2]

> O cruel adultère! ô vermisseau de terre![3]

In great contrast to the character of Nathan is that of the love-smitten king, Assuérus, in Act IV of *Aman*. He expresses himself in a *mélange* of Petrarchan and neo-Platonist imagery:

> Ce ne sont yeux aussi, mais deux Astres luisans
> Et l'heur et le mal-heur en mon cœur produisans,
> Qui d'un trait seulement me font mourir et vivre
> Et qui d'un seul attrait me forcent à les suivre;
> Bref qui tenans mon cœur en leur belle prison,
> Gouvernent maintenant à leur gré ma raison.
> Soit bénite à iamais ceste immortelle Idée,
> D'où ceste belle Grace au monde est procedée,
> Grace qui se ioüant peut surmonter les cœurs,
> Peut vaincre sans effort les plus braves vainqueurs.
> Aussi tous les parfums dont l'Assyrie est pleine
> Ne sentent pas si bon comme fait son haleine;
> Sa belle bouche aussi découvre en sou-riant
> Deux rangs bien égalés de perles d'Orient;
> Aussi le beau corail qui tient ces perles closes
> Fait honte au teint vermeil des plus vermeilles roses.[4]

Similarly, in *La Cartaginoise* and *La Reine d'Escosse*, the calm resignation with which the heroines face their death, though it may seem

---

[1] *Elizabethan and Metaphysical Imagery*, Chicago 1947.
[2] *David*, Act v; *P. de J.*, p. 230.
[3] *P. de J.*, p. 231.   [4] *Aman*, 1601 edition, A 1237–52.

so similar, is in fact brought about by completely different causes in each case. The difference between Stoic and Christian fortitude is underlined by the complete change of expression and imagery. Sophonisbe speaks simply; her Stoic phrases are unadorned:

> Mais bien, puis que le Ciel ordonne que ie meure,
> Il me fait un honneur que libre ie demeure,
> Sans que des fers honteux me rougissent le front.
> Possible un iour de moy les Numides diront
> Qu'une fin courageuse, une mort honorable,
> De ma vie innocente est l'acte plus loüable:
> La personne qui meurt gardant sa liberté,
> Trouve dedans la mort son immortalité.[1]

The Queen of Scotland, on the other hand, is upheld by her Christian belief in an after-life in heaven, rather than by a wish to remain immortal in the minds of men. Her speech is filled with ecstatic imagery:

> Puis qu'il faut tous mourir suis-ie pas bien-heureuse
> D'aller revivre au Ciel par cette mort honteuse?
> Si la fleur de mes iours se flestrit en ce temps,
> Elle va refleurir à l'éternel Printemps,
> Et la grace de Dieu comme une alme rosée,
> Distilera dessus sa faueur plus prisée,
> Pour en faire sortir un air si gratieux,
> Qu'elle parfumera le saint pourpris des Cieux . . .[2]

All this points to the fact that there was an accepted style for each kind of person, and, more important, for each kind of mood. Certain images came naturally to the author's mind when he was writing a certain kind of speech. This has relevance not only to the drama, but also to lyric poetry. How much of the poetry of this period was in fact written in this way, as an exercise in impersonation?

The drawback of practising the exercise of *prosopopœia* is, of course, that each speech stands on its own; often characters seem contradictory, for they speak in one way at one moment, and in another the next, with no explanation or description given of the change. One example of this is the first meeting between Massinisse and Sophonisbe, which has already been described. Massinisse is in one speech the courteous conqueror; in the next, the impassioned lover. Another is the scene of

---

[1] *La Cartaginoise*, Act v; *P. de J.*, p. 155.
[2] *La Reine d'Escosse*, Act v; *P. de J.*, p. 108.

David's repentance, in Act v of *David*. Nathan has only to speak of God's anger, and immediately David breaks out:

> I'ay péché contre toy, ma faute criminelle
> Ne merite rien moins que la mort eternelle.

This is the beginning, of course, of a long speech of repentance, which has been treated as though it stood entirely on its own; it is a paraphrase of Psalm 50. No attempt has been made to prepare us for this repentance.

The blame for such contradictions in character cannot, however, be laid entirely at the door of the rhetorical exercises. Certainly they created the climate in which such contradictions and *invraisemblances* were possible; but it would be equally easy, while practising such static creations of mood, at least to divide the various moods into different scenes, and avoid sudden clashes of mood within the same character on the stage. No, the added fact which, taken in conjunction with the attitudes induced by the rhetorical exercises, produced such scenes was, in fact, the Renaissance attitude to imitation.

The Renaissance dramatist tended to imitate 'set pieces' from his original sources, and to concentrate entirely on this imitation. And each 'set piece', in his eyes, was self-sufficient. Thus speeches which, in a historical source, had often been separated by explanation, and by other parts of the text, were, in a play, put next to one another. This, to modern eyes, makes certain scenes appear very *invraisemblable*.

In Montchrestien, further unlikely contradictions in his characters can be blamed on his blind following of his sources. *Vraisemblance* seems to have had no real importance or interest for him. Massinisse's sudden love for Sophonisbe, and his as sudden betrayal of her, seem to us most unlikely. Other dramatists tried to attenuate this *invraisemblance*. Trissino had tried to make his Massinisse more consistent in character (*a*) by his use of Appian, showing that Massinisse and Sophonisbe knew each other already, and had in fact been engaged; (*b*) by showing Massinisse strenuously opposing the arguments of Lelio and Scipione; and (*c*) by making Massinisse later repent of his fatal decision, and return, too late, to rescue Sophonisbe. Montreux, who was perhaps moving towards a seventeenth-century attitude to tragedy in this matter, created within his Massinisse a struggle between two opposing duties—that sworn to Rome, and that sworn to Sophonisbe. All his actions, being ruled by this struggle, were thus consistent. Montchrestien, however, used none of these solutions, because for him there was no problem. None of these things occurred in his sources, Livy and Petrarch; he therefore took the character as he found it with all its inconsistencies.

Montchrestien's outlook, like that of most other Renaissance dramatists, was ruled by the influence of the rhetorical exercise of *prosopopœia*. To express a single emotion, a single mood, in one speech; to place oneself inside a character for a single moment of time; to produce a speech rounded and complete in itself; all these aims of the rhetorical exercise tended to produce drama that was a series of 'set pieces' often unrelated to each other by anything but the general plot of the play. This explains the popularity of monologue in Renaissance drama; and it also explains why, in dialogue, the characters seldom seem to be listening to one another. Dramatic tension and characterization, two of the main attributes of modern drama, are not sacrificed, but ignored, in the pursuit of rhetorical ends; and other dramatic formulae, such as exposition scenes and *scènes à faire*, are put to far different uses than those which another century would tend to expect.

5. Lack of Concern with Non-Literary Matters

⚜

IN his concentration upon language and style, and upon the elaboration of certain themes within stylized forms, Montchrestien is typical of the tragedians of his day. In certain other respects, however, he is one of that small number who in fact devote themselves almost entirely to these linguistic and stylistic aims, and who avoid certain non-literary influences which might tend to detract from them. Many of the tragedians of the period, by overweighting their plays with such matters, destroyed that unity which French Renaissance tragedy demanded.

Two main mistakes had been the over-stressing of erudition through the introduction of long digressions which had no bearing on the play, and the intrusion of a polemical element, whether political or religious, into plays with a Biblical or contemporary subject.

Montchrestien avoids both of these mistakes; his erudition is diverted into other channels, his Biblical plays do not even solve for us the mystery of whether he was a Catholic or a Protestant, and his play on a contemporary subject takes care to present both sides of a very difficult problem. Indeed, despite certain claims that have been made, very little evidence is available in the plays as to any of Montchrestien's own personal opinions, and this being so, conjectures of any kind on this basis can only be dangerous.

(a) *The Absence of Erudite Digressions*

French Renaissance tragedy was created to appeal to a minority, an intellectual élite; in this it follows the Italian tradition, rather than that of the popular Spanish theatre. Minority appeal of this type was one of the guiding principles of the *Pléiade*, with whom so many of the early tragedians in the French language had close connections,[1] and whose

[1] e.g. Jodelle, Grévin, La Péruse, La Taille, Garnier, and even Théodore de Bèze, whose early poetic training had been in their company.

example was followed extensively later in the century. The case for this policy is stated by Joachim du Bellay in his *Deffence et illustration de la langue françoyse*: '. . . Seulement veux-ie admonester celuy, qui aspire à une gloire non vulgaire, s'eloingner de ces ineptes Admirateurs, fuyr ce peuple ignorant, peuple ennemy de tout rare, et antique sçavoir: se contenter de peu de Lecteurs a l'exemple de celuy, qui pour tous auditeurs ne demandoit que Platon . . .'

The minority at whom the tragedies were aimed consisted mainly of scholars, university audiences, and those members of the nobility who had some humanist education. The audience could be presumed to appreciate not only the new treatment of a story they knew well, but also the skilful use which the author made of classical techniques, both dramatic and rhetorical. Mythological references would be understood, quotations and borrowings recognized, variations of the rhetorical forms appreciated. Audience and author were on the same level of learning.

The stress upon erudition did, however, at times lead to abuses. The worst of these was the type of erudite digression which had no connection whatsoever with the theme of the play or, at most, a tenuous one. Such digressions spoil the shape of the play altogether, as did the religious digressions in some of the Protestant tragedies. It is above all in the weaker playwrights, however, that such digressions occur.

Montchrestien, like Garnier, is remarkably free of them. This does not mean that he is lacking in erudition; far from it. The sources which he uses for his plays denote a fairly wide knowledge. Plutarch,[1] Livy,[2] Homer,[3] Dares the Phrygian,[3] and Seneca[4] he could have read in translation. But he knew enough Latin to read Petrarch's *Africa*[5] and probably Roillet's *Aman*. He almost certainly read Trissino in Italian.[6] Among French writers, he had read Du Bartas,[7] Montaigne,[8] and Garnier.

A reading of his *Traicté de l'œconomie politique* shows us a wide acquaintance with the ancient philosophers and historians, and with classical mythology. (Though one must not exaggerate the knowledge which his quotations and references imply; to a certain extent they

---

[1] For *Les Lacènes*.　　　　[2] For *Sophonisbe*.　　　　[3] For *Hector*.
[4] *Passim*.　　　　　　　　　　　　　　　　　　　　[5] For *Sophonisbe*.
[6] For *Sophonisbe*. Fries, in the Introduction to his edition (Marburg 1886) shows that Montchrestien bases himself on the original Italian rather than on the French translations.
[7] For *David*, Chorus to Act II.
[8] For *Les Lacènes*. See G. E. Calkins in the Introduction to her edition (Philadelphia 1943).

could be explained by the use of one of the compendia of quotations popular at the time, and much of his other knowledge might come from works of reference, such as Charles Estienne's *Dictionarium historicum geographicum et poeticum*.) He quotes, among others, from Homer, Euripides, Hesiod, Plato, Aristotle, Thales, Xenophon, Suetonius, etc., and gives many evidences of his erudition upon such diverse subjects as navigation, canal-building, and the history of France. His digressions on more modern history, and especially upon the Indies, show a very competent knowledge, and some original ideas, upon the subject.

In this *Traicté* he makes long digressions of the type which he avoids in his plays. In the manner of Montaigne, he is continually wandering from his subject, and having to return abruptly with such phrases as: 'Je m'emporte hors des lices: reprenons le droict fil, et commençons comme par un autre chef.'[1] There are 35 pages of digression upon the history of navigating nations, 20 pages on the history of France, etc. Why, then, is his attitude so different in the plays? First, because prose writing had no fixed form at the time, whereas tragedy, with its concentration on form, could be destroyed by the overweighting of any one part. Secondly, because anything unconnected with the main theme of the play, or the moods it aroused, would detract from the audience's concentration on form and style.

Erudition is not lacking in Montchrestien's plays; the almost complete lack of exposition shows that the audience was expected to know the story already; the use of the larger rhetorical forms, and also of the tropes and figures, shows the author to have had a thorough rhetorical education; and the comparative lack of mythological references does not mean that the author is turning away from such obscurity, but merely reflects the trend of the time away from mythology and towards more concrete imagery from nature.

But there are no such digressions as we find, for example, in Rivaudeau's *Aman*. Here the chorus, telling Simeon of the banquet during which Vasthi was disgraced, describes at great length the tapestries on the wall of the banqueting-hall, which described scenes from Persian history. The monologue which opens the same play is a lesson in Jewish history.

In Act I of Trissino's *Sofonisba* there is an extensive digression upon Carthaginian history, in which we hear of Dido, of Hannibal, of the battle of Lake Trasimene, etc.

[1] p. 84.

The very few digressions which are to be found in Montchrestien all have close reference to the plot. Some are used for pathetic effect, to show the full tragedy of a character's life: these are the story of the death of Andromache's parents, told in Act I of *Hector*; the story of Queen Mary's past life, in Act III of *La Reine d'Escosse*; and the story of the love of Stratonice and Panthée, told by Stratonice in Act V of *Les Lacènes*. The others are used to contrast a person's former virtue with his present vice: *David*, Act I ('Suis-ie ce grand David . . .') and *La Cartaginoise*, Act IV (in Scipion's speech to Massinisse). These all have relation to the actual characters in the play. As will be seen later, many of these passages were introduced according to the needs of a rhetorical 'set piece'.

Montchrestien never made use of erudite prefaces as did some of the other playwrights of the century. With some of them, erudition runs completely amok. Rivaudeau and Matthieu, for example, in their plays on the subject of *Aman* and *Vasthi*, both devote long prefaces[1] to the difficult subject of finding out which king of Persia Assuérus was; their conclusions differ entirely. They each mention innumerable sources for their conclusions. Rivaudeau includes Thucydides, Herodotus, Josephus, Plutarch, Justinus, Philo, Zonaras, Sebastien Münster,[2] Ian Sleidan,[3] Carrio.[4] Matthieu has, among his sources, Thucydides, Herodotus, Diodorus Siculus, Strabo, Sulpicius, Clement of Alexandria, Tertullian, Justinus, Philo, Julius Africanus, Saint Jerome, Orosius, Isidore, Bede, Annius,[5] and Driedo.[6] What is the result of all this scholarship? Matthieu says, of Artaxerxes Mnemon: 'C'est celuy que nous cherchons, et qui fut le mary d'Esther, en l'histoire de laquelle on le nomme Artaxerxes.' Rivaudeau, writing over 20 years before Matthieu, had, however, claimed that Artaxerxes was the king in question. He throws scorn at those who believe in the claim of Artaxerxes Memnon:

I'ay cuidé passer soubz silence la miserable ignorance de ceux qui donnent ce discours à Artaxerxe Mnemon, arriere-fils du nostre . . . et encores le dis-ie à regret pour sentir en le comptant, la honte de celuy qui l'a pensé. C'est

[1] Rivaudeau, Preface to *Aman*, 1566. Matthieu, *Abrégé de l'Histoire des Roys de Perse, pour sçavoir quel fut Assuere* (before *Vasthi*), 1589.

[2] Sebastien Münster: Renaissance scholar, known as the German Strabo, d. Basle 1552.

[3] Ian Sleidan: Renaissance scholar, 1505–56.

[4] Carrio: Renaissance scholar, described by Scaliger as 'ce bougre larron de Carrio' (*Scaligerana*, p. 44).

[5] Annius: Giovanni Nanni, 1432–1502.

[6] Driedo: Jean Dridoens, a Belgian theologian, d. 1535.

abuser des lettres et des Muses et de la patience des hommes quand on tre-
busche si laidement et si deshonnestement!

These writers have gone to a great deal of trouble for little purpose.
The identification of Assuérus has little bearing on the play and its
problems.

As Montchrestien's plays were intended for performance, *arguments*
to the scenes, such as one finds for example in Matthieu, were of no use
to him. Many of Matthieu's *arguments* are of an erudite nature, e.g.
(from *Vasthi*): 'Toute ceste Scene est comme une Assueropedie, ou
institution du Roy . . .', 'L'academie des sages de Grece disoit qu'il
convenoit obeir aux Princes, ceder aux grands, et obtemperer aux Lois,
Vasthi ne fait ny l'un ny l'autre . . .', '. . . armee de deux sortes de
larmes que les Pythagoriens donnent aux femmes . . .', etc. In his contemporary play, *La Guisiade*, Matthieu describes in great detail the
hall in which the *États-généraux* actually took place, taking a page or
more to do so.

Such displays of erudition do not interest Montchrestien. His preoccupation is with language and rhetorical style, and with the stylized
forms into which it can be poured. His plays *are* erudite, but only in so
far as this does not interfere with his conception of dramatic construction.

(b) *The Absence of Polemical Writing in the Biblical Plays*

When one considers the subject-matter of three of Montchrestien's
six plays, i.e. *La Reine d'Escosse*, *David*, and *Aman*, the absence of
political or religious polemic is astounding; in a century of strong and
violent feelings, Montchrestien stands above factions; so much so, that
it is still a matter of doubt as to what his beliefs actually were.

However, a closer look at the religious drama of the century makes
Montchrestien's position much clearer. In those tragedies where polemic
has any large part, there usually results a neglect of dramatic form, of
balance, and of stylistic concern. Montchrestien was, as we shall be
seeing, concerned above all with tragedy as an art, aimed at the *illustration* of the language by various rhetorical and poetic means. And,
like the two other great writers of religious tragedy in this century, La
Taille and Garnier, he does not allow polemic to mar these aims.

Seidmann[1] divides the religious tragedy of this period into two main

[1] 'La Bible dans les tragédies religieuses de Garnier et Montchrestien', unpublished
Sorbonne D.U.P. thesis, p. 3.

groups: (a) 1551–83, the Protestant attack (stopped by the decree of the *Synode de Figeac* in 1579, which condemned biblical drama); (b) 1583–1601, the Catholic reply. The exactness of these divisions is shown, he says, by the presence of only two Catholic Old Testament plays in the first period,[1] and only one known Protestant biblical play in the second.[2]

As Seidmann states, the Protestant biblical drama had three main aims: to attack the Catholic adversary, to instruct morally, and to convert. Of these three aims the first had the most importance, and was expressed partly by attacks on the clergy, or the monks. Des Masures's Satan, for example, and Bèze's Satan (as a monk), both satirize the clergy and the religious orders. At the same time, reference is usually made to the small number of the elect, and to the difficulties they face. Thus Des Masures's Satan says:

> Ainsi fay-je, et feray qu'à estimer le prise
> Des Saints, encontre ceux que j'ay et auray pris,
> Le nombre des eleus seulement soit et vaille
> Un petit de grain, sous un grand tas de paille . . .[3]

The militant nature of this early Protestant drama led to a certain neglect of classical dramatic form. The plays of Bèze, Des Masures, Coignac, and La Croix hold in them much of the *mystère*: though much of this is due to the unbalancing effect of polemic, which has already been mentioned, it is nevertheless true to say that there was also, on the part of some of these writers, a conscious reaction against the forms bequeathed by pagan classicism.

In Coignac's *Desconfiture de Goliath*, and in La Croix's *Daniel*, Goliath and Nebuchadnezzar obviously represent the Pope, and the whole play is devoted in each case to an attack on the papacy, as is Philone's *Josias*.

On the other hand, a far more balanced, classical approach is shown by Jean de la Taille in his plays *Saül le furieux* and *La Famine*. There is no trace of polemical writing, and the author can concentrate fully on the construction of the play. Certain critics have, it is true, suggested that La Taille expresses specifically Protestant views in this play, by portraying Saul, the man deserted by grace. It is far more likely, however, that he saw in Saul the classical model of the man pursued by fate. The import of this play is not noticeably Christian; and little

---

[1] Adrien d'Amboise's *Holopherne*, Chantelouve's *Pharaon*.
[2] Philone's *Adonias*.   [3] *David Triomphant*, 585–8.

differentiates it, or its sequel, *La Famine*, from the tragedies of the time on secular subjects. Indeed, it is as much a secular subject as Montchrestien's *Aman* or *David*.

Between these two extremes lies Rivaudeau, whose play *Aman*, while constructed on a classical model, contains a certain amount of polemical writing.

Seidmann[1] and Loukovitch both insist that the Catholic theatre began with a *coup de maître* in 1583, Garnier's *Les Juifves*. The work is certainly a masterpiece, and Garnier, in his Preface, does ask us to draw a lesson from his work. We see God's terrible vengeance on the Jews who have abandoned their religion:

> Or vous ay-je icy représenté les souspirables calamitez d'un peuple qui a comme nous abandonné son Dieu. C'est un sujet délectable, et de bonne et saincte édification. . . . La prérogative que la vérité prend sur le mensonge, l'histoire sur la fable, un sujet et discours sacré sur un profane, m'induit à croire que ce traitté pourra préceller les autres . . .[2]

But the play itself does not reflect a polemical motive. It is a perfectly constructed classical play, and its plot, though taken from the Bible, is typical of secular tragedy. (Indeed, the subject may well have been chosen for its similarity to *The Trojan Women*.) Its characters speak in Biblical language, because they are Biblical characters; *prosopopœia* would demand as much. Polemic, as such, does not impinge upon the play itself; and Dr. Jondorf would appear to be right in her statement that 'Garnier is a "committed" artist, not to the extent of supporting a body of doctrine or partisan opinion, but in so far as he intends his plays to provoke some serious reflections on serious problems'.[3]

The Catholic plays which followed this contained much polemic, and were correspondingly at times irregular or unbalanced as plays. They had, as Seidmann says, the aims of 'combattre l'hérésie et enseigner la morale'. The authors concerned are Matthieu, Perrin, Virey, Ouyn, and Behourt.

Montchrestien, in his plays, *Aman* and *David*, shows no signs of attacking any political or religious faction; this is all the more surprising when one considers one of the two subjects he has chosen. *Aman* is one of the most suitable subjects for religious propaganda (the chosen people who are trodden underfoot, the king who puts his trust in evil counsellors, etc.). Thus Rivaudeau's play on this subject contains violent attacks on kings and priests, and encouragements to the chosen

---

[1] Op. cit., p. 4.   [2] Ed. Hervier, p. 2.   [3] Jondorf, p. 190.

people; Matthieu, the *ligueur*, on the other hand, found the message *he* sought in the same subject:

... Qui dira que ceste Tragedie composee en un siecle tragique soit à tort dediee à ceux qui sans masque et dissimulation se representēt auec tant d'autres sur le theatre de la France, pour faire veoir la prodigieuse *Tragedie du Schisme, du Discord, de la Desloyauté, de l'Heresie, quatre monstres cruels*, qui ensanglantent la Scene tant esleuee de ceste iadis tant florissante Monarchie?
... la malheureuse fin *d'un Prince*[1] *qui d'un pernicieux conseil charmoit iadis l'entendement d'un Roy* Payen, et disposoit de son authorité, selon la passion de son traistre et ambitieux esprit, *coniurant d'extirper l'union du peuple de Dieu*[2] ...[3]

The whole play, for Matthieu, is an attack on royal favourites, and particularly on d'Espernon, who had persuaded the king to denounce the *ligue*; the evils caused by heresy are stressed throughout the play.

Montchrestien's *Aman* contains nothing in the way of a political or religious message; he does not appear to have had any parallels in mind when describing the fate of the Jews, or the vanity of Aman, and we must take it that no such reference was intended. The theory that Montchrestien is here denouncing the Massacre of Saint Bartholomew has many times been denied, and rightly so; for there is nothing in the play to indicate this.

Though David had been used as a hero for plays by Des Masures, Coignac, and La Taille, the episode from his life shown in Montchrestien's play seems to have little value for a polemical attack.

While there is no polemical intention in these two plays, there also appears to be no specifically religious appeal in the choice of the stories. The book of Esther itself has two blemishes, the lack of a religious element, and the apparent delight in the wholesale slaughter of the Gentiles. Lods says of it: 'On ne peut se défendre d'une impression pénible en lisant ces pages consacrées à la glorification de la vengeance et des haines nationales. Le caractère de tous les héros du livre présente des côtés douteux et franchement antipathiques.'[4]

This book, despite these religious blemishes, contains one of the most pure examples of *hybris*, of the fall of a character through

---

[1] Presumably a parallel with d'Espernon. See Matthieu's *Guisiade*, written in the same year.
[2] The *ligue*.
[3] *Aux nobles et illustres consuls et escheuins de la ville de Lyon* (Preface to *Aman*). My italics.
[4] Lods, *Histoire de la littérature hébraïque et juive*, Paris 1950, p. 793 (quoted by Seidmann, p. 120).

overweening pride. For Montchrestien, the most important character is Aman, not Esther; the very title of the play, *Aman ou la Vanité*, shows us this, and Aman appears at the very beginning of the play. The first two acts are entirely devoted to him, and it is he who opens Act v. The middle of Act v is devoted to his first abasement, when he is forced to honour Mardochée; the end of the act is devoted to his final fall. The whole play, then, is planned to bring out to the full this message of the fall of vanity; Act III is the only act in which any specifically religious message is revealed, and in it Montchrestien is merely following the Bible. (He adds Mardochée's prayer from the Apocrypha, and a paraphrase of Psalm 78, but these appear merely to have been added as suitable 'set pieces'.) This act might seem necessary for the explanation of the action, of the intervention of Esther which is to bring about Aman's downfall; but it is also there for the sake of the 'set pieces' it provides. Act IV shows the influence of Esther's beauty on the king, and prepares the dénouement. In this play Montchrestien, by following the Bible, has given an essentially pagan impression; Racine, in his version, manages to add a Christian outlook.

In the same way, the title *David ou l'Adultere* clearly shows the aim of the author; we are to see the pernicious effect of love upon a king.[1] 'Si Faguet croit que le poète n'a pas eu la main heureuse dans le choix de ce sujet', says Seidmann, 'il faut lui donner raison si l'on considère qu'en développant cet épisode dans un drame, Montchrestien n'a pas su donner un caractère religieux à la pièce.'[2]

Rather than being the depiction of one of the elect fallen from grace, as the Preface would have us believe, this play is a picture of the great man destroyed by love, like Garnier's *Marc-Antoine*. The first four acts are almost pagan, while the religious element in the last act would seem to have been introduced because a prophet such as Nathan *should* produce a religious message. In other words, the practice of *prosopopœia* demanded it and there was a source for it. (This religious message, based on 2 Samuel 12 : 13–15, contains the death sentence of David's child for its father's fault.) In Act I, David realizes that he has been invaded by love. But there is no question of guilt, he does not feel that he would be better, and return to grace, if he suppressed his love; but rather that without it he would be lost. His consideration of it is pagan rather than Christian.

---

[1] The subject may also have been chosen from the purely sexual and sensational aspect, as, for example, were *Amnon et Thamar* and *Sichem Ravisseur*.
[2] Op. cit., p. 793.

In these early acts, if the message of a fall from grace, rather than the pagan theme of destruction by *eros*, was intended, surely the chorus should have conveyed it to us? However, the first chorus is on the force of love, the second a paraphrase of du Bartas on the institution of marriage, etc. In the play itself there is a passage of purely pagan *stichomythia* between David and Nadab.[1] David does not hang back from his crime for religious reasons, but from respect for law; here are his speeches from the *stichomythia*:

> Les loix n'accordent point cette licence aux Rois.
>
> Un legitime Roy selon elles doit viure.
>
> S'il veut se dispenser à commettre du mal,
> Le mesme à son exemple osera son vassal.
>
> Ce que l'on ne craint faire en autruy condamner,
> Est-ce pas contre soy le mesme arrest donner?
>
> Mais occir son ami, son fidele suiet,
> Ce n'est un coup de Prince, ains de tyran abiet . . .

The religious nature of Act v comes to us as a surprise. In following the Bible Montchrestien may have found such an ending necessary.

As well as being un-partisan, Montchrestien's religious plays are therefore essentially un-religious. He appears to have chosen from the Bible two stories which contain a classical tragic hero, and he deals with them from this aspect, including a religious element only where the Biblical story demands it.

(c) *Political Impartiality: La Reine d'Escosse*

The impartiality of Montchrestien in *La Reine d'Escosse* is even more unusual, for this subject would seem most eminently suited for polemic of some kind or another. Plays on contemporary subjects are rare in the sixteenth century; and when they do appear, the content is in almost every case political. Chantelouve's *Colligni*, Belyard's *Guysien*, Matthieu's *Guisiade*, Nérée's *Triomphe de la Ligue*, Brinon's *Tragédie des Rebelles*, and others, all take contemporary situation sand use them for an attack upon one or other of the groups, political or religious, of the time. The only play upon a contemporary subject which does *not* have such a political content is Roillet's *Philanire*,[2] which does not deal with the great, but with ordinary people.

---

[1] *David*; P. de J., pp. 215–16.
[2] Bounin's *La Soltane*, though contemporary, is distant in place.

Matthieu, in the third edition of *La Guisiade*, shows his political leanings by the very dedication 'au tres-Catholique et tres-genereux Prince, Charles de Lorraine, protecteur et Lieutenant general de la Coronne pour le Roy tres-Chrestien *Charles X*, par la grace de Dieu Roy de France'. In the 'Discours sur le suiet de ceste Tragedie', he says:

> L'Enuieuse ialousie qu'Henry troisiesme Roy de France et de Pologne, portoit aux genereuses entreprises, et heureuses proüesses d'Henry de Lorraine, Duc de Guise, se changea en telle rage et despit, que le succes de ceste Tragedie monstre . . .

Most of this 'Discours' is devoted to the question of perfidy (and of Henri III's in particular). The play itself is an attack on the King and on his favourite d'Espernon of whom Matthieu says in the Argument to Act III:

> Le Poëte à contre-cueur fut contraint de mettre entre la Majesté et la grandeur de ceux qui ioüent ceste Tragedie, un homme de si petite valeur qu'est d'Espernon; mais l'opinion que tout le peuple de France a tres asseuree de ses deportemens, et qu'il alluma sur tous le Roy à ceste sanglante deliberation contre la maison de Lorraine, l'a fait entrer en ce troisiesme acte, côme un desesperé, un sorcier, auec toute sa daemonomanie . . .[1]

D'Espernon even seems to share the author's opinion of him, for his first words are:

> I'ay bien ce don du ciel d'estre né d'un bon pere:
> Mais ie n'en vaus pas mieux, car trop ie degenere
> De l'ayeule vertu, et ie ne voy en moy
> Des Nobles Nogarets, ny l'honneur ny la foy . . .[1]

But in case his message is not conveyed by the text itself, Matthieu devotes the whole 'Argument' at the beginning of Act IV, a page and a half,[2] to a long contradiction of the arguments he will be putting into the mouths of the king's advisers. Accusations of perfidy, of murder, of anti-Catholicism, are hurled throughout the play at Henri III, who was still alive when the first edition of the play appeared.

This one play is but one example of the polemical use to which such plays on contemporary subjects were put; it is typical of all the others. Thus Chantelouve's *Colligni* (1575) is made to exclaim:

> Je demande à part moi de renverser la Foi
> Du Pape et de Calvin et fuyant toute Loi

[1] p. 35.   [2] pp. 61–2.

> Qui vueille retenir ma main sous son empire,
> Moi seul exempt de Loi, estre Roy je desire.
> Je feins d'estre bien fort Chrestien Réformé
> Pour mieux surprendre ainsi nostre Roy désarmé.[1]

In Belyard's *Le Guysien, ou Perfidie tyrannique commise par Henry de Valois* (1592), Henri III is described as 'ce meurtrier, . . . ce perfide Heretique'. Nérée's *Triomphe de la Ligue* (1607) is a Protestant, anti-*ligueur* pamphlet. An interesting point is the mention of Marie Stuart in Act IV. Fonteny's *Cléophon* (1600) is Royalist and Catholic. Billard's *Henri IV* is Catholic, but devoted mainly to a mourning of the great king, and a praise of the queen as the new regent. Brinon's *Tragedie des Rebelles* (1622) and P.M.'s *La Rocheloise* (1629) are both directed against the rebels.

The death of Mary Stuart was a most burning question in the Catholic–Protestant controversy, especially in France, where her mother's family had inspired some of the plays that have just been described. It seems incredible that Montchrestien should have chosen this subject, if he had no interest in politics; yet he seems to regard the subject primarily as providing an example of a Stoic death,[2] and also as a tragedy of fate rather than of human malice. Certainly he deals with the subject completely impartially, going out of his way to provide us with a full description of Elizabeth's reasons for the execution.

Another play in which Mary Stuart's name appears is Nérée's *Triomphe de la Ligue* (1607), in which Visteie, 'harengueur seditieux' (a Jesuit), and Giesu, 'Roy imaginaire' (Guise), mourn her death (Act IV); the picture given of her is that of a political intriguer. Another possibility for a playwright would have been to make of her a martyr.

However, in Montchrestien, we are given in full both Catholic and Protestant points of view, and both are shown to a certain extent to be wrong. For though the subject may originally have been chosen for its truly tragic end, the detail with which we are shown the complications of the political scene at the beginning (which is a departure from the author's usual custom) might well seem to denote a positive attempt on the author's part to show that the blame could be equally divided. But, as we have already seen, this balanced discussion is based on imitation of a 'historical' source, Matthieu, so the author's aims are not

---

[1] Act I.
[2] Cf. Du Vair on Mary's death, Oraison 31 (quoted by Willner, p. 27): 'Mais si en ceste horrible tragedie nous avons quelque enseignement de l'inconstance et vicissitude des choses humaines, nous avons une beaucoup plus profitable instruction et consolation en l'admirable patience et incomparable constance de ceste Royne.'

necessarily justice to both sides, so much as imitation of a suitable source of political discussion. Be the reasons what they may, Montchrestien's play is nevertheless free not only of polemic, but also of any kind of *parti pris*.

Elizabeth starts by deploring her position, 'exposée au danger / Du prison domestique et du glaiue estranger . . .'.[1]

The sword of Damocles is continually hanging over her head; the kingdom is in perpetual danger from Spain:

> L'Espagnol non content de son Monde nouueau,
> Veut son Throsne en ce lieu planter sur mon Tombeau.
> Où la force ne vaut l'artifice il employe
> Pour remettre ma vie et mon Estat en proye . . .[2]

It is this background of danger which explains the attitude of Elizabeth, and even more so that of her *Conseiller* and her people, who persuade her to do the deed she dreads. For, as the *Chœur des Estats* points out in Act II, Mary presents another danger from within:

> Voyez l'esclat brillant des cuirasses Françoises,
> Escoutez les tambours des bandes Escossoises,
> Et les pifres d'Espagne; aujourd'huy son danger
> Suscite tout le monde, et pour la dégager
> On va couurir la mer de voiles et de rames,
> Emplir nos riches ports et de fer et de flames,
> Cependant parmi nous ce tison consommant
> Ira de tous costez les Ligues allumant,
> Et la peste mortelle enclose en nos mouelles
> Causera plus de mal que les guerres cruelles.[3]

The whole tragedy is based on a fatal misunderstanding; Elizabeth, in Acts I and II, and Mary, in Acts III and IV, say things about each other which are mutually contradictory; the fact that they never meet heightens this effect of misunderstanding.

Elizabeth complains of Mary's plots against her, after her kindness:

> Quoy que de sa prison l'ennuyeuse longueur
> Peust un iuste courroux allumer en son cœur;
> Par mon doux traitement elle deuoit l'esteindre,
> Se plaignant en son mal de ne s'en pouuoir plaindre:
> Mais l'on m'a rapporté qu'en ce dernier effort,
> Elle brigue mon Sceptre, et minute ma mort.
> Seroit-ce donc l'amour, Ame ingrate et legere,
> Que me iuroit sans fin ta bouche mensongere?[4]

[1] B 3–4.   [2] B 19–22.   [3] B 477–86.   [4] B 47–54.

She claims[1] that Mary is aiming at the destruction of England and the massacre of its inhabitants.

But in Mary's attitude we find, instead of rebellion, resignation. The words 'l'on m'a rapporté' in the passage above, seem to show the basis of the misunderstanding. Each fears the other, and misjudges her. Elizabeth judges Mary as inhuman and perfidious:

> O cœur trop inhumain pour si douce beauté,
> Puis que tu peux couuer tant de desloyauté,
> D'enuie et de despit, de fureur et d'audace,
> Pourquoy tant de douceur fais-tu lire en ta face?[2]

In reply, Mary speaks of the cruelty and perfidy of the English:

> Peuple double et cruel, dont les suprémes loix
> Sont les loix de la force et de la tyrannie,
> Dont le cœur est couué de rage et felonnie,
> Dont l'œil se paist de meurtre et n'a rien de plus cher
> Que voir le sang humain sur la terre espancher.[3]

All this, after Elizabeth's hesitation at spilling blood! The misunderstandings go still deeper, when the *Conseiller* refers to Mary as 'homicide, . . . femme meschante . . ., desloyale', without any contradiction from Elizabeth, who merely remarks that 'elle est hors de nos loix', and only to be ruled by God. Mary calls upon her husband's spirit to deny these very charges.

Elizabeth's mistrust of Mary is equalled by the latter's misjudgement of the English queen. After we have heard Elizabeth saying how little she desires Mary's death, we are surprised to hear the latter exclaim:

> Ma sentence est donnée, il me faut preparer.
> On veut fraper le coup, ie ne le puis parer.[4]

Elizabeth speaks of her clemency in several places (e.g. B 242, 244, 262), but Mary believes her to be furious, and after her blood:

> *Les esprits furieux* aux prieres sont sours.[5]

> *A qui veut se vanger* tout autre respect cesse.[6]

Above this scene of misunderstanding, we see the tragic struggle of the English queen with her duty, a higher force to which she finally gives in; and, on the other hand, the calm acceptance by the Scottish queen of her undeserved death. The play is essentially two tragedies, joined by a fine thread.

[1] B 81–100.   [2] B 75–8.   [3] B 826–30.
[4] A 819–20.   [5] B 870.   [6] B 852.

Political necessity, and tragic misunderstanding, are overshadowed by a higher fate, which rules both the queens. This fate has prevented Elizabeth from freeing Mary:

> Et voulant mille fois sa chaine relascher,
> Ie ne sçay quel destin est venu m'empescher.[1]

Mary's first monologue is a lamentation of her treatment by this same fate, which has pursued her from her birth. We hear of her mother's flight from Scotland, and of Mary's marriage to François II, who immediately died:

> O fortune volage, est-ce ainsi que ta rouë
> Des reines et des Rois inconstamment se iouë![2]

She returns to Scotland, to meet new disasters:

> Sur le triste moment qu'au monde ie fus née,
> Le Ciel à souffrir tout m'auoit bien condamnée![3]

Even her shipwreck in England comes about by chance:

> Une fiere bourrasque à nos vœux importune
> La vient ietter aux bords des barbares Anglois.[4]

There seems to be a positive intention to show the innocence of both queens in this play. Use of a specific source may, in fact, show the aims of an author; though these aims were most probably in no way political. We are shown this crushing force of fate, helped by misunderstanding and by political necessity. There is no sign of political or religious polemic; one can discount Mary's mention of 'la folle opinion d'une rance heresie'.[5] It is used in the same way as Aman's imprecations against the Jews (as being natural to the character), and is counter-balanced by Elizabeth's Protestant sentiments in the other acts.

(d) *Sententiae*[6] *and the Moral Aim*

In a long and detailed thesis, *Montchrestiens Tragödien und die stoische Lebensweisheit*, Dr. Kurt Willner expresses the opinion that Montchrestien, in his plays, puts forward an ordered scheme of life, and that his aim is definitely moral; the *Lebensweisheit* expressed is, according to him, an original mingling of traditional neo-Stoic and

---

[1] B 43–4.   [2] B 755–6.   [3] B 767–8.
[4] B 824–5.   [5] B 772.
[6] See note on the form of *Sententia*, at end of chapter.

Christian principles, the whole being based upon personal experience of life and upon personal opinions.

This belief is almost certainly mistaken; Montchrestien does not appear to be attempting to convey an ordered *Weltanschauung* such as Willner provides. Even if he were, the examination of the *sententiae* in his plays would have little value in an attempt to assess the author's views. *Sententiae* are for him, as for other dramatists, one more type of stylized ornamentation, one more detail from the books of rhetoric; their use is one more form of imitation of the ancients. Other aspects of the logical and rhetorical training given to the authors during their years at school and university make it unlikely, and impossible to prove, that any of the characters speak the opinions of the author.

In the manuals of rhetoric which were used at this time, the *sententia*, or *gnome* is listed as one of the principal ornaments of style. That the dramatic theorists regarded it above all as a form of ornament is shown unconsciously by their manner of referring to it. Laudun Daigaliers, for example, couples *sententiae* with similes as 'ornements de poesie': 'Il faut qu'en la Tragedie les sentences, allegories, similitudes et autres ornements de poesie . . . y soient fréquentes';[1] '. . . Les sentences, similitudes, figures et autres ornements de poësie . . .'.[2]

Though Scaliger regards their role as more important, seeing them as the columns on which the play rests—'. . . Sunt enim quasi columnae aut pilae quaedam totius fabricae illius . . . quibus tota tragoedia est fulcienda . . .'[3]—this role is a purely structural one, having relevance to form rather than content.

The *sententiae* are thus principally ornaments of language; and, like all the other ornaments, metaphors, similes, and so on, they can be taken from other authors. Many of them are extremely derivative, expressing *lieux communs* used by the ancients, or by other authors of the Renaissance. Many, indeed, have been taken from commonplace-books, whether printed or compiled by the author himself. Apart from these traditional themes, the neo-Stoic and Christian ideas which Montchrestien expresses were also current at the time. He draws on all these different sources, and makes no attempt to formulate these borrowed ideas into a system of thought.

Many of the *sententiae* upon which Willner's argument is based are taken from the classics, either directly or via other playwrights of the

---

[1] Laudun Daigaliers, *Art poëtique françois*, 1597, Livre v, Ch. 4 (Lawton, p. 95).
[2] Ibid., Livre v, Ch. 8 (Lawton, p. 98).
[3] Scaliger, *Poetices Libri Septem*, 1561, lib. iii, cap. xcvii (Lawton, p. 95).

sixteenth century. Thus, for example, all the ideas expressed on pages 38 and 39, in the section 'Das rationale Denken: Stoische Vernunft-auffassung', have been expressed before, by Jodelle and Garnier. Compare Montchrestien's

> Un Prince vertueux doit en toute saison
> Regler ses actions au compas de raison:
> Car qui lasche son cœur aux transports de son ire
> Est vassal de soy-mesme et Roy ne se peut dire.[1]

with these two passages from Garnier's *Juifves*:

> Un monarque irrité
> A tousjours, se vengeant, trop de sévérité.
> L'on ne voit a grand'peine homme qui s'y tempere:
> S'il ne se faict raison, c'est qu'il ne le peut faire.
> Mais un roy qui peut tout n'a qu'à se retenir
> Si quelqu'un l'a fasché, de ne le trop punir.[2]
>
> C'est plus de se domter, domter ses passions,
> Que commander monarque à mille nations.[3]

Similarly, Willner's next quotation, in which Montchrestien refers to 'la divine Raison',[4] can be placed beside Jodelle's:

> Or la raison, par qui enfans des dieux nous sommes,
> Suit plustost le parti des grands dieux que des hommes.[5]

The necessity for reason to rule the passions, an idea expressed on the next page of Willner's thesis, page 39, is to be found again and again in the plays of this century: e.g. 'Celuy commande plus qui vit du sien contant / Et qui va ses désirs par la raison domtant'.[6]

In the section 'Mensch und Schicksal' (pp. 33–7), we find the same situation. Accusations of fate, of the type described in this section, were regarded as typical of tragedy, as we can see in this statement of Jodocus Badius Ascensius: 'Nam reges et principes qui se primum perbeatos et perquam felices arbitrantur, in fine tragoediarum in extremam miseriam redacti exclamationibus et dedignationibus caelum et terram confundunt, omniaque et caelestia et terrestria incusant.'[7]

---

[1] *La Cartaginoise*, 128.
[2] *Les Juifves*, 273–8.
[3] Ibid., 1017–18.
[4] *Susane*, ii. 308.
[5] *Didon*, 671–2.
[6] Garnier, *Cornélie*; ed. Pinvert, p. 101.
[7] *Praenotamenta*, Cap. iv (Lawton, p. 28).

Montchrestien's accusations that fate rewards the wicked and punishes the just—

> Tel souvent n'a failli qui souffre le dommage.[1]

> Immuables decrets du Ciel tousiours mouvant,
> Qui du bien et du mal ne prenez connoissance;
> Par vous seuls l'innocent qui le bien va suivant,
> Jouissant de la vie a moins d'esiouissance.[2]

—are paralleled by those of Garnier and of Seneca:

> Ses aveugles presens, jettez à l'avanture
>   Honorent plus souvent
> Un homme vicieux qui de vertu n'a cure,
>   Qu'un homme bien vivant,
> Et ceux que le désir méchamment ensorcelle
>   D'un illicite honneur
> En leurs faits violens ont presque tousjours d'elle
>   Une heureuse faveur.[3]

> O Fortuna viris invida fortibus,
> Quam non aequa bonis praemia dividis.[4]

In the section 'Erkenntnis' (pp. 49–55), we find the ideas of Montaigne upon self-knowledge. But, as Willner himself admits, this idea goes even further back, to Epictetus and Marcus Aurelius. The later ideas in this section, on the ultimate necessity of death for everyone and on the vanity of earthly things, are so widespread as *lieux communs* that it is hardly necessary to mention examples.

The Christian ideas which Montchrestien expresses, and to which Willner draws attention in his Chapter XIII (pp. 171–90), are in no way original or unusual.

These examples show that most of the thoughts expressed by Montchrestien can be traced to other sources. This in itself would not conclusively disprove Willner's theory, for from these derivative sources it would be possible to build up a new view of life. But in Montchrestien's case the diverse sources are not used to form a connected *Lebensweisheit*. They are used as the occasion demands, without thought for the contradictions they will create, and thus we find, if we attempt to disentangle a system of thought, nothing but a hopeless muddle, a mixture of classical, neo-Stoic, and Christian ideas.

---

[1] *Les Lacènes*, III. 182. [2] Ibid., IV. 192.
[3] Garnier, *Porcie*; ed. Pinvert, p. 52. [4] Seneca, *Hercules Furens*, 524–5.

In this mixture there are a great many contradictions, the most striking of which occur when Christian and pagan ideas come into contact. The mistrust of the gods which we have seen expressed in Willner's chapter 'Mensch und Schicksal' stands as a great contrast to the feelings of the chorus in Act IV of *Aman*:

> Atten du Ciel ta delivrance,
> Espere le salut de Dieu,
> Tout le bien provient de ce lieu,
> Et sa crainte donne asseurance
> Aux cœurs naturellement bas,
> Contre les frayeurs du trespas.

Another great contradiction is to be found in the author's view of man's ultimate goodness or evil. In his chapter 'Der Mensch ist von Natur aus gut', Willner quotes the following two passages:

> Que l'ame a de peine a mal faire!
> Elle sent dix mille combats
> Qui la poussent de haut en bas
> Par maint et maint discours contraire.

> O qu'il est aux mortels mal aisé de mal faire!

Willner claims that these lines are compatible with the Christian idea of grace; be that as it may, they are definitely incompatible with the ideas on original sin expressed by Nathan in *David*:

> Que le vice est commun à nous, malheureux hommes!
> Nous pechon à toute heure, et tout ce que nous sommes
> Ne cesson d'attirer sur nos chefs odieux
> L'effroyable courroux qui fait trembler les Cieux.
> Monarque tout-puissant, sans ta divine grace
> L'homme fait tousiours mal quelque chose qu'il face;
> Si tu ne tiens la main à ce monceau de chair,
> Il est au premier pas tout pres de tresbucher.[2]

Such contradictions are common; it seems impossible that Montchrestien should have intended to state any particular view of life.

Apart from the diversity of the sources, there are two other important reasons for these contradictions; they are both connected with the rhetorical and logical training which Montchrestien, and most of the other authors of the century, probably underwent at school and university.

[1] *La Reine d'Escosse*, III. 89.   [2] *P. de J.*, p. 229.

As we have seen, *prosopopœia* was one of the great rhetorical exercises. The great set speeches in the plays of Montchrestien show the influence of this exercise in portrayal of a mood; the set speeches in his sources, Livy and Petrarch, show the same preoccupation. As Aphthonius says: 'Ethopœia (id est, ut ita dicamus, imitatio) est expressio morum personae subiectae.'[1] The student had to put himself completely inside a character and imagine what he (or she) would say under given circumstances.

Milton, who had himself received a training in rhetoric, was to defend Aeschylus against the theories of Salmasius in the following words, which are equally applicable to Montchrestien and the tragedians of the Renaissance: 'We must not regard the poet's words as his own, but consider who it is that speaks in the play, and what that person says; for different persons are introduced, sometimes good, sometimes bad, sometimes wise men, sometimes fools, and they speak not always the poet's own opinion, but what is most fitting to each character.'[2]

Though characterization is weak in these plays, in the sense that the characters change little and, when they do, change abruptly, the depiction of *mood* is convincing: Nathan speaks as one would expect an angry prophet to speak, and Aman is typical of the proud pagan; within stylized limits, this depiction is convincing. But one could not expect the words of Nathan to agree with those of Aman, nor those of Scipion with those of the amorous David! *Sententiae* need not even be moral, when the character who expresses them is immoral:

> Il vaut mieux perdre autruy que se perdre soy-mesme.[3]

Formally, this is a perfect *sententia*.

Dialectic, as it was understood at the time of the Renaissance, was a dialectic of probability; one started from two probabilities, and tried to reach a probable truth. Mixed with this concept, however, one finds the idea of *persuasion*, taken over from traditional Rhetoric; each person in a dispute must try to persuade the other that he alone was right.

Inventio and *dispositio*, the two parts of ancient Rhetoric which had been taken over by Renaissance Logic, consisted of the choice and the arrangement of the arguments found in the *loci*. In the disputes on

[1] Aphthonius, *Progymnasmata* (trans. Agricola, ed. Lorichius).
[2] Milton; Columbia edition, vii. 307. Quoted by D. L. Clark, *John Milton at St. Paul's School*, p. 244.   [3] *David*, Act III; *P. de J.*, p. 215.

general subjects which are to be found throughout the tragedies of the Renaissance, the *sententiae* are often analogies formed by what has been found in the *loci*.

As, in these arguments, everyone is trying to persuade the other that he is right, how can we find the author's own thought? These disputes are pure exercises in argument, in which the author pretends to support both views. The subjects of discussion are usually fairly general, like the subjects given in the study of Logic, e.g. justice versus clemency, the advantages and disadvantages of suddenly changing one's mind, the reasons for and against suicide, etc.

Often, in these disputes, you find completely opposite views side by side (above all in stichomythia); for example:

Hector: L'ordinaire des Dieux c'est d'aider aux meilleurs.

Priam: A tous bons et mauvais ils versent des malheurs.[1]

or:

Reine: Le temps au sage esprit sert parfois de raison,
La volonté se tourne avecques la saison,
Et le Pilote seul est digne de loüange
Qui peut tendre la voile ainsi que le vent change.

Chœur: Quand un dessein est pris il ne le faut changer,
Si par ne le point faire on se met en danger.[2]

Such examples show how impossible it is to attribute such *sententiae* to the author's own views.

Willner, in his thesis, places much importance on the way in which Montchrestien's prefaces stress the moral aim of his tragedies, as do the *vers liminaires* by Bosquet. This stress, however, is typical of much of the theoretical writings of the rest of the century. We have already seen, in other cases, the possibilities of discrepancies between theoretical writings and theatrical practice in this era; so such theoretical statements need not necessarily be taken as being an accurate assessment of theatrical intention. By tradition the theatre of the sixteenth century was a moralizing genre, and by tradition statements of intent on these lines were made in prefaces. Horace had stressed the moral aim of literature, and for the ancients, tragedy set forth an example of the frailty of fortune. The Renaissance theorists, and the dramatists themselves, express the same view; but is it by this time merely a tradition? Certainly most of the dramatists of the age appear concerned

---

[1] *Hector*, Act II; *P. de J.*, p. 23.   [2] *La Reine d'Escosse*, Act II; *P. de J.*, p. 84.

above all with form and style, of which the moralizing *sententia* was a part. Rarely does there seem any hint of a coherent moral message on the part of these authors.

It must be stated here that the evidence I have used to attack Willner's theories is essentially negative, and that when assessing an author's personal theories and commitments in this way, one must work in probabilities. It is improbable that Montchrestien had a theoretical system such as Dr. Willner suggests; but this by no means proves definitely that *none* of the opinions in his plays reflect personal opinions of the author. All that one can say is that *proof* of any such connection is now impossible.

Dr. Jondorf, in her thesis on Garnier, is more convincing than Dr. Willner, and Garnier is a more convincing case than Montchrestien. The balance of probability in this case is greater; but even here it is still merely probability. 'Buchanan, La Taille and Garnier are all interested in the political commitments of their characters',[1] says Dr. Jondorf, and warns us of the danger, because of the example of Seneca, of presuming that 'all French writers who follow Seneca in embodying political material in their plays do so for the same, mainly rhetorical purpose'.[2] This is, of course, a danger, as are all presumptions.

Dr. Jondorf's comparison of Garnier and Montchrestien would seem to me to carry a good deal of weight: '. . . Garnier is a "committed" artist, not to the extent of supporting a body of doctrine or partisan opinion, but in so far as he intends his plays to provoke some serious reflections on serious problems. Montchrestien has no such concern; his preoccupation is with language, which he handles with skill, producing effects of splendour, violence or gentle beauty.'[3]

It is impossible to find any system of moral teaching in the tragedies of Montchrestien, except in so far as the Stoic fates of the heroes stand as examples to the beholder, and in so far as the tragedies reflect the general Stoic tendencies of the time. The *sententiae*, with their numerous contradictions, were obviously regarded as purely formal, i.e. as a form of stylistic ornament. None of the words spoken by characters can be regarded as necessarily expressing the opinions of the author; and the *sententiae* in the Chorus are usually extremely derivative *lieux communs*.

In his tragedies, then, Montchrestien has avoided anything unconnected with the plot, or with the rhetorical development of themes

[1] Jondorf, p. 28.   [2] Ibid, pp. 35–6.   [3] Ibid, p. 190.

and emotions arising from that plot. Erudite digressions are not introduced for their own sake; though this omission does not detract from the erudite nature of this form of tragedy. Polemics, whether political or religious, are not a feature of Montchrestien's biblical and contemporary plays; each subject is treated as an example of a tragic fate, and of the hero's reaction to it; nothing else is necessary. In all this, Montchrestien is not necessarily typical of the whole of Renaissance tragedy; but he is true to its main objectives, and typical of what is best in contemporary practice.

Note on the form of the sentententia (see p. 96)

Schérer quotes the Abbé d'Aubignac as saying that *sententiae* are '. . . propositions générales qui renferment des vérités communes, et qui ne tiennent à l'action théâtrale que par application et par conséquence'. Schérer goes on to say that, though these propositions must be strictly general, the mind must be able to link them up with the action. He defines the *sententia* as a complete phrase, which can stand by itself; not even a conjunction such as *ainsi* may attach it to what has gone before.

This is an excellent, and strict, definition of the *sententia*. But many of the phrases put in inverted commas by Renaissance dramatists, who were not so strict in their definitions, are excluded by it. For example, the following marked *sententiae* in Montchrestien are invalidated by the words in italic:

> C'est bien un ordinaire
> De sentir *tels effets* d'un Prince debonnaire,
> D'un bon arbre bon fruit . . .

> Les douleurs de l'esprit n'ont point d'*autre* remede.

> L'eau qui *la* peut esteindre est celle de la raison.

> C'est un feu d'artifice, on ne s'*en* peut deffaire.

> *Taschez-y* tout soudain, *vous* verrez tout soudain
> Mourir *sa* chaude ardeur; l'essay n'en sera vain.

On the other hand, some unmarked lines are true *sententiae*; for example, the following, of which line three is the only one so marked in the text:

> Quand l'esprit est privé de ce que plus il aime,
> Il ne sçauroit autant exprimer qu'endurer:
> Car tousiours sans parole est la douleur extréme.

Though, as can be seen from this, the system of marking *sententiae* is not to be trusted, it is on the whole true to say that inverted commas *do* mark what the tragedians believed to be general maxims, even if they do not all conform to Schérer's strict definition of the *sententia*. Thus any passages so marked can be taken to be of general import, and are of use in this study.

6. 'Set Pieces'

ITHIN the plays of Montchrestien, as in those of the other Renaissance dramatists, there are various stylized forms that serve as a framework for that display of style and language which was the dramatist's primary aim. These forms are of varying types; they range from the large blocks of monologue, *tirade*, *récit*, and chorus to the rapid crackle of *stichomythia*; but their main common characteristic is stylization and a lack of dramatic *vraisemblance*. The whole of Renaissance dramatic composition was directed towards the production of such 'set pieces'; let us now look more closely at these forms themselves, both in their external relation to the play around them, and in their internal construction.

(a) *The Monologue*

Monologues, for various reasons, take up a preponderant part of the space in Montchrestien's tragedies. All the plays, and most acts, begin with one. Sometimes the speaker is alone; but at other times he has silent companions, who later join him in a dialogue. The presence of other characters does not prevent these speeches from being monologues; for the speaker is not addressing his companions, but is speaking to himself alone.

The two types of opening monologue are, then, those in which the speaker is alone on the stage, and those in which he has silent companions. In the first type, the monologue often continues for a few lines after the speaker has caught sight of a new arrival, sometimes in order to describe him (or her):

> *Massinisse*: La voy-ie pas venir? Quelle rare merueille!
> L'Afrique n'eut iamais une grace pareille!
> Et croy que si l'Amour defaisoit son bandeau
> Il aimeroit luy-mesme un visage si beau.
> (*La Cartaginoise*, C 1010–13)

Massinisse then addresses the new arrival, so that a dialogue ensues. At times, however, the speech is considerably lengthened, becoming a tirade addressed to the other character who has just appeared. Such continuations are to be found in Act IV of *La Cartaginoise*, where Scipion addresses 24 lines to Siphax before the latter speaks, and later in the same act, where Scipion's short monologue is extended by 89½ lines addressed to a silent Massinisse. At other times, however, the monologue comes to an abrupt end when a new character speaks, having just appeared on the stage; in Act II of *La Cartaginoise* Sophonisbe speaks immediately after Massinisse's monologue. The character who spoke the monologue may even go off without speaking to anyone, as does Mardochée at the beginning of Act III of *Aman*.

The other type of monologue, that spoken in front of a silent companion, is usually presumed to have been heard by him, even though the speech is a soliloquy. This we see, for example, in Act I of *La Reine d'Escosse*, where the Conseiller carries straight on from Elizabeth's last statement, and has obviously heard what she has been saying. The silent companion is sometimes addressed, towards the end of the monologue speech; at other times he speaks without our being warned that he is there. It is difficult to know what the silent character is meant to do during the speech, much as in the case of the *tirade*.

Monologues, as I have said, are very common. There is one at the beginning of every play, and one at the beginning of every act except Act II of *La Reine d'Escosse* and Acts II and V of *Hector*. They are also very common within the acts, especially in *Les Lacènes* and *Aman*. In *La Reine d'Escosse*, Act IV is entirely a monologue. The *Mégère* and the *Ombre de Thericion* enjoy monologues quite outside the action of their respective plays.

Not only are monologues common; they are also, at times, very long. Montchrestien, it is true, cuts them down a little between the versions of his plays, as he was to do with his *tirades*. But the general impression, to a modern reader, is still one of great length. This is, in fact, true of all Renaissance dramatists; though by the turn of the century occasional apologies or justifications for the practice appear in prefaces. Montchrestien himself, in the preface to the 1596 *Sophonisbe*, justifies his long *tirades* by the example of his predecessors. Claude Billard de Courgenay, in the Preface 'Au Lecteur' to the 1612 edition of his tragedies, justifies the length of his monologues by the necessity to describe completely emotions which cannot be contained in a shorter space:

Je t'adüoueray encor' auoir par fois rendu mes monologues un peu longs: non que ie sois si mauuais Cappitaine, que ie ne sçache fort bien me retrancher dans une meschante place, lors que le temps, et la necessité le requierent: mais par ce qu'ils sont la naifue representation de nos pensées, nos esperances, et nos desseins, qui bien souuent nous entretiennent plus long temps, qu'une simple tirade de cent, ou deux cents vers.

At first sight, M. Schérer's description of the monologue in the seventeenth century, in his *La Dramaturgie classique en France*, would seem to conform with the Renaissance view: 'La fonction essentielle du monologue est de permettre l'expression d'un sentiment. . . . Le monologue permet au dramaturge, non seulement de faire connaître les sentiments de son héros — facilité que lui offre tout dialogue — mais de les chanter.'[1]

And this characteristic of the monologue does indeed remain to a certain extent in the seventeenth-century monologue, even though, probably for this reason, monologues become a good deal rarer. At the same time, the seventeenth-century monologue came to be used for various additional functions. The monologues of Racine, for example, became an essential part of the action; they often pushed characters from one course of action to another, for within the monologues an inner struggle was fought out which often ended in an important decision. At the same time, there were two other seventeenth-century uses of the monologue which had a bearing on the dramatic construction of the play—exposition and the skilful *liaison* of scenes.

In the sixteenth century, however, none of these additional uses of the monologue were of any importance.

Montchrestien has no need for exposition in his plays, so even though they may open with a monologue, this monologue is usually used for purely lyrical purposes. As for *liaison* of scenes, it is only rarely that we find the monologue used in such a way in Montchrestien, and even then this does not appear to be the primary purpose (e.g. Mardochée's prayers in Act III of *Aman*, which are primarily lyrical 'set pieces'). Only in Act IV of *La Cartaginoise*, where the introduction, between the versions, of Scipion's second monologue makes the exit of Siphax and the entrance of Massinisse much smoother, does the monologue seem to be being used in this way.

The sixteenth-century monologue is essentially the lyrical expression of feelings. As such, it is static, expressing the situation, and not attempting to change it. Admittedly, this situation may be one of doubt, as in Act I of *La Reine d'Escosse*, but no solution is reached within the monologue.

[1] J. Schérer, *La Dramaturgie classique en France*, p. 246.

These monologues usually express a single emotion on the part of the character involved. The most common emotions expressed are pride and anger (*Aman, Assuère*), Stoic resignation (*Stratonice, La Reine d'Escosse*), and grief (*Sophonisbe, Andromache, Heleine*). This static nature of the monologue is in accordance with the practice of *prosopopœia*, i.e. the setting forth, in a 'set piece', of the emotions which a person *might* have felt in certain circumstances. Grief is certainly the most popular of the emotions chosen for depiction in the books of *Progymnasmata*, as one can see from the titles in Aphthonius (Lorichius's edition) and Libanius (Morel's translation), which include:

Libanius:

Quibus verbis ante Hectorem iacentem Andromachi uti potuisse videatur.
Quid Niobe liberis amissis dicere potuerit.
Altera Ethopoeia eiusdem Niobes.
Quid pronunciarit Menelaus cum Agamemnonis interitum cognovit.
Quid dixerit Achilles super Patroclo.
Quid Achilles amans diceret post caedem Penthesiliae.
Alia eiusdem.
Quae verba Aiax efferre valuerit post insaniam.

Aphthonius:

Quae verba dicere posset Niobe, iacentibus liberis.
Qualia verba dixerit Hecuba post excidium Troianum.
Quae verba Andromache captiva, patria solo everso, et marito occiso potuisset dicere.
Quae dixerit Andromache, interfecto Hectore.
Quae dixerit Medea, suos mactatura filios.
                    (from Libanius)
Quaenam dixerit Cornelia, cum audisset victum a Caesare Pompeium.

Prosopopœia was one of the freer rhetorical exercises, in that it had very little of a set plan. It did not, like other exercises, aim at logical argument, but rather at the elaboration of an emotion. The kind of verbal elaboration caused by stylistic rhetoric is thus in no way a contradiction to its plan, as it was at times in the *tirade*; rather, it is a natural extension of the prosopopoeic monologue.

For most rhetoricians *prosopopœia* had no inner plan. Aphthonius, however, stated a very simple plan, which was later elaborated by Lorichius. Many of Montchrestien's monologues of grief do in fact seem to follow this vague plan.

The speech, says Aphthonius, should be divided into three parts: '. . . Proque capitibus, divides tribus ipsam temporibus: praesenti, praeterito et futuro.'[1] Let us take, as an example in Montchrestien, the first speech of the *Reine d'Escosse*.[2] This is, indeed, divided into these three parts, in the same order.

Lorichius, in his *scholia* to Aphthonius, defines the first section thus: 'In praesenti, instantis fortunae permutatio, et aerumnae recensentur.'[3] This *exordium* on present ills usually took the form of exclamations of grief, e.g.:

Andromache: O me miseram, quae divitiis et honore sidera iampridem adibam, nunc maximas in aerumnas praecipitata sum.[4]

Aiax: O recentem furorem! O praesentem resipiscentiam![5]

The Queen of Scotland similarly begins by exclaiming on her misfortunes:

> De qui me dois-je plaindre? O ciel, ô mer, ô terre!
> Qui de vous trois me livre un plus âpre guerre? . . .

. Soon she turns to the past, as one would expect. Lorichius says of this second section: 'In praeterito potissimum ea conferuntur cum infortuniis parentum vel maiorum.'[6]

Though the return to the past was usually concerned with the speaker himself either comparing past joys with present griefs, or complaining of the perpetual ill-will of the gods against him, on occasion writers made use of this further extension of Lorichius, and related the misfortunes of parents and ancestors as well. Montchrestien conforms by relating the misfortunes of Mary's mother as well as those of the queen herself. The narration of all these past events takes up most of this long speech. As a form of *récit*, this section makes use of many of the ornaments typical of the Senecan messenger speech[7]—descriptions, reported speech, etc.

Of the third section, Lorichius merely says: 'In futuro, rerum eventus, malorum fines adducuntur, vel consilia, quorum ratione tantis malis succurri possit.'[8]

Most speeches of grief end with this look to the future. Mary ends

[1] Aphthonius, *Progymnasmata* (1583), p. 167ᵛ.
[2] *La Reine d'Escosse*, Act III; *P. de J.*, pp. 90–3.
[3] Aphthonius, op. cit., p. 172ʳ.
[4] Ibid., p. 178ᵛ.
[5] Libanius, *Exempla Progymnasmatum* (1606), p. 166.
[6] Aphthonius, op. cit., p. 172ʳ.
[7] See the section on the *Récit*.
[8] Aphthonius, loc. cit.

her speech by looking to the future not with hope, but with calm resignation in the face of an inevitable fate:

> Ie ne dois plus sortir d'une prison si forte
> Ou si i'en doy sortir la mort en est la porte
> On veut frapper le coup que ie ne puis parer:
> Et bien, c'est fait de vivre, il m'y faut preparer.

The conclusion of the speech consists of a couple of *sententiae*:

> Le mal impatient s'irrite davantage;
> Nous n'avon rien d'humain plus grand que le courage.[1]

Not all Montchrestien's monologues of grief, naturally, follow this plan so rigorously; but very few of them stray far from it.

Not only speeches of grief conform to the pattern; among other types of speech one may count Massinisse's speech of thanksgiving to the gods.[2] He starts by thanking them for present favours; soon he turns to his former misfortunes, and to the aid which the heavens brought to him; he ends the speech by turning to the future, and promising to sacrifice continually to the gods:

> Comment donques pourray-ie, ô seigneurs immortels
> Humblement prosterné devant vos saints Autels,
> Rendre un hommage digne à vos graces propices?
> Est-il pour tel effet assez de sacrifices?
> Tant d'obligation ne s'aquitte en un jour.
> Aussi l'an desormais ne fera son retour,
> Qu'en ce temps fortuné d'avantures si belles,
> Ie ne vienne invoquer vos bontez eternelles,
> Et que le Bœuf muglant par le Prestre amené
> N'ait le front sourcilleux de Laurier couronné.

This speech, too, ends with *sententiae*:

> C'est raison que l'honneur retourne à qui le donne,
> Tout se fait par destin comme le Ciel l'ordonne.

This inner plan of the *prosopopœia* is of no real importance; what is important is the outlook which the use of this rhetorical exercise induced in the author. Not only is it an explanation of the superabundance of monologues in Renaissance tragedy; it also makes clear the reasons for the static, lyrical nature of these monologues, and for their depiction of one specific emotion or mood.

---

[1] *P. de J.*, p. 93.   [2] *La Cartaginoise*, Act II; *P. de J.*, pp. 126–8.

(b) *The Tirade*

Even in situations which would seem potentially dramatic, the sixteenth-century custom was for the characters to address each other in long, extended speeches. While one speaks, the other waits patiently to reply. An extreme example of the stylized use of this technique is the *Sophonisbe* of Montreux, where each scene begins with such long tirades; though gradually, in each scene, the speeches became shorter and shorter, until we arrive at quick-fire *stichomythia*. In the Scipion–Siphax scene in Montreux's Act I, there is the following sequence of speeches: 114–128–40–4–40–34–4–8–2–6–8–4–4–4–4–4–4–4–4–(then 3 pages of 1-line stichomythia)–8–12. The Massinisse–Misipsa–Gelosses scene (Act III) follows much the same pattern: 128–71–1–76–40–88–4–4–4–4–4–4–4–(4 pages of stichomythia).

The *tirade*, and *stichomythia*, are the two extremes, both of them used extensively by Renaissance dramatists, who were looking, not for *vraisemblance* in dramatic technique, but for stylized methods within which they could show their linguistic virtuosity.

Dramatic impact was not Montchrestien's main aim; he follows the Renaissance technique of the *tirade*, lessening the dramatic impact, but improving the rhetorical flow.

A good example is the first meeting between Massinisse and Sophonisbe; here Montchrestien finds the *tirades* ready-made in his source, Petrarch, and reproduces them at great length. In the 1596 version, Sophonisbe's plea lasts for 148 lines, Massinisse's reply for 36; Sophonisbe's thanks thereupon take 44 lines.[1] Admittedly, by 1604, these *tirades* have been shortened to 98, 28, and 30 lines respectively. But the technique is exactly the same, and shortening must be taken as part of the general policy of concision between the versions.

The *tirades* are self-contained, and very seldom show a change of mood within themselves: this technique, then, tends to lead to *invraisemblance*, as, if there is a change of mood, this remains unexplained. The author's aim is the portrayal of the mood, rather than an explanation of the change which leads to it.

One of the difficulties inherent in the *tirade* is, of course, the question of what the other person does during it. During Sophonisbe's plea, does Massinisse show himself gradually falling in love with her? And if so, how? Does Sophonisbe show her acceptance of Massinisse's offer during his *tirade*? And again, how?

[1] A 703–938.

I think it must be taken that the author had no thought of *vraisemblance* in this scene; he saw in it merely an excuse for several extended *tirades*: (*a*) The clement conqueror, (*b*) The pleading captive, (*c*) The man overcome by love, (*d*) The grateful captive. These *tirades* are self-contained, in the manner of the exercises of *Progymnasmata*, and he does not have any thought of showing us the gradual awakening of the emotions involved. The *tirades* are an excuse for rhetorical development, and thus an end in themselves. The other character on the stage appears to be forgotten during these speeches; perhaps he retires to the back of the stage.

In the preface to the 1596 edition of *Sophonisbe*, Montchrestien excuses this use of the *tirade*: 'Quand à ce que les personnages introduits en la mienne parlent longuement, sans entrerompre le fil de leur discours; sçache que ie ne l'ay fait sans exemple.'[1] There are many scenes of this type. For example, there is the scene between Scipion and Siphax in the same play. After Scipion's monologue, he continues his speech without a pause, addressing Siphax (34 lines in 1596, 24 in 1604).[2] Siphax then makes a long *tirade* (44 lines in 1596, the same in 1604);[3] after Scipion has given a short order to untie him, Siphax continues with a speech of thanks. Similarly, the scene in *La Reine d'Escosse* between Elizabeth and the 'Chœur des Estats'[4] starts with long statements of their cases by each of them.

The inner form of the *tirade* can be ruled by several things. It may closely follow a model in another author; it may be based upon a traditional form, such as the tyrant speech or the depiction of a dream. And from time to time, when the situation demands it, a *tirade* will conform to one or other of the *Progymnasmata*. Scipion's speech to Massinisse, in Act iv of *Sophonisbe*, for example, follows fairly strictly the exercise of *Locus Communis*. He wishes to condemn Massinisse's actions with regard to Sophonisbe and force him to give her up; the argument takes the following form:

(1) *Exordium* (A 1546–56)
He invokes their old friendship, held together by virtue.

(2) *A contrario* (A 1557–67)
A great man should subdue his passions, however strong they may be.

---

[1] p. 15 (Fries, p. 43).
[3] A 1470–1512, C 1154–97.
[2] A 1434–69, C 1130–53.
[4] *P. de J.*, pp. 82 ff.

(3) *Ab expositione* (A 1568–75)

But some people's passions overwhelm them; this is bad.

(4) *A comparatione* (A 1576–95, A 1596–1609, A 1614–17)

Three comparisons support this message: (*a*) Runaway horses wrecking a carriage, (*b*) A ship dashed to pieces by the wind, (*c*) A woman's sweet voice is like a bird-decoy, attracting us into a trap.

(5) *A sententia* (A 1618–57)

'Le passage du cœur à l'amour il faut clore . . .' A general discussion of the dangers of love. The only digression is one short comparison with Hannibal, who proves this general rule (A 1634–7).

(6) *A vita antecedente* (A 1658–67)

Massinisse's past life, and its contrast with his present situation.

(7) *Ab exclusione misericordiae* (also *A vita antecedente*) (A 1699–1709)

Sophonisbe's past deeds, which show her to have no claim for pity:

> Cete fine femelle, ô gentil Massinisse
> Qui porte plus d'apas, de rets, et d'hameçons
> Que Thetis dans son flot ne porte de poissons,
> A detourné de nous Syphax ce chef de guerre . . .
> . . . céte femme mechante . . .

Massinisse must therefore resign himself to giving up Sophonisbe. Further reasons are given:

(8) *A legitimo et iusto* (A 1688–97)

> Tu sçais bien que Syphax étant le prisonnier
> Du peuple porte-loy lon ne pourroit nier
> Que sa femme, ses biens, ses cités et sa terre,
> Retournent aux Romains par le droit de la guerre.
> Si tot donc que i'aurai receu commandement
> Du Senat et du peuple, il faut que prontement
> J'envoye ou mene à Rome et Syphax et sa femme
> Afin qu'obeissant ie n'encore aucun blame.
> Tu le sçais Massinisse, il faut qu'un bon bourgeois
> Revere le Senat et obtempere aux loix.

(This is the only part of the speech to be placed differently from in the rhetorical models; it appears before the *exclusio misericordiae*.)

(9) *Ab utili* (A 1712–7)

It is important to Massinisse's career that he should give her up.

(10) *A facili et possibili* (A 1718–25)

Rather than bear passive suffering like Prometheus, he must take upon him the strength of Hercules in order to break loose. (In 1604, however, this section runs:

> Tel parfois est tombé, lequel se relevant
> Tient plus ferme debout qu'il ne fist paravant.)

(11) *Conclusio ab eventuro* (A 1725–35)

> ... Plutôt Atropos
> Le corps de Sophonisbe envoye sous la lame,
> *Que ces yeux vos vainqueurs trionfent de vôtre ame.*
> Plutôt encor' Jupin face un but à ses dars
> De son chef déloyal, et plutôt mille pards,
> Mille ours, mille lions, éperonnés de l'ire,
> En déchirant son corps écueillent son martire,
> *Qu'elle étrange de nous un magnanime Roy,*
> *Le support des Romains, des ennemis l'effroy;*
> *Qui charitable aux siens, aux haineux redoutable,*
> *N'a rien fors que soi-meme a soi-meme semblable.*

As can be seen, this speech, in the 1596 edition, follows the scheme of the *Locus communis* extremely closely. Though the 1604 speech is greatly shortened, it follows the same plan, the only major change being the combination of the two sections *Ab expositione* and *A comparatione* (C 1258–67).

This speech is, however, also a good example of the deformation of formulary rhetoric by stylistic rhetoric.[1] The basic plan of the speech is distorted by the vast addition of three comparisons (41 lines) and by 40 lines of *sententiae*, and later by two more comparisons (20 lines). In the original plans comparisons or *sententiae* would be short and pithy. On the smaller scale, the continual use of various other figures of thought, especially the hyperbole, tends to detract from the value of the argument. It is no longer a trenchant argument; it has become an excuse for literary delight.

Use of the strict rhetorical models is only to be found where the dramatic situation lends itself to it; the free form of *prosopopœia* is far

---

[1] See Chapter 2.

more common. However, there are several examples of the use of other *progymnasmata* in Montchrestien's works.

For example, Stratonice's speech in Act II of *Les Lacènes*[1] follows the model of *Refutatio*. Stratonice wishes to deny the likelihood of Ptolemy's having freed the Spartans:

(1) *Exordium a reprehensione*
One cannot believe a 'lasche Tyran':

> Le croire desormais c'est par trop s'abuser
> Luy qui le temps plus cher despend à courtiser
> Une vile putain dont l'œil seul le gouverne . . .

(2) *Ab expositione*
Could such a man 'penser rien de si beau' as setting their husbands free?

(3) *Ab incredibili, ab impossibili*
How could such an evil prince change his mind? Why should he set them free?

> . . . Mais le meschant ne veut,
> Tant il se plaist au mal! faire le bien qu'il peut.
> Attendez-vous plustost de voir que les Rivieres
> Rebroussent contremont leurs bruyantes carrieres,
> Que l'Aigle nage en l'onde et le Dauphin en l'air,
> Qu'un iour libres de fers il nous laisse en aller.

(4) *Ab obscuro*
'Un bruit mensonger' . . . Archidamie, her listener, is being led astray by false hopes. Stratonice has 'soupçons ambigus'.

(5) *Ab inconsequenti*
Panthée's behaviour before he left her does not fit in with all this.

(6) The sections *Ab indecoro* and *Ab inutili* cannot apply in this case.

(7) *Peroratio*
A prayer to the gods to have pity on them.

Occasionally, even in short speeches, we find fragments of progymnasmatic schemes. Thus, when Priam exclaims against Achilles, during the messenger speech in Act V of *Hector*, he pronounces the

---

[1] *P. de J.*, pp. 171–3.

first part of a classical *vituperatio*; but the messenger speech has to continue, and so the incipient formal *tirade* is broken off:

> Va meschant, va felon, Thetis n'est point ta mere,
> Bien que les flots cruels soient tousiours ton repaire
> Bien que le vieux Pelé pour son fils t'ait receu,
> Dans le cœur d'un Rocher Caucase t'a conceu
> Et puis une Tigresse oubliant son engeance,
> De sang plus que de lait te nourrit en l'enfance . . .[1]

One must not exaggerate Montchrestien's use of progymnasmatic models other than *prosopopœia*. These other types of speech (*laus*, *vituperatio*, *locus communis*, *chreia*, *refutatio*, etc.) could only be used in certain circumstances; many of the *tirades* in Montchrestien's plays have no connection with them whatsoever; in others the traditional pattern is so varied as to be almost unrecognizable. The use of these models is, however, one more example of the emphasis laid on stylization, as a frame for the development of language.

The *tirade*, then, a long speech made by one character to another, is essentially devoted to the development of one theme. It contains no dramatic progression within itself. As with the monologue, this is mainly a result of a training in the rhetorical exercises, and particularly in that of *prosopopœia*.

The *tirade* is static, and an excuse for rhetorical elaboration, lengthy imagery, etc. Often it follows a strict formal pattern, whether based on another literary model or on one of the progymnasmatic exercises. This pattern is at times distorted or almost destroyed by the over-elaboration of certain parts of it, owing to the influence of stylistic rhetoric.

The use of the *tirade* in potentially dramatic scenes may lead to *invraisemblance* in modern eyes, for it portrays static moods without attempting either to explain changes of feeling, or to give the impression of true conversation. In fact, one often feels oneself to be in a Chekhovian world where people do not listen to each other, or even speak to each other, but each continues with his own preoccupations.

(c) *Stichomythia*

In contrast to conversations consisting of *tirades*, in stichomythic conversations the protagonists are usually fully aware of each other. In

---

[1] *P. de J.*, p. 64.

fact, in the best examples this is a technique which perfectly conveys the cut-and-thrust of logical argument.

Stichomythia is a form found originally in Greek tragedy, which was taken over first by Seneca, and then by the Italian and French tragedians of the Renaissance. Strictly speaking, it is a dialogue, in which each reply consists of one line only; but by extension it has come to mean any dialogue in which the replies are of a regular length; one can thus have half-line, two-line, three-line, or even four-line examples of stichomythia. (In Montchrestien we find one example of eight-line stichomythia.)

Regularity is the essence of the definition of this form; for it does not mean merely a conversation of short replies. Many such conversations, by their irregularity, do not deserve the term of stichomythia. There is such a thing as irregular stichomythia; but there must be within it a general tendency to regularity, otherwise it is nothing more than ordinary dramatic conversation.[1]

The purposes of this form gradually changed during its history. In Greek tragedy, its most common use was for the conveying of information. Usually it consisted of question and answer, e.g.:

Medea: Salve propago providi Pandionis
　　　　Aegeu, unde in istud contulisti te solum?
Aegeus: Phoebi vetustum deferens oraculum.
Medea: Cur umbilicum faticanum adisti soli?
Aegeus: Prolis cupido consulere adegit deum, etc.[2]

In Seneca, stichomythia retains this use, e.g.:

Andromache: An aliqua poenae pars meae ignota est mihi?
Helena: Versata dominos urna captivis dedit.
Andromache: Cui famula trador? ede; quem dominum voco?
Helena: Te sorte prima Scyrius iuvenis tulit.[3]

But in Seneca another use, which had been fairly unimportant in Greek tragedy, becomes predominant. Stichomythia becomes the vehicle for close-knit dispute, in which one person takes up the arguments of the other, and contradicts them; e.g.:

Nutrix: Caeca est temeritas quae petit casum ducem.
Clytaemnestra: Cui ultima est fortuna, quid dubiam timet?

---

[1] As, e.g., in Grévin's *César*, which contains no stichomythia.
[2] Euripides, *Medea*, 665–9 (in Buchanan's translation).
[3] Seneca, *Troades*, 973–6.

Nutrix: Tuta est latetque culpa, si pateris, tua.
Clytaemnestra: Perlucet omne regiae vitium domus.
Nutrix: Piget prioris et novum crimen struis?
Clytaemnestra: Res est profecto stulta nequitiae modus.»
Nutrix: Quod metuit auget qui scelus scelere obruit.»
Clytaemnestra: Et ferrum et ignis saepe medicinae loco est.»
Nutrix: Extrema primo nemo temptavit loco.»
Clytaemnestra: Rapienda rebus in malis praeceps via est.»

As can be seen, when stichomythia was used in this way, it could often make use of *sententiae*, which were used to contradict one another.

This use of stichomythia was the more popular with Renaissance dramatists. Almost all their examples of the form are arguments. It was an opportunity for them to make use of their logical and rhetorical training; in these arguments they could speak for both sides. Often, one can feel the author's mind perusing the *loci* from which he will draw the arguments for his characters. Towards the end of the century argument becomes, in the Ramist manner, an accumulation of examples.

Stichomythia can be extremely effective; it varies the tempo of a scene, coming as a contrast with the long *tirades* typical of Renaissance drama. However, if used too much, as it is in many cases, it becomes monotonous and repetitive. It is easy to see why it appealed to Renaissance dramatists; the stylized rigidity of the form could not have failed to impress them.

Some authors, such as Garnier, use stichomythia a great deal, and use it well; others, such as Montreux, use it too much. Some, like Jodelle, use it sparingly, while Grévin uses it not once.

In some of Montchrestien's plays, stichomythia is used a great deal; in others, it is relatively unimportant:

In *Aman* there are no examples.

In *David* there is one lengthy example.

In *Les Lac'nes* there are three very short examples.[1]

In *La Cartaginoise* there are a few examples.

In *La Reine d'Escosse* there are three long examples (one of them is vast).

In *Hector* there are innumerable examples, some of them very long indeed.

---

[1] There is also an example of four-line stichomythia (p. 188) in the form of the lyric lamentations of Cratesiclea and the Chorus (i.e. in stanzas, for a divided chorus).

Why is there this discrepancy between the plays? The absence of stichomythia in *Aman* and in most of *David* could be accounted for by the fact that there is no opportunity for it in the biblical story, which the author is following fairly strictly. But *Les Lacènes* is a subject eminently suited to this procedure; and in it all we find are three very short examples:

(1) Nine single-line speeches in the Cléomène–Panthée scene in Act I.

(2) Later in the same scene, the sequence 1–1–1–3–1–1–1–1–1.

(3) In Act II, between Cratesiclea and the chorus, the sequence 1–1–2–1–1–1–2.

La Reine d'Escosse, with its great need for argument, justification and explanation on the part of the two queens, demands the stichomythic treatment, and receives it. In Act I, the Queen of England and her Counsellor hold an immense stichomythic conversation which lasts for five pages, as they argue whether to kill Mary or not. In Act II, Mary's followers try to encourage her, and there is a dialogue of twenty-two one-line replies and four two-line replies. In Act II, the Queen of England and the *Chœur des Estats* exchange twelve one-line replies.

Of the 1601 plays, *La Reine d'Escosse* is the only one which contains much stichomythia; and this because the subject demands it. *Hector*, the new play of 1604, contains a vast amount of stichomythia; in fact, it is used almost too extensively. Not an act goes by without its use, and it is used in each case at inordinate length.[1]

This suggests a possible explanation for the discrepancy between the plays; that Montchrestien was more attracted by stichomythia as time went by. Certainly this theory would seem to be corroborated by a comparison of the different versions of the plays; for Montchrestien, in his revisions, tends to regularize what had been ordinary conversation into regular stichomythia. Take, for example, *Sophonisbe* (*La Cartaginoise*). Much of the stichomythic material to be found in the 1604 edition was originally, in the other editions, so irregular as almost to be ordinary conversation. In the 1596 version, for example, the Massinisse–Scipion dialogue in Act IV ran as follows: $1\frac{1}{2}-\frac{1}{2}-1\frac{1}{2}-\frac{1}{2}-$ $1-1\frac{1}{2}-1\frac{1}{2}-1-5-1\frac{1}{2}\frac{1}{2}-1-2-1-4-1$. This could never be considered as stichomythia. However, in 1601 it became: $\frac{1}{2}-\frac{1}{2}-1-1-1-1-1-1-1-6-1-$

---

[1] In Act I, three pages (pp. 5–7); in Act II, eight pages (pp. 17–20, 22–5); in Act III, four pages (pp. 31, 35–7); in Act IV, four pages (pp. 46–7, 49–50); in Act V, five pages (pp. 56–60). (*P. de J.*)

1–1–1–1– 1–1–6, and in 1604 it became: $\frac{1}{2}$–$\frac{1}{2}$–1–1–1–1–1–1–6–1–1–1–
1–1–2–2–1–6.

Similarly, a conversation in Act I, in which the Nurse tries to persuade Sophonisbe to tell her about her dream, is transformed from 2–2–$\frac{1}{2}$–1$\frac{1}{2}$–1–1$\frac{1}{2}$–1$\frac{1}{2}$–1, to 1–1–1–2–1–1–2, which is far more regular.

So Montchrestien shows a tendency to regularize conversation into stichomythia; and his last play, *Hector*, is full of stichomythic conversation. The discrepancy between the amount of stichomythia used in his different plays could be explained by the difficulty of changing plays that had already been written, in order to bring them into line with the new tendency.

How does Montchrestien's use of stichomythia compare with that of other authors in the century? Certainly, he makes it more regular than does Garnier, who often intersperses his examples with odd half-lines;[1] on the other hand, he never reaches the extremes of regularity of Jodelle, who, in the three-cornered one-line stichomythia between (*a*) Cléopâtre, (*b*) Eras, and (*c*) Charmium, in Act I of *Cléopâtre*, makes them speak strictly in the following order: a.b.a.c.a.b.a.c.a.b.a.c.a.b. a.c.a.b. Jodelle's stichomythia is usually of one type in each case. Thus in Acts I and III of *Cléopâtre* it is all one-line, and in Act IV all two-line.

Montchrestien's introduction of stichomythia is never as stylized, either, as that of Montreux, who usually starts his scenes with very long speeches, and then descends gradually to quick-fire stichomythia. Montchrestien's scenes are never as regular as this; stichomythia and speeches alternate, not in any predetermined order, but rather as the need arises.

The *Oxford English Dictionary* describes stichomythia as 'characterized by antithesis and rhetorical repetition or taking up of the opponent's words'. In this it is wrong, as these are not *essential* characteristics of stichomythia; and, indeed, the statement is not generally true of Greek tragedy. Renaissance dramatists, however, took up these characteristics a great deal, and many of them used them far too frequently and in too stylized a manner. It is interesting to see Montchrestien avoiding the pitfalls of excess into which so many others fell.

For repetition and antithesis became one more element in the stylization of the stichomythia, so that, for example, the passage in

[1] e.g. *Porcie*, Act II, Porcie–Nourrice: 1–1–$\frac{1}{2}$–$1\frac{1}{2}$–1–1–$\frac{1}{2}$–$1\frac{1}{2}$–1–1–(gap)1–$\frac{1}{2}$–$\frac{1}{2}$–1–2–2–
2 (gap)–1–1–1–$\frac{1}{2}$–$\frac{1}{2}$–$\frac{1}{2}$–$\frac{1}{2}$–1–(gap)–1–1–1–2–2–1–1–$\frac{1}{2}$–$1\frac{1}{2}$–1–1–1–. . . . (The parts I have italicized are irregular.) Montchrestien very rarely uses the half-line, and cuts out examples of it between the editions.

Act I of Jodelle's *Cléopâtre*, which has already been mentioned, runs like this:

Cléopâtre: Que gaignez-vous, helas! en la parole vaine?
Eras: Que gaignez-vous, helas! de vous estre inhumaine?
Cléopâtre: Mais pourquoy perdez-vous vos peines ocieuses?
Charmium: Mais pourquoy perdez-vous tant de larmes piteuses?
Cléopâtre: Qu'est-ce qui adviendroit plus horrible à la vue?
Eras: Qu'est-ce qui pourroit voir une tant despourvuë? etc.

Garnier's use of repetition is less glaring; in him it is quite common, but the effect is nevertheless more striking than in Jodelle, e.g. in *Marc-Antoine*:

Eras: C'est mal fait de se perdre en ne profitant point.
Cléopâtre: Ce n'est mal fait de suyvre un amy si conjoint.
Eras: Mais telle affection n'amoindrist pas sa peine.
Cléopâtre: Sans telle affection je serois inhumaine.
Charmium: Inhumain est celuy qui se brasse la mort.
Cléopâtre: Inhumain n'est celuy qui de misères sort.
Charmium: Vivez pour vos enfans.
Cléopâtre: Je mourray pour leur père.
Charmium: O mère rigoureuse!
Cléopâtre: Espouse débonnaire!
Eras: Les voulez-vous priver du bien de leurs ayeux?
Cléopâtre: Les en privé-je? non, c'est la rigueur des dieux.

Such repetitions and antitheses are rare in the original stichomythia of the Greeks and Seneca. On the very few occasions where Seneca repeats a line, the repetition stands by itself, and is effective through the unusual nature of the usage. For example, in *Hercules Furens*:

Lycus: Quemcumque miserum videris, hominem scias.
Amphitryon: Quemcumque fortem videris, miserum neges.[1]

Though the argument in Montchrestien's stichomythic dialogues is often quick and sharp, he very rarely uses such repetitions or antitheses; when he does, they are isolated examples, as in Seneca. They never pile up, as in Jodelle and other dramatists; they gain their effect from sparing use amid other stichomythic exchanges.

In *Hector*, the play which is most filled with stichomythia, there are only five examples of such close repetition:

p. 6 Dieu qui nous l'a donné le nous peut conserver.
Dieu qui nous l'a donné pourra nous en priver.

---

[1] Seneca, *Hercules Furens*, 463–4.

p. 24 Le conseil sans la main est une ame sans corps.
La main sans le conseil iette aux vents ses efforts.

p. 25 C'est comme aux assiegeans on hausse le courage.
C'est comme l'assiégé resiste d'avantage.

p. 31 Il mourra sans renom qui . . .
Il viura sans repos qui . . .

p. 49 Par mon authorité ie ne l'ay peu tenir.
Par vostre authorité faites-le reuenir.

Such examples are therefore rare; and they are never collected in stylized lists as in Jodelle.

Sententiae are often used in stichomythic arguments, and this can have some bearing on the role of the *sententia* in drama, as we have seen.

In Montchrestien's first five plays, then, regular stichomythia is rare, except in *La Reine d'Escosse*, where the subject and the source specifically lend themselves to such treatment. Within the various versions of the plays, however, and particularly in *Sophonisbe*, we can trace a gradual stylization of conversation taking place, and by the time we reach *Hector*, Montchrestien is extensively using stichomythia. *Hector* is also the most regular of his plays, so it would seem that to the end of his dramatic career Montchrestien is progressing even further towards regularity and stylization, and that the play *David* had been a mere excursion into the irregular.

Montchrestien's stichomythia itself is sparing in its use of repetition and antithesis, and does not reach the excesses of stylization to be found in Jodelle and in Montreux. In a three-sided conversation, characters speak in whatever order they please. In a scene, there is no stylized pattern of development from tirades to stichomythia, but both are used where the situation demands them.

Though a progression in stylization, his use of stichomythia is also a progression towards movement. In his hands it is a supple and often subtle instrument. The very regularity of a stichomythic conversation can have a cumulative effect on the mind of the listener, and occasional surprises within the regularity can focus the attention on important facts. It is the perfect form for regular logical argument.

(d) *The Récit*

The *récit* is the most varied of the stylized 'set pieces'. It contains narrative, description, extended similes, and at times reported speech;

the procedures, the very framework, are traditional and stylized; and within this framework the poet is free to expand, to describe, to digress. It is a perfect vehicle for *illustration* of the language.

At times the *récit* was used too much, as one can see, for example, by a glance at Rivaudeau's *Aman*. Here hardly any of the action takes place on the stage, and every potentially dramatic scene is retailed to us by a messenger.

Rivaudeau's play, however, is an extreme example; such excessive use of the *récit* was forced upon the author by his extremely strict views upon the Unity of Time. (He stated that the action should be completed in exactly the same time as the play took to be performed.) Usually a far more sparing use of the *récit* was made; and by the end of the century authors had come very close to what Schérer describes as the seventeenth-century classical view of the place of the *récit*: 'Les récits seront donc fréquents dans le théâtre classique. Mais ils ne seront point préférés par principe à la représentation des actions; c'est le contraire qui est vrai. Chaque fois qu'on le peut, on doit montrer l'événement lui-même; quand c'est impossible, on se résout à le raconter.'[1]

This is not to say that sixteenth-century dramatists did not enjoy using the *récit*; they delighted in it for all the reasons given above. But the greater ones, i.e. Garnier, La Taille, and Montchrestien, realized also the value of actually performing a dramatic scene upon the stage. Vauquelin de la Fresnaye was to state quite clearly the place of the *récit*:

> Qu'aux yeux elle sera de tous representée,
> Ou bien, faite desja, des joueurs recitée;
> *Et bien que ce qu'on oit emeuue beaucoup moins*
> *Que cela dont les yeux sont fidelles tesmoins,*
> Toutefois il ne faut lors montrer la personne,
> Quand la honte ou l'horreur du fait les gens etonne.[2]

Thus an actual scene was to be preferred to a *récit*, but there were certain circumstances in which a *récit* was the best course to take. *Récits* could be used when some obstacle stood in the way of the actual representation of the scene, e.g. (i) *The Unity of Time.* A *récit* would be needed to describe anything that took place before the action of the play. (ii) *The Bienséances.* Nobody should be killed or seduced on the stage, nor should anybody fight. (iii) *Vraisemblance,* as in the case of a full-scale battle.

---

[1] *La Dramaturgie classique en France*, pp. 229–30.
[2] Vauquelin de la Fresnaye, *Art poëtique*, ii. 387–92.

Montchrestien, in his *Aman*, shows us how this subject can be treated dramatically, with almost no *récits*. (There are only the dream *récit* and the ten-line description of Aman parading Mardochée through the city, which is not a true *récit*.)[1] This story, as told in the Bible, is extremely dramatic, and Montchrestien gives us the scenes which Rivaudeau, mainly because of his restriction of the Unity of Time to the length of the representation, has to describe in *récits*. None of these scenes would be forbidden by any rule other than that of Unity of Time.

To recapitulate the categories of necessary *récits*, these would be: (i) *Récits* of exposition, caused by the Unity of Time. As Montchrestien has no need of an exposition, on the whole he does not use this type of *récit*. (ii) The *dénouement récit*, caused by the *bienséances*. This is usually the description of someone's death. It does not necessarily, however, take place in the last act. Just as in Garnier's *La Troade* there are several such *récits*, so in Montchrestien's *Les Lacènes* we find two, in Acts III and V, though that in Act III qualifies as a battle *récit*. Other examples of *dénouement récits* are to be found in *Hector*, Act V, *David*, Act IV, and *La Reine d'Escosse*, Act V (the first two both qualify as battle *récits*). Sophonisbe commits suicide on the stage, so Montchrestien cuts out Trissino's *dénouement récit* from *La Cartaginoise*. (iii) The battle *récit*, caused by the rule of *vraisemblance*. There are three in *Hector* (Acts III, IV, and V), for the battle is perpetually raging off-stage, and the fortunes are continually changing. We find one in Act I of *La Cartaginoise*, one in Act III of *Les Lacènes*, and one in Act IV of *David*.

These are the three types of necessary *récit*. Yet there is a fourth category of *récit* which is very important in the Renaissance, and of which we can find examples in almost all dramatic authors. This is the dream *récit*, which was very popular. Its character made both its framework and its internal form different from other types of *récit*, as we shall see. In Montchrestien, examples of it can be found in *Hector*, *Aman*, *Les Lacènes*, and *La Cartaginoise*.

In Montchrestien there is only one *récit* which lies outside these four categories. This is Nadab's description of Bethsabée's anguish at her pregnancy.

---

[1] As Schérer says (op. cit., p. 235): 'Toute mention d'un événement non représenté sur scène n'est pas un récit. Le vrai récit doit ... *avoir une certaine forme*; il faut qu'il attire l'attention par quelque ampleur, qu'il soit un morceau d'éloquence. Trois vers faisant allusion à un événement qu'on n'a point vu ne font pas un récit.'

The Frame of the Récit

The *récits* are sometimes important for the effect they have on those to whom they are addressed. The three *récits* in *Hector* are all of this type. That in Act III spurs Hector to fatal action; he is so stirred by it that he leaves the stage without a word. The one in Act IV serves to raise the hopes of Priam, Hecube, and Andromache (and allows them to express a different mood), only for them to be dashed again by the *dénouement récit* in Act V. Similarly, that in Act III of *Les Lacènes* is important not only in itself, but also for the effect it has on Cratesiclea, who thinks at first that Pheax is bringing good news. The *récit* in Act IV of *David* is remarkable for showing us how unmoved David is by it, or apparently so. Other *récits*, however, which are made to the Chorus, are interesting only in themselves. They are aimed at the audience, and the Chorus acts as a kind of prompter and intermediary, rather than as an interested listener. Whereas one of the rules of seventeenth-century tragedy was to be that the hearer on the stage should be vitally interested in the *récit*, in the sixteenth century the *récit* was often aimed at the audience, and the Chorus could be used as auditor.

As M. Schérer points out,[1] the *récit* itself is surrounded by various fixed *formulae*, which introduce and punctuate it. Montchrestien's usage is not only interesting in those cases where he keeps to these formulae: it is also fascinating when he departs from them. There are often valid reasons for this, which are worthy of note. The accepted formulae are as follows:

(*a*) Normally, for a *dénouement récit*, the messenger (who is usually either anonymous, or a very unimportant character, who may not even appear elsewhere in the play) appears, and bewails fate in general terms: e.g. Seneca, *Troades*, 1056:

> O dura fata, saeva miseranda horrida! . . .

Or Garnier, *Marc-Antoine*, Act IV:

Dircet: Accident lamentable. O céleste courroux!
   O dieux trop inhumains!

Often he accuses the fate which causes him to bring this message; e.g. Seneca, *Hippolytus*, 991-2:

> O sors acerba et dura, famulatus gravis,
> Cur me ad nefandum nuntium casus vocat?

---

[1] Op. cit., pp. 235-9. Some of the 17th-century formulae do not apply in the 16th century, so the pattern is somewhat different, as we shall see.

Or Garnier, *Porcie*, Act IV:

Messager: Helas! n'avoy-je pas assez
　De quoy me malheurer en mes malheurs passez,
　Si mon désastre encor', pour recharge nouvelle,
　Ne me faisoit porter ceste triste nouvelle?

The messenger in Act V of *Hector* follows this pattern:

> Quel trait d'aspre douleur trauerse mon courage!
> Ie suis bien malheureux d'apporter le message
> De ton dernier desastre . . .

Similarly, Pheax, in Act III of *Les Lacènes*, speaks to himself at his first appearance:

> Malheureux Messager d'un malheureux message,
> Pourront bien tes soupirs accorder le passage
> Aux accens de ta voix qui tremble encor d'effroy,
> Pour avoir veu mourir mon cher Maistre et mon Roy.

But here there is an important change in the procedure. We, the audience, are already told the reason for his sorrow, and the full message. But those on the stage are not; they have not yet heard him. Cratesiclea still believes that 'Quelque bonne nouuelle il nous vient aporter', so this change in the traditional order of events provides some dramatic irony as the situation is gradually revealed to Cratesiclea.

When speaking to the Chorus, Montchrestien's messengers seem far less grief-stricken. Thus, in Act V of *La Reine d'Escosse*, the messenger merely says:

> Vous venez a propos, dolentes Damoiselles,
> Pour entendre par moy de piteuses nouuelles,

while the messenger in Act V of *Les Lacènes* declares his admiration for what has happened.

(*b*) After this first lamentation, the hearer usually asks the cause of it, whereupon the messenger quickly states what has happened. As M. Schérer says, it is important that this should come before the *récit* itself:

Celui qui fait un récit, au théâtre, ne peut pas, en général, suivre un ordre strictement chronologique. Si la personne qui l'écoute s'intéresse vraiment à son récit . . . elle doit être impatiente de connaître tout de suite le fait nouveau qu'annonce le messager. Un héros est-il mort, par exemple? La rhétorique peut détailler complaisamment les causes et les circonstances de cette mort, et ne finir qu'avec le dernier soupir du héros; mais l'intérêt dramatique exige que les personnages en scène et le spectateur sachent tout de suite que le héros est mort . . .[1]

In cases where this revelation is left out in sixteenth-century plays, this shows the unconcern of the author for such matters of *vraisemblance*, and his interest, above all, in the *récit* as an opportunity for rhetoric.

One must note, however, M. Schérer's phrase, 'Si la personne qui l'écoute s'intéresse vraiment à son récit'. In the cases where this is so (as we have seen, it was an essential in the seventeenth century, but not in the sixteenth), the news is told immediately. (*Cartaginoise*, Act I; *Hector*, Acts III, IV, and V; *Reine d'Escosse*, Act V (the chorus here consists of the Queen's companions).)

In Act III of *Les Lacènes* there is a short period of suspense, as we have seen. There are two examples, in Montchrestien, of a *dénouement récit* where we do not learn the full truth beforehand. The one is in Act V of *Les Lacènes*. The chorus is curious, but is not intimately involved. (Cratesiclea's and Stratonice's companions died with them, so this must be a different chorus which is merely there in order to 'hear' for the audience.) When the messenger declares his admiration for the Spartan women, the chorus does not specifically ask *what* has happened, but says: 'De grace di nous donc cette chose incroyable', whereupon the messenger launches into his *récit*.

The other example is in Act IV of *David*. The messenger comes to tell us of the death of Urie. Montchrestien here leaves out the prior revelation of this death for what may be a subtle purpose. We know the importance to David of Urie's death as opposed to the fate of the army as a whole. David, who has ordered that death, wants to know if he has succeeded. But he cannot ask about it, and has to ask a general question; the messenger does not realize the importance to the king of the death of Urie, and starts by giving a long description of the battle.

(c) After this first revelation of misfortune or death, there has to be some excuse for the messenger to give the details. Usually the hearer asks for more details, often in a merely mechanical phrase: e.g. Seneca, *Hippolytus*, 999: 'Mortis effare ordinem.' At other times a reason is given, e.g. Seneca, *Troades*, 1066–7:

> Gaudet magnus aerumnas dolor
> Tractare totas. Ede et enarra omnia.

Many sixteenth-century tragedians ignore such a preparation, and rush straight into the *récit*, neglecting all *vraisemblance* (for there is, in

---

[1] Op. cit., p. 237.

reality, no need for the messenger to give more details, unless asked).
Montchrestien, however, usually gives this preparation. In Acts IV
and V of *Hector*, Priam prompts the messenger to begin:

> Comme l'as-tu connu, di le nous, ie te prie?[1]

> Messager, pour nous voir en ces extrémitez
> Ne laissez de poursuiure et sa mort nous contez [2]

In *La Reine d'Escosse* the messenger gives his own reason for describing Mary's death in detail: he does it in order to console the lamenting chorus. In Act I of *La Cartaginoise*, Sophonisbe asks for details:

> Et comment, ie te prie, a-il peu nous surprendre?

In Act III of *Les Lacènes*, Cratesiclea wishes to know whether her son died stoically or not, and in Act V the chorus is moved by curiosity to hear the details of what has aroused the messenger's admiration. In Act IV of *David*, the king says: 'Au reste, rien du fait ne palie et ne cache . . .', hoping that the messenger will say something about Urie, but unable to ask for that specific piece of information directly.

(*d*) It was usual, when the hearer was keenly interested in the *récit*, for him to interrupt it at various points, partly in order to break up the vast expanses of unbroken rhetoric. But Montchrestien does not seem to have been very keen on this usage; possibly he felt that it broke up the interior form of the *récit*. Of the three interrupted *récits* that we find in his plays, one, that in *Sophonisbe*, Act I, has the interruption removed between 1596 and 1601. Of the others, one is in the *récit* in *David*, Act IV, where the king, to feign interest in the battle (and not in the death of Urie, which has not yet been revealed by the messenger), makes a long comment on Joab's faults in tactics. The other example is the *récit* in Act V of *Hector*, where Priam breaks in twice, inveighing against the treachery and cruelty of Achilles.

(*e*) At times the words of the hearer after the *récit* are important in showing us the effect it has had. (In other words, the *récit* is usually the opportunity for a *tirade* of grief.) Here, again, *David* is very interesting. After hearing of Urie's death, David, in place of the usual lamentations, speaks the following glib, sententious lines, which finish the scene:

> Ce dommage est fort gand, mais quoy? le sort des armes
> Tombe comme par chois sur les meilleurs Gensdarmes,
> Leur vaillance les perd; on diroit que la mort
> Espargne le poltron et poursuit le plus fort.

[1] P. de J., p. 52.   [2] Ibid., p. 62.

Hector's reaction to the Act III *récit* is translated purely by action, as he rushes off the stage without a word.

Dream *récits* have a slightly different outer framework. First, they are usually made by one of the main characters. Second, they are often preceded by vague forebodings and prophecies of disaster, followed by a request on the part of the hearer for a description of the dream. Andromache's dream *récit* in Seneca's *Troades* follows this pattern; Andromache foretells new disaster, and her audience, the anonymous *Senex*, finally asks her: 'Quae visa portas? effer in medium metus.'[1] Often, in Renaissance tragedy, the *récit* is preceded by a long argument in *sententiae* and *lieux communs* on the value of dreams as omens.

This is the case for Sophonisbe's dream. She and the Nurse discuss it in the following manner:

Sophonisbe: Vaines! non sont Nourice. Il est vraiment certain,
 Qu'un songe est prophetique, et qu'il n'est iamais vain.
Nourice: Il faut donc confesser que tout cela qu'on songe
 Est pure verité: non, ce n'est que mensonge . . . etc.[2]

Finally the Nurse asks her:

 Dites moi, s'il vous plait, ce songe qui vous ronge.[3]

The dreams of Mardochée and of Cléomène do not have this outer framework. They are given to us gratuitously, one of them to round off the play *Aman*, the other in the opening monologue of *Les Lacènes*. Andromache's dream in *Hector* is very interesting for its variation on the traditional technique. Andromache tells the nurse of her dream, and receives the usual reply:

 Un songe n'est que vent, n'y mettez nulle foy.[4]

After a little more dialogue, the nurse says:

 Dites moy vos ennuis pour vous en consoler,
 La tristesse s'allege en luy donnant de l'air.[4]

So far we seem to be following the traditional pattern, and the spectator, or reader, awaits the usual exhibition of stylized but brilliant verbal virtuosity. But the author appears to be playing with us: Andromache hesitates, and says that she must see Priam. It is only after a while, in

---

[1] Seneca, *Troades*, 437. [2] *Sophonisbe*, 1596, 345–8.
[3] Ibid., 353. [4] *P. de J.*, p. 18.

the next scene, that we hear the *récit*, after we have gone through the whole process once more, with Priam asking her:

> Chaste espouse d'Hector, raconte les douleurs
> Qui tirent de tes yeux ceste source de pleurs.[1]

The framework around Montchrestien's *récits* fills, on the whole, the same role as that around the *récits* of other Renaissance dramatists. Around dream *récits* there is the usual discussion on the efficacy of dreams; around other *récits* there are the usual introductory exclamations and inquiries. Montchrestien follows, too, the sixteenth-century practice of occasionally providing *récits* addressed to the chorus; here the prospective audience is in fact the actual theatrical audience or the reader. The chorus cannot be expected to have the same intimate interest in the content of the *récit* as a protagonist of the play would have, and so the framework is occasionally varied accordingly.

At times, because of the hallowed framework of the *récit*, an author is able, by changing it slightly, to achieve surprising effects. This happens, in Montchrestien, in Act III of *Les Lacènes*, where those on stage do not hear the messenger's lamentations, and are thus for a while misled, and in Act IV of *David*, where the king's equivocal position makes him unable to ask for the information he wants, and forces him to comment on what to him is unimportant information. The fact of having a stylized framework can therefore make departures from that framework most effective.

The *récit* itself, within this framework, was for the Renaissance dramatist another set piece, sufficient in itself.

The Form of the Récit

The interior form of the *récit*, in Renaissance tragedy, follows very closely the model of Seneca, rather than that of the Greek tragedians. The Greek messenger speech had essentially been a straightforward narrative, moving quickly from one event to another, the poet endeavouring to convey a clear message to the listener; the few decorative elements were subsidiary; similes were terse and striking, seldom lasting for more than a line; people and places were described with similar terseness. The tightly-knit narrative kept the listener's attention from beginning to end, as it swirled him along with irresistible force.

With Seneca, however, the aim was completely different. The form of the *récit*, which had been so free in Greek times, became more and

---

[1] Ibid., p. 20.

more stylized. Similes became an excuse for long digressions, as did descriptions. The scene was set in time or place by a digression of many lines. The characters in the *récit* pronounced long *tirades*. The whole *récit* became far more static, far more ornamental. Seneca, the rhetorician, saw in it an opportunity for linguistic and rhetorical display, rather than for dramatic narrative.

The difference can be seen if we compare the description of the monster in the messenger speech from the *Hippolytus* of Euripides and Seneca. Euripides, concerned with the narrative above all, gives no clear description, but merely states the impression of horror which this monster aroused:

> The wave belched forth a bull, a monster fierce,
> With whose throat-thunder all the land was filled,
> And echoed awfully, as on our gaze
> He burst, a sight more dread than eyes could bear.[1]

Seneca, on the other hand, takes the opportunity for a long digression. First he arouses our horror by a couple of rhetorical tricks:

> Os quassat tremor.
> Quis habitus ille corporis vasti fuit![2]

Then he proceeds to a long and detailed description of the animal:

> Caerulea taurus colla sublimis gerens
> Erexit altam fronte viridanti iubam;
> Stant hispidae aurea, orbibus varius color,
> Et quem feri dominator habuisset gregis
> Et quem sub undis natus—hinc flammam vomunt
> Oculi, hinc relucent caerula insignes nota;
> Opima cervix arduos tollit toros
> Naresque hiulcis haustibus patulae fremunt;
> Musco tenaci pectus ac palear viret,
> Longum rubente spargitur fuco latus.
> Tum pone tergus ultima in monstrum coit
> Facies et ingens belua immensam trahit
> Squamosa partem. Talis extremo mari
> Pistrix citatas sorbet aut frangit rates.[3]

Such long descriptions are common in sixteenth-century *récits*. There

---

[1] Euripides, *Hippolytus*, 1214–17 (Loeb translation).
[2] Seneca, *Hippolytus*, 1034–5.
[3] Ibid., 1036–49.

is a good example in Sophonisbe's dream *récit*, where after ten lines
of description of a monster, she declares:

> Nourice ie ne veux d'un diligent pinceau,
> Peindre ce monstre horrible en ton foible cerveau
> Je pourrois imprimer en ta vieille poitrine
> L'horreur qu'en y songeant mon esprit s'imagine.[1]

Even more common than such descriptions are the long Homeric
similes which abound in these *récits*. Again, such digressions are purely
Senecan. Where Euripides's similes rarely last more than one line, e.g.:

> As shipman tugs against the oar.[2]

or:

> For like two charging hosts her torment came,[3]

Seneca's are expanded to a great length, e.g.:

> Silva iubatus qualis Armenia leo
> In caede multa victor armento incubat
> (Cruore rictus madidus et pulsus fame
> Non ponit iras; hinc et hinc tauros premens
> Vitulis minatur dente iam lasso piger)—
> Non aliter Atreus saevit atque ira tumet.[4]

This is the most typical form for the extended simile; it starts, in
this case, with the straightforward comparison (two lines), continues
with an explanatory expansion, in parenthesis (three lines), and then
connects the whole thing with the main action of the *récit* (non
aliter . . . etc.).

Montchrestien's *récits* are full of such similes, many of them con-
forming to this strict plan, e.g.:

> Comme quand un faucon soustenu de ses aisles
> Descouvre le voler des faibles Colombelles,
> Qui retournent des champs et coupent seurement
> La vague remuant du venteux élément,
> Il se laisse tomber sur la bande timide;
> La pluspart fuit legere où la crainte la guide,
> Proye à d'autres oiseaux, mais celles-là qu'il bat
> Et de bec et de mains sur terre il les abat:
> Hector fondant de mesme en l'Argolique armée . . .[5]

---

[1] *Sophonisbe*, 1596, 379–82.   [2] Euripides, *Hippolytus*, 1221.
[3] Euripides, *Medea*, 1185.   [4] Seneca, *Thyestes*, 732–6.
[5] *Hector*; *P. de J.*, p. 62.

and also:

> Comme quand un torrent chet des hautes montagnes
> Il se fait à l'instant Roy des basses campagnes;
> Nulle digue ne peut sa fureur arrester,
> Qui s'efforce tant plus on luy veut resister:
> Les pauvres Laboureurs esmeus de leur dommage
> S'opposent, mais en vain, à ce cruel ravage.
> Tout est envelopé dessous les flots troublez,
> Qui ravissent les ponts, les arbres, et les bleds:
> De mesme nos Guerriers . . .[1]

Besides these long, extended similes, there still exist the short, striking ones used by both Greek and Latin dramatists, e.g.:

> Il tombe sur terre
> Comme un chesne abattu des trois dards de tonnerre.[2]

Scholl claims[3] that Montchrestien uses more of these long comparisons than his predecessors. Certainly, the few that he cuts out between the different editions of *Sophonisbe* were probably suppressed more because of the general compression of the play than because of a dislike for this type of image.[4] In Act I of *La Cartaginoise*, in the 1604 edition, there is a very long image of this type, which lasts for fourteen lines; it deals with the mariner driven by the storm.

The stylization of the inner composition of the Senecan messenger speech is stressed by the opening, where the scene is set, either in space or in time. Often there is a long description of the place where the action is to take place. Thus, in Seneca's *Troades*, the description of the death of Astyanax starts with a twenty-line description of the scene:

> Est una magna turris e Troia super,
> Adsueta Priamo, cuius e fastigio
> Summisque pinnis arbiter belli sedens
> Regebat acies. Turre in hac blando sinu
> Fovens nepotem, cum metu versos gravi
> Danaos fugaret Hector et ferro et face,
> Paterna puero bella monstrabat senex . . .[5]

As can be seen, the description of the scene often contains its former history. Similarly, in Seneca's *Thyestes*, the messenger's speech starts

---

[1] *Les Lacènes*; *P. de J.*, p. 182.   [2] Ibid., p. 183.
[3] *Die Vergleiche in Montchrestiens Tragödien*, Munich, 1894, p. 67.
[4] See Appendix 1.   [5] Seneca, *Troades*, 1068–74.

with *forty-two* lines of description of the scene.[1] The sixteenth-century dramatists often use this method of opening the *récit*; but only very rarely do they go to such lengths. More usually, the place-setting occupies four or six lines, as, for example, in Garnier's *Les Juifves*:

> Derriere le chasteau, où le bruyant Oronte
> Coule en le traversant d'une carrière prompte,
> S'estend une grand'place enfermée à l'entour
> D'une longue muraille, où flanque mainte tour.
> Là, les rois syriens, quand ils vouloyent s'esbatre,
> Enfermoyent les lions, pour les faire combatre.[2]

Where Montchrestien uses this type of opening, he is similarly short: e.g. *La Reine d'Escosse*, Act v:

> Une grand'salle estoit funebrement parée,
> Et de flambeaux ardans haut et bas esclairée.
> D'une noire couleur esclatoit le paué,
> L'eschaffaut paroissoit hautement esleué.
> Là des peuples voisins se fait une assemblée,
> Qui de tel accident estoit beaucoup troublée . . .[3]

Another type of opening is that of a stylized description of time. This type of introduction is usually fairly short,[4] e.g. Andromache's dream in Seneca's *Troades*:

> Partes fere nox alma transierat duas
> Clarumque septem verterant stellae iugum.[5]

---

[1] Seneca, *Thyestes*, 641–82.
[2] Garnier, *Les Juifves*, 1891–6.
[3] *P. de J.*, p. 108.
[4] However, occasionally in Renaissance tragedy one finds passages which compete, for garrulous periphrasis, with Shakespeare's humorous lines in *Hamlet*:

> Full thirty times hath Phoebus' cart gone round
> Neptune's salt wash . . . etc.

e.g. Matthieu, *Clytemnestre*:

> Dix fois Ceres avoit retondu sa perruque . . .
> Dix fois Phebus avoit logé chez les bessons,
> Dix fois de belles fleurs la Printaniere Flore
> Avoit coiffé nos champs, et dix fois douze encore
> Diane avoit changé de cornes son croissant,
> Diane honneur du bois et du ciel blanchissant,
> Dix fois le bon Denis avoit dansé en cuve,
> Espurant la liqueur que l'univers abreuve . . .

[5] Seneca, *Troades*, 438–9.

Montchrestien uses the time-opening quite extensively, at times with the traditional references to the sun, e.g. *Les Lacènes*, Act III:

> A peine le Soleil auoit laissé derriere
> Une egale moitié de sa longue carriere.[1]

and *David*, Act IV:

> Ià le Soleil doroit le coupeau des montagnes . . .[2]

or *Sophonisbe*, Act I:

> Ja le coq matineux disoit bon iour au iour,
> Appelant au combat les coqs qui tour a tour,
> Saluent le leuer de la vermeille Aurore,
> Qui reconduit sur nous le char qui nous redore . . .[3]

Of course, there is often no indication of time, for the messenger may have come straight from the scene he describes, as in Acts III, IV, and V of *Hector*.

Another type of digression with the *récit* is the speech, whether it is given as reported speech or otherwise. This is common in the *récits* of both Greek and Latin tragedy, though in the Greek such speeches are very short. Here the devices of spoken rhetoric vary the otherwise epic form of the *récit*. The speeches are usually made by the person who is about to die, or by a general before a battle; their content is often Stoic and proud. The effect on the spectators is usually described. The characteristics of these speeches are the same as those of the *tirade*.

Thus Cléomène, in Pheax's *récit* in Act III of *Les Lacènes*, makes a speech of 52 lines before the Spartans' bid for liberty. The speech is, as most are, given in direct speech. He spurs them on to action:

> Marchon, braves Guerriers, ou l'honneur nous conuie.[4]

After the speech, we hear that:

> A ces propos hautains ses compagnons aimez
> Furent d'un vif esprit chaudement allumez . . .[4]

In the last *récit* of *La Reine d'Escosse* there are four speeches. Firstly,

---

[1] *P. de J.*, p. 180.   [2] *P. de J.*, p. 222.
[3] *Sophonisbe*, A 355–8.   [4] *P. de J.*, p. 181.

in eighteen lines, she tries to console her companions; this does not have much effect, however:

> Quand elle eut dit ces mots à ses tristes seruantes,
> Pour son cruel depart plus mortes que viuantes,
> S'accreurent les souspirs en leurs cœurs soucieux,
> Les plaintes en leur bouche, et les pleurs en leurs yeux.[1]

Later, she speaks (in nine lines) as she mounts the scaffold, looking forward to the martyr's sacrifice. These words are addressed to the heavens:

> Ces mots sur des soupirs elle enuoyoit aux Cieux,
> Qui sembloient s'atrister des larmes de ses yeux.[1]

Only very rarely are the speeches given in indirect speech. The herald's speech in Act I of *Sophonisbe* is transformed from indirect to direct speech between 1601 and 1604.

It is in this form of digression that *sententiae* come into their own. For it is rare for them to be used in the ordinary *récit*; in a reported speech they can be used as freely as in a normal speech.

The *récit*, then, is a stylized form, of epic quality. It sets out to describe things that cannot be performed upon the stage. Montchrestien's *récits* on the whole fill the same role as those of other tragedians of the Renaissance. The plays are not over-filled with them; they fulfil certain accepted functions, either essential to the plot, or, as in the case of dream *récits*, because they conform to an accepted formula. Occasionally there is what one might call a luxury *récit*, such as that of the 'Ombre de Thericion' in *Les Lacènes*.

The outer framework of the *récit*, the conversation before, during, and after it, is normally extremely stylized. Such stylization makes an occasional variation in the formula very effective.

The inner form of the *récit* is varied, but stylized in its variations. On to the epic basis are attached lyrical dramatic and rhetorical elements.

The *récit* in the Renaissance is essentially a static form of 'set piece', like that of Seneca, for the news it delivers would be just as effective if told in a few lines. The length of the *récit* is devoted to an elaboration of the facts; the story is told in full, and to it are added long descriptions, images, and rhetorical speeches. This is perhaps the richest of the 'set pieces'.

[1] Ibid., p. 109.

(e) *The Chorus*

The chorus had, in Renaissance tragedy, two distinct roles: that of a composite character, who could take part in the dialogue, and that of a lyric interlude, dividing the acts (and at times the scenes). In many authors of this period the same chorus could perform both roles. Garnier, for example, though he often has two or three different *chœurs* in a play, nevertheless lets them each perform both roles. Montchrestien, on the other hand, presents us on the whole with two completely different types of chorus, each with a different function. One is impersonal, and performs the role of an interlude, usually making moral judgements with general reference to the plot; the other takes the part of a composite character. Only at one point, in Act III of *Aman*, do we find a chorus which appears to fulfil both functions.

In this separation of the two functions of the chorus Montchrestien would appear to be unusual. For though both roles of the chorus were typical of ancient tragedy, there was no sharp differentiation of the two types, and the same group of people could perform both tasks. This was also true in the case of most Renaissance dramatists.

The distinction, in Montchrestien's mind, between the two types of chorus, is shown most clearly on the occasions when they speak one after the other. For on such an occasion he repeats the heading '*Chœur*', a procedure which would be completely unnecessary if the two functions were not to be clearly differentiated. There is an example of this in Act v of *Aman*, where, after the Assuérus–Aman scene, the interlude-chorus speaks, in the usual manner, four lines of general moral import relating to the scene we have just witnessed:

> La Fortune de Cour est semblable à la rouë,
> Dont le plus haut endroit vient d'un tour en la bouë.
> Qui s'enfle trop du vent de cet honneur mondain,
> A la parfin en creve ou se void en desdain.[1]

Here the interlude-chorus is filling a function which we shall find to be typical; it facilitates a change of place by commenting generally on the situation. But now the chorus continues; and in the Petit de Julleville edition its situation appears ludicrous, because it becomes the children of Israel, unaware of recent events, who are bewailing their lot, and Aman's fury against them. They receive with surprise a messenger's news of Aman's abasement, and Mardochée's honours; in fact, they refer to this as a 'changement du sort du tout inespéré!'

[1] *Aman*, B 1435–8.

Indeed, in Petit de Julleville's edition the chorus's position seems ludicrous, and Montchrestien's work slovenly. It is only when we turn to the original edition that we find that Montchrestien, after the four lines of interlude-chorus, had carefully inserted again the heading *Ch.*, thus making it quite clear that the scene had now changed, that the interlude-chorus had served its purpose, and that a chorus of Israelites had appeared on the stage as a composite character. Petit de Julleville's deletion of this word has made a nonsense of the whole scene.

There is a similar repetition of the word *Chœur* in Act III of *Hector*, where the character-chorus attempts to console Helen in twelve lines, and then the interlude-chorus is announced by this means.

Formally, the two different types of chorus are usually differentiated by the fact that the interlude-chorus is in stanza form, or in some metre other than the alexandrine, while the character-chorus retains the alexandrine used for the speech of other characters. There are, however, occasional exceptions to this. The character-chorus may on occasion lament or pray in lyrical stanza form, as a kind of 'set piece'. There is one such lament in Act IV of *Les Lacènes*, consisting of seventeen quatrains of alexandrines; and there is a prayer in Act III of *La Reine d'Escosse* consisting of six stanzas (10.10.6.6.) (though this might in fact be taken as an interlude-chorus).

Strictly speaking, the character-chorus is no concern of this chapter; but it would perhaps be as well briefly to touch on this aspect of the chorus, before dealing with the interlude-chorus in its role as a 'set piece'.

Jacques Peletier du Mans said of the chorus: 'Le Chore en la Tragedie (nous disons Keur aux eglises) est une multitude de gens, soit hommes ou femmes, parlans tous ensemble.'[1]

Grévin disagrees with this, splitting his chorus into parts, which converse with each other. Montchrestien's chorus, on the other hand, speaks with one voice, except in the extraordinary lament in Act IV of *Les Lacènes*. This, though in alexandrines, is in stanza form. Each quatrain, except one, is headed *Chœur* for the first ten quatrains (the one exception is a quatrain marked '*Cratesiclea*'). After this there is a group of four quatrains under one heading, then another group of three. This scheme is true of all editions. The chorus must at this point be divided into at least two parts, which reply to each other.

In two of Montchrestien's plays, *Sophonisbe* and *David*, there is no character-chorus at all, and the other plays use it in varying degrees. It

---

[1] *Art poëtique*, livre ii, ch. 7.

is possible, indeed, to have two character-choruses in the same play, as in *La Reine d'Escosse*, where there is both a 'Chœur des Estats', which speaks with Elizabeth, and the 'Chœur' of Mary's companions; and as in *Les Lacènes*, where a different chorus appears in the last act, to hear of the fate of the Spartan women.

Montchrestien's use of the character-chorus follows a surprisingly similar pattern to the development of the use of stichomythia which we have already seen. There are no examples in the *Sophonisbe* of 1596 (or in the later versions of this, naturally enough); there are no examples in *David*; and there are merely two brief appearances in *Aman* (in Acts III and V). In the other two 1601 plays, however (*La Reine d'Escosse* and *Les Lacènes*), there is quite extensive use of the chorus as character, and by the time of the 1604 *Hector*, we appear to have a chorus which is almost permanently on the stage, observing and commenting on the action.

In *Les Lacènes* the chorus of Spartan women only appears with the women characters, who are in a different place of captivity from the men. Then, in Act V, there is another and more detached chorus, which receives the messenger, and comments on his *récit* of the death of the other chorus.

In *La Reine d'Escosse* one of the choruses has a far more active role. Whereas Mary's companions are essentially *confidantes*, who try to give her hope in Act III, express horror at Davison's message in the same act, and listen to the messenger in Act V, the 'Chœur des Estats' is partly instrumental, in Act II, in persuading Elizabeth to kill Mary. It is a second attempt, following on that of the Conseiller in Act I, to win her over. Admittedly, at the end of the act the victory seems uncertain; but we see from later events that the persuasion has been successful.

In *Hector*, the character-chorus appears to be continually on the stage, observing and commenting on the action. It speaks in every act, and no mention is ever made of its entry or exit. At times it acts as *confidant*, e.g. for Cassandre and for Hector in Acts I and III, and for Andromache in Act IV. It is also part of the audience for all three *récits*. Elsewhere, it observes and comments, e.g. Heleine's tirade, and the chorus's comment on the Priam–Hector argument in Act II.

Thus Montchrestien seems gradually to have used the character-chorus more and more, until in 1604, in *Hector*, where it appears to remain on the stage throughout.

Let us now consider the interlude-chorus, which can be considered as yet another form of 'set piece'.

'Chorus est pars inter actum et actum', says Scaliger.[1] It thus represents any imaginary time which passes between the acts, and also helps
us to move more easily, in our imagination, from place to place. The
practical side of a performance is taken into account by Daigaliers, who
suggests that the Chorus is there '. . . pour que le Theatre ne demeurast
vuide et que le peuple fust distraict'.[2]

Garnier, in the *Argument de Bradamante*, a play in which there is no
chorus between the acts, is worried by this practical side, and says:
'Et parce qu'il n'y a point de Chœurs, comme aux tragédies précédentes,
pour la distinction des actes, celuy qui voudroit représenter cette
Bradamante sera, s'il luy plaist, adverty d'user d'entremets, et les
interposer entre les actes pour ne les confondre, et ne mettre en con-
tinuation de propos ce qui requiert quelque distance de temps.'

Scaliger adds: 'In finem tamen Fabularum etiam Choros videmus',
whereas Daigaliers claims '. . . chacun acte a ses chœurs apres, excepté
le cinquième qui n'en doit point avoir ...',[1] even though he himself has
gone against this dictum in his own plays. Certainly, there is no need
for a Chorus at the end of the play, according to the needs defined by
Daigaliers and Garnier.

Montchrestien on the whole conforms with Daigaliers, for, though
the chorus has the last word in four of his plays, in each case it is the
character-chorus; in *La Reine d'Escosse* it laments after hearing the
messenger's speech, in *Les Lacènes* it comments on the situation for
six lines in general terms, after the *récit*; in *Hector*, having been present
for the lamentations of Andromache, Priam, and Hécube, it comments
for twelve lines; and in *Aman* we have the nearest approach to a final
Chorus, a paraphrase of Psalm 124, consisting of six *sixains* of alexandrines. (It is, however, recited by the 'Chœur des Fidèles'.)

Each of these endings (except, of course, the paraphrase of the
psalm) finishes up with a kind of moral, a sentential summing-up of
the point of the play. These are of the usual Stoic nature, for example:

La Reine d'Escosse

    » De moment en moment on voit tout se changer;
    » La vie est comme une ombre ou comme un vent leger,
    » Et son cours n'est à rien qu'à un rien comparable.

Les Lacènes

    » De là nous apprenon que contre toute rage
    » La vertu se maintient sans endurer d'outrage.

---

[1] *Poetices libre septem*, Paris 1561, liber i, cap. ix (quoted in Lawton).
[2] *Art poëtique françois*, Paris 1598, livre v, ch. vii.

» Soient tous les vents du monde émeus pour l'esbranler,
» On ne la voit iamais çà et là vaciller;
» Mais plus ferme qu'un Roc elle est tousiours toute une
» Aux orages divers qu'apporte la fortune.

Hector

» Que le bon-heur publique est foible et vacillant,
» S'il dépend de la main d'un seul homme vaillant,
» Qui s'offre à tous hazards sans crainte de la Parque.
» Mortels, voyez ici que pour estre Monarque,
» Empereur, Capitaine, on ne vit pas plus seur
» De tromper les ciseaux de la fatale sœur,
» Qui sans aucun respect en la tombe devale
» La houlette champestre et la verge Royale.

In the play *La Cartaginoise*, which has no character-chorus to perform this function, Act V ends with an 'Epigramme' which does fulfil it:

EPIGRAMME

Sophonisbe s'estant à son vainqueur rendue,
Il ne la peut sauver en ayant volonté:
Aussi tost qu'elle en a la nouvelle entendue,
Mourons, dit-elle donc, c'est là trop arresté:
Si ne c'est en gardant la chere liberté,
Ce sera pour le moins apres l'avoir perduë.

David is the only play which ends with the speech of a character (Nathan). In this, as in many other aspects, it differs from Montchrestien's other plays.

A progression in Montchrestien's dramatic art is marked by the introduction of choruses in the *middle* of acts, where the scene changes, to aid our imagination in moving from place to place.[1] There were examples of this already in 1601 (e.g. *David*, Act V), but by 1604 it has become the general rule, the only blatant example of lack of its use being in Act II of *Les Lacènes*, where the Stratonice–Archidamie scene takes place directly after the Cratesiclea–Chœur scene. However, these two scenes may possibly be happening in the same place, even though there is no *liaison des scènes*; in 1604 Cratesiclea says in her last speech 'Couron viste a l'autel . . .' (instead of the 1601 'Reschauffon les autels'), thus getting herself and her companions off the stage before the others come on (though they may have been there already, during the previous scene).

[1] See Chapter 7, 'Stage Representation'.

In Montchrestien the chorus of lyric interlude is always impersonal, speaking in general statements, commonplaces, *sententiae*, etc. In the plays of earlier authors, however, the distinction between the two types of chorus was less sharp, and the interlude-chorus had often been a chorus of definite people, who had the interests of one or other of the characters at heart. The verses spoken by the chorus were often bound up with the action of the play, as in Jodelle's *Cléopâtre* or Garnier's *Hippolyte*; on the other hand, they were at times more general, as in Garnier's *Marc-Antoine*, where there are more references to the general effects of civil war and to unspecified grief, than to the action of the play itself. Whereas in Montchrestien the interlude-chorus is always the unspecified 'chœur', in other authors this is not always the case.

Montchrestien's interlude-chorus is indefinite, and very much the voice of the author. Its connection with the plot is at most very slight, its sayings being general moral *sententiae*, whose only connection with the plot are the general values which are treated in both.

The author is here ruled by the current sixteenth-century misinterpretation[1] of the passage in Horace's *Ars Poetica* relevant to the role of the chorus:

> Actoris partis chorus officiumque virile
> Defendat.[2]

'Actoris' was mistaken for 'Autoris', and the chorus was thus understood to take the place of the author, rather than to take the role of an actor. Peletier, in his *Art poétique*, tells us: 'Il doit tousjours être du parti de l'auteur: c'est à dire qu'il doit donner à connoitre le sens et le jugement du poëte: parler sentencieusement, craindre les Dieux, reprendre les vices, menacer les mechans, ammonester à la vertu. . . .'[3]

The moral nature of the chorus had also been stressed by Horace; but nobody had ever gone quite as far as Montchrestien in converting the chorus into a purveyor of general moral lessons.[4] In the 1604 edition *sententiae* are, in the usual manner, marked by inverted commas, and each interlude-chorus is an unrelieved sea of these signs.[5] Exceptions are rare; and even unmarked passages are usually sententious in import.

---

[1] Due to a variant text.

[2] *Ars Poetica*, 193–4. [3] *Art poëtique*, 1555, livre ii, ch. 7.

[4] The value of these as views of the author is discussed elsewhere.

[5] Not all the lines so marked conform to M. Schérer's rigid formula for the *sententia*. (See Schérer's *Dramaturgie classique*, and my section on *sententiae*.) However, lines so marked are always general statements, which have no specific connection with the play.

In Montchrestien's plays there are occasional, but only very slight references to the action of the play in the interlude-chorus; in *La Cartaginoise*, at the end of Act II, two stanzas are devoted to the surprising reconciliation of Massinisse and Sophonisbe; two stanzas at the end of Act III warn Massinisse not to let love run away with him. Similarly, at the end of Act III of *Les Lacènes*, three stanzas praise the courage of the Spartans for breaking out, and after the first act of *David* two stanzas compare the king's former to his present state. The history of marriage, after Act II of *David*, has no connection other than general to the plot. In *Aman*, after Acts I and II, the references to 'O toy potiron d'une nuit, / Que l'orgueil a si fort seduit', and 'Pan, si tes plumes t'orgueillissent . . .', do not necessarily refer to Aman personally; for the chorus in both cases is referring in general terms to pride, ambition, and presumption.

The chorus, as a lyrical interlude, presents an opportunity for the author to expand at length upon a given subject. In Montchrestien's case, it enables him to present a calm and measured treatment of a moral or philosophical subject, rather than a study in mood. As such, it is a contrast both in aim and in subject-matter with the tirade and the monologue.

It presents, also, an opportunity to escape from the alexandrines into various other metres and stanza forms. Here it must be admitted that Montchrestien does not go so far in his experimentation as do other sixteenth-century dramatists. Many of his choruses consist simply of quatrains of alexandrines. His other main metre is the octosyllabic, of which he constructs stanzas of four, five, six, or even eight lines, but without varying them with lines of any other length, except after the first act of *Hector*, where there are sixains of 6.8.6.8.6.6, and in Act V of *Les Lacènes*, where there are sixains of 8.8.6.8.8.6. The only real originality seems to be Montchrestien's use of the seven-syllable line (Choruses to Acts II and IV of *La Cartaginoise*) and one or two other isolated examples. (Quatrains 6.10.10.6 after Act I of *La Cartaginoise*, quatrains 12.6.12.12 after Act II of *Hector*, quatrains 12.6.12.6 after Act I of *La Reine d'Escosse*, a prayer of quatrains 10.10.6.6 in Act III of the same play, and cinquains 12.12.6.12.12 after Act IV of *David*.)

But while Montchrestien is not metrically adventurous, his choruses nevertheless present a difference in mood from that of the rest of the text of the plays, forming lyrical interludes which can view the overtones of the plot from a detached viewpoint. The chorus devotes itself to the discussion of eternal values, usually by use of *sententiae*. Though these eternal values have reference to the plot, it is an implicit, rather than an explicit reference. The interlude-chorus is an anonymous body, completely separate from the character-chorus.

(f) *Conclusion*

The stylization of the 'set pieces' stems partly from the classical models (above all Seneca), and partly from the outlook derived from the rhetorical exercises used in Renaissance education—exercises complete in themselves, and having no progression of mood.

These 'set pieces' lie at the basis of Montchrestien's dramatic technique. All is subordinated to them, and they in turn dutifully serve the author's primary purpose, which is the rhetorical development of certain emotions and ideas.

Vraisemblance is subordinated to stylization; the characters address each other in long tirades, argue in regular stichomythia, and retail important news at great length, with a wealth of detail. In the monologues and tirades, feelings are static and unchanging; in the *récits*, the narration of the event is continually interrupted by long descriptions, similes, and reported speeches. The chorus elaborates the statement of eternal truths.

Within these 'set pieces' the author's language and style can be set out to their best advantage; the aims of Renaissance tragedy are fully achieved by the use of these stylized forms.

7. Stage Representation

ARIOUS questions must be asked about Montchrestien's plays:
Were the plays performed? If so, on what type of stage? How
common are changes of place within the acts? How does Montchrestien engineer these changes of place? To what extent does
Montchrestien bother about 'justification' (in the seventeenth-century
sense) for the entrances and exits of his characters?

(a) *Performance of the Plays*

Were the tragedies of the sixteenth century intended to be performed, or not? In the long-standing controversy over this question,
Lanson[1] and Haraszti[2] appear to have won the day. It is now certain
that many of these tragedies were performed, and that many of them
were written for that purpose. Among those known to have appeared
on the stage are Montchrestien's *Sophonisbe* (some time before 1596)
and *L'Escossoise* (in 1601, 1603, and 1604). As the performances of
the latter are known to us purely by chance, because of a diplomatic
incident, it is probable that the other plays were performed as well.

But what form did these performances take? Rigal, who originally
believed that the tragedies were written purely for reading,[3] was
eventually forced, by the weight of evidence, to abandon this position;
but he still claimed that they could never have been written for a true
performance, and that there must have been some form of 'récitation',
or 'lecture dialoguée'.[4]

One of the main considerations which brought him to this conclusion
was the apparent impossibility of many of the scenic directions, and

---

[1] G. Lanson, 'Études sur les origines de la tragédie classique en France', *R.H.L.F.*
(1903), pp. 177 ff., 413 ff.

[2] J. Haraszti, *R.H.L.F.* (1904), pp. 680 ff.

[3] In *Alexandre Hardy et le théâtre français à la fin du 16ᵉ siècle et au commencement du
17ᵉ siècle*, Paris, 1889, and also in his chapter in Petit de Julleville's *Histoire de la littérature
française* (vol. 3, p. 268), and in *Le Théâtre français avant la période classique*, Paris, 1901.

[4] See E. Rigal, *De Jodelle à Molière* ('La mise-en-scène dans les tragédies du 16ᵉ siècle')

especially the presence of the chorus in many places at once. This difficulty is at once removed, in the case of Montchrestien, however, when one understands the impersonal nature of the interlude-chorus, which stands outside time and place. Rigal's mistake becomes clear if we look more closely at the examples he has taken from Montchrestien's plays; he imagines that the chorus must at all times be a character. He describes the chorus in *Sophonisbe* as being 'composé des sujets de Sophonisbe',[1] whereas there is no character-chorus in this play; he then complains because he thinks that it sings 'chez Massinisse, où sa place ne saurait être'. The same mistake is made about *L'Escossoise*, where he thinks that Mary's companions sing 'chez Elizabeth au premier et an second acte'. Again, in *Les Lacènes*, he believes that the chorus of young Spartan women 'entend et loue l'héroïque résolution de Cléomène'. It is small wonder that, with this view of the chorus, Rigal should believe that

souvent même, l'auteur ne se demande pas où se passe son action et ne s'inquiète pas des contradictions que contient son texte. . . . Que ces pièces aient ou n'aient pas paru sur une scène, à vrai dire il n'importe guère. Ce qui importe, c'est que la plupart de celles qui ont paru sur le théâtre n'ont pu y être que récitées; c'est que leurs auteurs n'avaient pas l'idée de ce qu'est une véritable représentation.[2]

Now, though Rigal's reasons for reaching this conclusion are often unsound, this does not necessarily mean that the conclusion itself is in all respects wrong. Very often, indeed, in the works of sixteenth-century dramatists, one gains the impression that they are not worrying very much about the exact location where their action is taking place. That this does not, however, cut out the possibility of a 'real performance' (whatever that may mean) is something which Rigal seems to ignore.

So we have no real proof as to the nature of the performance of the plays themselves in the sixteenth century; all we can be certain of is the fact that many *were* performed (though of course others, such as those of Matthieu, were clearly written for reading).

As for the lack of concern for details of stage production, which Rigal ascribes to the authors, for some of them this is certainly true. But of such men as La Taille, Garnier, and Montchrestien, the statement is far from the truth. Montchrestien took great care to improve

---

[1] Ibid., p. 118.   [2] Ibid., pp. 137–8.

the stageability of his plays by the changes he made between the successive versions.

(b) *The Type of Stage*

Apart from a *récitation dialoguée*, Rigal appears to envisage only two possible types of performance; for him, the play must either take place on the medieval *décor multiple*, or conform strictly to Unity of Place.[1] He ignores the possibility of the stage representing one place at a time, with that place changing at various times during the play (as, for example, in the plays of Shakespeare). He also ignores, as so many sixteenth-century critics have done, the fact that the Unity of Place, despite one solitary, puzzling mention in Jean de la Taille's *Art de la tragédie*, had no place in sixteenth-century dramatic practice.

If we rule out the possibility of a *lecture dialoguée*, then, we are left with a choice between the medieval type of stage, made up of compartments, and a single stage representing a place which may from time to time change. Seiver and Calkins both believe that a stage of compartments was used, though one of a slightly different type from that of the medieval stage.

However, if we look at the play *Aman*, which Rigal describes as 'une de celles dont on est le plus tenté, au premier abord, d'expliquer la disposition par le système décoratif du moyen âge',[2] and for which Seiver provides a whole scheme of compartments, we can see clearly that Montchrestien's stage was in fact probably single, and that he made every effort, while keeping close to the Bible, to be *vraisemblable* with relation to changes of place. The stage represents an indeterminate place; 'change of place' is thus a comparative term, for while we realize that the new place must be different from the last, it is doubtful whether any scenery changes.

In Acts I and II of *Aman* there is no difficulty to prevent a single stage, as there is no place-change within the acts. Seiver, however, linking the two acts up, imagines that 'the staging for these two acts may be envisaged as composed of two sections, i.e. a place or antechamber adjoining the King's room . . .'.[3]

For the third act, Seiver envisages '. . . a three-divisional aspect of the stage, i.e. on each side of the stage a room, one the quarters of

---

[1] See *De Jodelle à Molière*, p. 41.
[2] Ibid., p. 129. Rigal, however, believes that Montchrestien 'est gauchement resté fidèle au récit du Bible', and has not even thought about *vraisemblance*.
[3] Seiver, *Aman*, p. 16.

Esther, and the other those of the King and his suite; in the middle would be situated an indefinite place or square'.[1]

If we number these compartments A, B, and C, the act can be divided as follows:

A	C	B
(Quarters of Esther)	*(Indefinite place or square)*	*(Quarters of King and his suite)*
	1. Mardochée's monologue	
2. Sara and Rachel see Mardochée	2. Sara and Rachel see Mardochée[2]	
3. Sara and Rachel speak to the queen		
4. Esther is left alone: monologue		
5. Sara and Rachel return with Mardochée's message, and Esther sends Athach to him		
	6. The chorus	
	7. Mardochée's prayer	
	8. Athach's interview with Mardochée	
	9. Mardochée's third prayer	
	10. Athach returns after speaking to Esther	

Seiver's plan has several drawbacks; nor can they be dispelled by our believing that the author is unthinkingly following the Bible. If this is a multiple stage, then Mardochée would remain on stage throughout scenes 3, 4, and 5; but if this is so, why do we not see Sara and Rachel speaking to him, when they have been sent to him for that purpose by the queen? Similarly, if Esther is still in her apartment in scenes 6–10, why do we not see Athach speak to her, when he is sent by Mardochée? We see Athach sent off by Esther in Scene 5; what does he do until he appears to Mardochée in Scene 8? Stand half in one compartment, and half in the other?

A simpler explanation of this act would be that it consisted of two large scenes, both of them in undetermined places in the vicinity of the palace. These two places are not both on the stage at the same time, but appear one after the other. In the first, we see Mardochée praying; he goes off the stage as the maids arrive. (No mention is made at any point of their being in a different place, or of their seeing him through

---

[1] Ibid., p. 17.
[2] This scene could be in either A or C.

a window. They can be presumed to be in the same place as Mardochée for a moment.) The Queen then comes to this same place:

Rachel: Mais i'apercoy la Reine,
Haston de luy conter son incroyable peine.[1]

The Queen sends the maids after Mardochée, and in a while they return. She then sends Athach to him.

The place now changes, and we see Mardochée and the chorus in prayer. Athach appears, is sent to Esther, and then returns.

If Montchrestien had been unthinkingly following the Bible, as Rigal suggests, we would have seen each interview in turn; there would have been no need for the maids to *describe* their interview with Mardochée, and Athach his with the Queen. The story has been fitted into these two long scenes; though the gap between them is not filled, as it should be, by the interlude-chorus, but by the character-chorus.

In Act IV, Montchrestien's growing desire for *vraisemblance* in changes of place is shown by the changes between the successive versions of the play. Seiver believes that the King's remark just after Esther's monologue, in the 1601 edition, means that Esther is in one compartment, and that the king has seen her, through a window, from the other:

Mettant sans y penser la teste à la fenestre,
I'ay veu ma belle Esther comme un Soleil paroistre.[2]

This same 1601 edition, however, seems to point far more clearly to a change of place, on a single stage, made possible by Esther's departure from the stage:

Or allon, chères sœurs, allon trouver le Roy.[3]

The king then comes on, describes Esther at great length, as she was *when he saw her a minute ago*:

Quel paradis d'amour *vient ores de* s'ouvrir.[4]

Finally, on her reappearance, he says:

Mais la voici venir . . .[5]

Such a change of place, unaided by interlude-chorus, is typical of the stage Montchrestien's development had reached in 1601. By 1604,

[1] *Aman*, B 747–8.   [2] A 1228–9.   [3] A 1221.
[4] A 1225.   [5] A 1259.

however, when he wishes a character to *reappear* immediately after a change of place, he usually inserts an interlude-chorus, or uses some other means of avoiding the abrupt change of scene.

In this instance, he includes various changes in the 1604 edition which transform the action so that no change of place is necessary. In particular, he makes use of the sixteenth-century convention (which we have already seen in relation to our study of the monologue) whereby a person can remain for some time on the stage without being noticed by the other. This is a convention used, for example, in Garnier's *Les Juifves*, where the Queen of Babylon speaks quite a long monologue before noticing Amital and the chorus. (It is interesting that in Montchrestien's plays, when one character finally sees the other, he almost always says 'Il faut que je m'avance' (*David*; *P. de J.*, p. 222), 'Amis avancez-vous' (*Les Lacènes*; *P. de J.*, p. 198), 'Il vient a nous' (*La Cartaginoise*; *P. de J.*, p. 123), or something similar. A man can remain unseen or unnoticed for some while.)

In 1604, therefore, Esther must be presumed to be on stage with the king from the start. Her monologue is shorter than in 1601, and when she finally decides to act, she does not suggest that they should all go off and find the king, but merely '. . . marche avant ie te prie'[1] (a statement similar to 'Amis avancez-vous' etc.).

The king suddenly notices her as she advances, and, instead of saying

Quel paradis d'amour *vient ores de* s'ouvrir,[2]

(or that he has just seen her from his window) indicates that he is actually seeing her at that moment:

Quel paradis d'amour *est* a mes yeux ouvert.[3]

Two lines later, by using the present tense again, he shows that she is on the stage with him:

1601: *I'ay veu* ma belle Esther comme un Soleil paroistre.[4]
1604: *Est-ce* ma belle Esther que i'aperçoy paroistre?[5]

As they are both on the stage, his monologue of description cannot be long, so it is shortened from 34 lines to 6; at the end of it, instead of saying:

Mais la voici venir . . .

[1] B 1176. [2] A 1125. [3] B 1177.
[4] A 1228. [5] B 1179.

indicating that her sudden appearance on the stage prevents him continuing with this long speech about her, he says:

> Mais la voici bien pres . . .

indicating that he has merely been able to say 6 lines about her while
she was crossing the stage, and that she is now too close for him to
continue.

In Act v of *Aman*, there are three changes of place, but nothing to
suggest a change of compartments. Two of the changes are helped by
the interlude-chorus.

In the other plays also there are occasional hints of the unlikelihood
of a compartment stage, one of the most obvious cases being Act III of
L'Escossoise, where the appearances of Davison, the Queen, and the
chorus, all point rather to a single stage, on which changes of place are
similar to those we have been describing, than to any use of compartments.

It would appear that Montchrestien had in mind a single stage. This
stage would have to be very simple, as far as scenery was concerned,
because of the swift changes. Probably it would be almost completely
bare, especially as the productions of Montchrestien's plays were either
by the University (as is probable in the case of *Sophonisbe*'s pre-1596
performance) or by travelling actors (as in the case of *L'Escossoise*).
Gone are the lavish court productions of the mid sixteenth century,
such as that at Blois in 1556.[1]

(c) *Changes of Place within the Act*

Though changes of place do occur within the acts of Montchrestien's
plays, he seems nevertheless, during the course of the new versions, to
be trying to avoid this practice more and more; and indeed, by the time
we reach the 1604 play, *Hector*, he has reached the point where no such
changes occur, though the devices to avoid them are rather *invraisemblable*, in that all the characters come on the stage at the very moment
that the author requires them to, and give no reason whatever for their
appearance at that moment. Changes of place are avoided by similar
means in Act III of *Sophonisbe*, where Massinisse says:

> Je cours en advertir ma plus chere moitié . . .
> *Mais la voici venir.*[2]

---

[1] See Lanson, art. cit. *R.H.L.F.* (1903), 196.   [2] *Sophonisbe*, 1596 edn.

and in Act v of *David*, where Nathan, after his monologue, says he is
going to see the king:

> Je m'en vay l'aborder; *à propos ie le voy*.[1]

In Act III of David, however, there is an extremely skilful avoidance
of change of place. David and Nadab have been talking together, and
Urie has then to speak a monologue; it would seem natural to change
the place of action. However, David finishes his conversation with the
words:

> Mot mot, mon cher Nadab, retiron nous d'icy,
> Il nous pourroit ouïr; regarde, le voicy.
> Couron, couron bien tost luy dresser sa dépesche.
> Le dessein estant pris rien plus ne m'en empesche.[2]

Thus David and Nadab leave the stage as Urie appears, justifying
their departure by what the Abbé d'Aubignac would call a 'liaison de
fuite'. David's reappearance is justified by the same reason, as he now
knows where Urie is, and having prepared his *dépesche*, comes to bring
it to him.

Aman, from its subject, is the play in which the most changes of place
must occur. However, as we have seen, such changes are far fewer than
Seiver would have us believe, and certainly far fewer than a close,
unimaginative following of the Bible, as suggested by Rigal, would
necessitate. Montchrestien has managed to place most of the changes
in the intervals, but four of them, in the 1604 edition, occur within
acts. In *L'Escossoise* there are two mid-act changes, in *Les Lacènes*
a possible three, while *Sophonisbe* and *David* have one each.

Often, in the 1601 edition, there is no indication of the changes;
one character stops speaking, and another one starts in a different
place. Thus, in Act v of *La Cartaginoise*, Sophonisbe starts speaking
immediately after Hiempsal's speech in the scene before; and Hiempsal
returns to the stage again soon afterwards. In Act III of *L'Escossoise*, the
Queen starts her monologue directly after Davison has finished his;
and in Act IV of *Aman* Assuérus begins to speak immediately after
Esther's monologue.

By 1604, however, Montchrestien seems to have decided that such
abrupt changes are both bewildering and *invraisemblable*, particularly
in a case where a character reappears in the new place. In this case he

---

[1] *David*; *P. de J.*, p. 230.
[2] *David*, Act III; 1601 edn. The procedure is the same in the 1604 version.

inserts an interlude-chorus, to bridge the gap in time and place, as in Act III of *L'Escossoise* and Act V of *La Cartaginoise*; or else he changes the action so that the place does not change, as in Act IV of *Aman*. (Sometimes he had used an interlude-chorus in this way in 1601 as well, as in Act V of *Les Lacènes*, after Ptolemée's speech, or in Act V of *David*, before Nathan's remonstrance, or in Act V of *Aman*, after the Aman–Sares scene, and again after the Assuérus–Aman scene.)

Another procedure for facilitating change of place is for people to mention the fact that they are leaving the stage, just before the change. Where Cratesiclea, in Act II of *Les Lacènes*, had, in 1601, merely said:

> Reschauffon les Autels d'hosties allumées,

in 1604 she says explicitly:

> Couron viste à l'autel.[1]

In one or two cases it is difficult to tell whether there is a change of place, or merely an imperfect *liaison de scène*, with one group of characters going off, and another coming on, in the same place. This is so in the case I have just mentioned from *Les Lacènes*, and the same is true in Act V of the same play, where Stratonice may depart to her death after her monologue, leaving the character-chorus (who may have been on the stage with her) to wait for news.

By 1604, only one definite case is left of a change of place which is facilitated neither by an interlude-chorus, nor by the stated departure of the characters from the first scene. This is in Act V of the *Reine d'Escosse*, where the character-chorus speaks as soon as the *Maistre d'Hostel* has finished his monologue.

(d) *Liaison des Scènes*

Throughout this chapter I have been using the word *scène* in the seventeenth-century sense, as the point in an act when a new character appears, or another goes off.

It was not yet the custom, in the sixteenth century, to mark each change of personnel on the stage as a new scene; thus it is at times difficult, in the absence of stage-directions, to tell exactly when the change occurs. In the different versions of Montchrestien's plays there appears to be a gradual attempt on the part of the author to improve the entrances and exits of his characters.

[1] *Les Lacènes*; *P. de J.*, p. 171.

In many sixteenth-century plays these are ill prepared, if at all. Montchrestien at times shares this fault; for example, at the end of Act IV of *Aman* we suddenly realize that Aman is on the stage, even though he has not spoken; and in Act V Mardochée suddenly appears in the same way. Often, too, we can only tell of the departure of a character from a change of tone on the part of someone on the stage; in Act V of *Aman* we only realize that Assuérus has left the stage because of the vigour with which Aman's fury is expressed at what has just happened.[1] *Justification* in the seventeenth-century sense is usually sadly lacking,[2] and characters give no reason for their wanderings on and off.

Justification in this sense cannot have seemed necessary to Montchrestien, for he makes no attempt to improve it between the versions of his plays; in 1604 appearances are still heralded by phrases such as 'Mais voy-ie pas le Roy?'[3] or 'Mais voici pas quelqu'un qui s'en vient devers nous?'[4] There is a steady improvement, however, in the preparation of entrances and exits, by exact phrases which tell us when a character is coming on or going off.

There are several examples of such improvements in the various versions of *Sophonisbe*. In Act III, the heroine appears in 1596 unheralded, whereas in 1601 and 1604 Massinisse says: 'Mais la voicy venir.'[5] In Act IV, Massinisse's entrance, unheralded in 1596, is announced by Scipion in 1601 and 1604; after speaking about Massinisse in his monologue, he then says: 'Qu'il survient à propos.'[6] A short time before this, in the same act, Siphax's exit, which had not been clearly marked in 1596 and 1601 (thus making it possible that he was still on the stage when Massinisse appeared), is made definite in 1604, when Scipion begins his monologue with the words: 'Remene le soldat et sans luy faire tort.'[7] In Act V of the same play, Hiempsal's entrance, unheralded in 1596, is greeted in 1601 by the words: 'Mais ie le voy Hiempsal adressons nous a luy.'[8]

Despite such changes, there are still many unprepared entrances and exits in the 1601 version, many of which carry over into the 1604 version. In *Hector*, however, the new play which appears for the first time in 1604, Montchrestien seems to be making a conscious effort to let us know when people come and go. There are still occasional

---

[1] *Aman*, A 1503, B 1415.
[2] Except in Act III of *David*, which we have just discussed.
[3] *David*; *P. de J.*, p. 210.   [4] *La Reine d'Escosse*; *P. de J.*, p. 107.
[5] *Sophonisbe*, B 1117.   [6] Ibid., B 1329.
[7] Ibid., C 1210.   [8] Ibid., B 1731.

surprises; Hécube speaks, in Act II,[1] when we did not even know she was on the stage; but the over-all impression is one of great care. If we discount the Chorus, which remains always on the stage,[2] and the opening monologues (during which other people may be on the stage, as we have already observed), we see that the entrances and above all the exits are very carefully marked.

In Act I, after Cassandre's monologue and scene with the chorus, the approach of Hector and Andromache is announced by the words:

> Mais voici pas Hector? C'est sans doute luy-mesme,
> Qu'Andromache poursuit eschevelée et blesme.[3]

In Act II, after the dialogue between Andromache and the Nurse, Priam's arrival is announced:

> Voyez Priam à temps avec deux de vos frères.[4]

Hector is later greeted by Priam:

> O mon plus ferme appuy, te voilà donc armé.[5]

Act III is the most carefully organized. Hector, after his dialogue with Antenor, sends him off with the words: 'Va, mon cher Anthenor.'[6] He himself remains on the stage, and converses with the Chorus; he is about to go off, when they announce the arrival of the messenger:

> *Hector*: Marchons pour en sçavoir.
> *Chœur*:   N'allez ia plus avant,
> Voici l'un de vos gens qui nous vient au devant.[7]

Hector's precipitate departure after the *récit* is described by the messenger himself:

> Où court si tost Hector transporté de colère?[8]

and the messenger departs with the words:

> Allez donc l'assister, car au camp ie recours . . .[8]

The Chorus, who are thus left alone on the stage, soon see Helen approaching:

> Mais voilà pas Heleine? elle approche vers nous.[8]

---

[1] *Hector*, Act II; *P. de J.*, p. 26.   [2] See Chapter 6, 'Set Pieces'.
[3] *Hector*, Act I; *P. de J.*, p. 7.   [4] Ibid., Act II; *P. de J.*, p. 19.
[5] Ibid., p. 22.   [6] Ibid., Act III; *P. de J.*, p. 33.
[7] Ibid., p. 37.   [8] Ibid., p. 39.

Act IV starts with Andromache's monologue; Cassandre is presumably on the stage during it. Eventually Andromache addresses Cassandre, and there is a scene consisting of these two characters and the Chorus. At the end of it, Andromache sees Priam: 'Voici venir Priam . . .'[1]

Priam and Hécube come on, talking together. After a short conversation, they notice Andromache and Cassandre:[2]

> Je voy son Andromache et Cassandre avec elle.[3]

They call them over: 'Mes filles, venez ça.'[3]

In this scene, though Cassandre presumably remains on the stage, she does not say anything (in order to obey the rule of three speakers).

Eventually they all see Antenor approaching, and then listen to his *récit*.

Act V starts with a dialogue between Priam and Hécube. They decide to go and see what is happening, but then they see Andromache coming towards them:

> Arrestez, Andromache arrive devers nous.[4]

After a while, they all see the messenger coming. Andromache faints, and is carried off:

> Retirons la, mes sœurs, dedans ceste maison.[5]

However, her return at the end of the act is unprepared.

From the changes between the versions of the other plays, and from the comparative care taken in *Hector*, we can see that Montchrestien came to consider that the careful marking of entrances and exits was important, though he saw no need for *justification* of these entrances and exits.

We know that two of Montchrestien's plays were performed, and may presume that the others were as well. The improvements he makes in various aspects of construction certainly seem to point to a concern with stage performance: e.g. (*a*) He attempts to make changes of place more *vraisemblable*, by inserting an interlude-chorus, or by making sure that one group of characters retires before the others appear. (*b*) He

---

[1] Ibid., Act IV; *P. de J.*, p. 46.
[2] In accordance with the stage convention which allows people to remain on the stage unnoticed.
[3] Ibid., p. 47.
[4] Ibid., Act V; p. 60.
[5] Ibid., p. 61.

attempts to mark more clearly the precise moments of entrances and exits, by means of stage directions in the speeches themselves.

He is not interested, however, in *justification* in the seventeenth-century sense, and characters always seem to appear on the stage just when they are needed. In this way he manages at times to avoid awkward changes of place within the acts: *Hector*, his last play, contains no such changes.

It is likely that the stage the author has in mind is a single stage, and not a stage of compartments. There is little evidence of the existence of any form of scenery. The performers were probably either University people (as in the case of the first performance of *Sophonisbe*), or travelling actors (as in the case of *L'Escossoise*).

8. Style

※⩥⟨※⩤⩤

RENAISSANCE dramatic technique was devoted to the development of certain ideas and emotions within the framework of static, stylized 'set pieces' similar to the rhetorical exercises. The author's poetic style, in this manner, became the most important feature of his work, by which it must stand or fall.

Montchrestien's style and language are essentially those of the late sixteenth century. Any influence which Malherbe may have had on them must have been very slight;[1] indeed, the existence of any *rapport* between the two writers seems extremely unlikely.

Lanson describes Montchrestien as 'un de nos derniers et plus exquis lyriques, avant le règne du bon sens eloquent'. In its richness and variety Montchrestien's style is of the Renaissance; in its balance and clarity we see evidence of the rhetorical training of the period; and Renaissance poetic is above all typified by a stress upon ornamentation such as we see in Montchrestien's plays.

Montchrestien is, with Garnier, the most accomplished poet of the Renaissance tragedians. Jean de la Taille may provide more dramatic impact; but such impact has little place in Renaissance theories of drama. The rhetorical development of style and language is the main aim; and, where Jean de la Taille is but a mediocre poet, Montchrestien, practising with great perfection the lessons of rhetoric, provides the listener with some of the most magnificent poetry of the period.

The measure and balance of his style stem from the intelligent use of the rhetorical figures of diction; the richness of its ornamentation from a similar use of the tropes and the figures of thought. On the whole, he does not use them excessively; and especially in the case of the figures of diction, they do not draw attention to themselves. As we read in the *Rhetorica ad Herennium*: '. . . Si crebro his generibus utemur, puerili videmur elocutione delectari; item, si raro interseremus has exornationes et in causa tota varie dispergemus, commode luminibus distinctis inlustrabimus orationem.'[2]

---

[1] See Appendix I, *Malherbe Correcteur de Tragédie.*
[2] *Rhetorica ad Herennium*, IV. xxiii. 32.

(a) *Measure*

The use of the alexandrine, usually with caesura after the sixth syllable, naturally leads to speeches consisting of balanced periods and regular *isocola*. That this trend is conscious, however, can be seen by the avoidance of awkward enjambments (except in particular circumstances) in the course of the changes between the editions:[1] by the perpetual balancing of antitheses, synonymies, and chiastic phrases; and by the frequent use of repetition, whether of words or of ideas.[2]

Rhythmical balance of this kind is, of course, most common in speeches of argument or persuasion, or in those which reflect a mood of calm resignation. In the former, the true origins of rhetoric as the art of persuasion are to be found; in the latter, the character can methodically formulate his reasons for receiving the blows of fate with such courage. Speeches of violent emotion demand a different kind of pattern; but they are few, and the main impression with which one is left after reading these plays is that of a calm and measured statement both of ideas and of emotions.

As an example, let us take a passage from the scene between the Queen of England and her *Conseiller* in Act I of *La Reine d'Escosse*. Elizabeth finishes her first speech with the following words, referring to Mary:

> Tes yeux qui tous les cœurs prennent à leurs appas,
> Sans en estre troublez, verront-ils mon trespas?
> Ces beaux Astres luisans au ciel de ton visage,
> De ma funeste mort seront-ils le présage?
> N'auras-tu point le cœur touché d'affliction,   5
> Voyant ceste belle Isle en desolation,
> En proye à la discorde en guerres allumée,
> Au meurtre de ses fils par ses fils animée?
> Verras-tu sans douleur les soldats enragez
> Massacrer à leurs pieds les vieillards outragez,   10
> Égorger les enfants presence de leurs peres,
> Les pucelles forcer au giron de leurs meres,
> Et les fleuves encor regorger sur leurs bords
> Par les pleurs des vivans et par le sang des morts?

[1] See Appendix I, *Malherbe Correcteur de Tragédie*.

[2] Repetitions are in no way avoided, as Lebègue seeks to suggest. (See Appendix I.) They are used a great deal, in the manner common to the Renaissance. All forms of rhetorical repetition are used (*epanaphora, conduplicatio, gradatio, traductio, antanaklasis,* etc.).

Se ceste volonté barbarement cruelle   15
Peut tomber en l'esprit d'une Reine si belle,
Si le cœur d'une femme ayant la mort au sein
Ose encor' concevoir ce furieux dessein;
Ie croiray desormais que les Ourses cruelles
Dépouillent les fureurs qui leur sont naturelles;   20
Et que la femme née à la benignité
Environne son cœur d'une aspre cruauté.[1]

In this passage the thought progresses smoothly in almost perfect *isocola*. Firstly, Elizabeth asks whether Mary can possibly wish to bring about such destruction (1–14); secondly, she states that if this is so, she must have the soul of a wild beast (15–22). The question is divided into two parts; the question of Elizabeth's death (1–4), and that of the destruction of the country by civil war (5–14). Each of these is again divided, by the use of synonymy; i.e. each part of the question is repeated in similar words.

Lines 3 and 4 are thus a repetition of lines 1 and 2, in different words; 'tes yeux' become 'ces beaux Astres', etc.; this figure of diction, synonymy, or *interpretatio*, was considered very important as a re-inforcement of a statement.[2]

The second half of the question (5–14) is also divided into two parts by the use of synonymy, though this time the two parts are not exactly equal in length (5–8, 9–14). Again, there is a very close similarity between the statements of the question (N'auras-tu point le cœur touché d'affliction, voyant . . .', 'Verras-tu sans douleur . . .'), but this time there is a progression; the second part is a more detailed picture of the horrors which have been hinted at in the first. Each part is rounded off by a satisfying figure, which by its very regularity shows that the question has ended; a telling repetition in the first case ('Au meurtre de ses fils par ses fils animée'), an even more striking antithesis in the second, strengthened by the hyperbolic image within which it is contained ('Et les fleuves encor regorger sur leurs bords / Par les pleurs des vivans et par le sang des morts').

The statement with which the speech ends is again formed of regular *isocola*; a conditional clause (two lines) followed by another (two lines); a statement (two lines), followed by an antithetic corollary (two lines).

This whole passage, then, flows relentlessly to its conclusion; its balance and measure add to the effectiveness of its impact.

[1] *La Reine d'Escosse*; *P. de J.*, p. 73.
[2] The *Rhetorica ad Herennium* says of it: 'Necessum est eius qui audit animum com-moveri cum gravitas prioris dicti renovatur interpretatione verborum (IV. xxviii. 38).

The *Conseiller*'s speech continues in the same way:

> Le masque est ià levé, la chose est trop connuë:
> L'œil qui ne la void point est voilé d'une nuë;
> L'esprit qui ne la croid soy-mesmes se dément;
> Le cœur qui ne la craint n'a point de sentiment;
> Il s'endort misérable, et l'orage tempeste   5
> Qui doit à l'impourveu fondre dessus sa teste.
> Il ne faut plus, Madame, en demeurer ici;
> Embrassez de vous mesme et de nous le souci:
> Car si le bien public doit estre votre envie,
> Il faut aussi pour luy conserver vostre vie.   10
> Ainsi pourrez vous rendre esteins plustost que nés
> Les barbares desseins de ces fiers Basanés;
> Ainsi vous nous pouvez apporter asseurance,
> A l'Escosse dommage, et terreur à la France;
> Là où si vous mourez c'est le souhait des Rois,   15
> La fin de nostre Foy, le tombeau de nos loix . . .[1]

Here, the first six lines tell us that the danger must be known to all; this point is stressed by reference to the stupidity of anyone who does not realize it. In the first line there are two parallel statements, divided by the caesura. Lines 2, 3, and 4 are parallel to each other, stressing how unobservant or stupid the man must be who does not see the danger; the progression 'œil–esprit–cœur', the repetition of the phrase 'qui ne la' in all three lines, and the similar sound of the verbs 'void–croid–craint', contrive to give an incantatory effect. Lines 5 and 6 are an extension of line 4, strengthening by means of a vivid metaphor the man's stupid obliviousness of danger.

Lines 7–8 are an exhortation to the Queen to take action. As such, the phrases are short and clipped. Lines 9–10 give the reasons why she should act; they are in the form of a perfect *isocolon*.

Lines 11–14 contrast, in a very regular way, the results of action and inaction in this case. The case for action is given by the two parallel clauses beginning with 'Ainsi . . .'; they are rounded off neatly by a chiasmos: 'A l'Escosse dommage, et terreur à la France.' The case against inaction is given in the last two lines; 'Là où' comes as a contrast after the repetition of 'Ainsi'; and the three parallel half-line phrases round off the train of thought, in preparation for the extended simile which is to follow.

Such measured expression is not only suitable to argument or to the

[1] *La Reine d'Escosse*; *P. de J.*, pp. 73–4.

stressing of an idea; it can be used in any speech where the speaker can
be presumed to be in a calm mood. Thus, in Massinisse's speech in Act II
of *La Cartaginoise*:

> I'estois à peine encor' en la fleur de mon âge,
> Que ie me vis bani de mon propre heritage,
> Desnué de moyens, d'ennemis traversé:
> Quantes fois estendu dans le creux d'un fossé
> Ay-ie passé la nuict, pour lict la dure terre,   5
> Pour courtine le Ciel, pour chevet une pierre?
> Quantes fois ay-ie pris sur le dos d'un vert pré
> Le repas maigre et sobre et toutes fois agré?
> Et quantes fois changé les exquises delices
> Aux travaux de la guerre, aux rudes exercices?   10
> Or le Ciel tout-puissant mon Thrône a restabli
> Mon propre deshonneur m'a de gloire anobli . . .[1]

Here lines 2 and 3 provide an example of triple *disjunctio*, which the
Rhetorica ad Herennium describes as 'ad festivitatem . . . apposita';[2]
within this *disjunctio*, in line 3, there is a balanced *chiasmos*. Lines 4–10
consist of a repetition, in the form of *epanaphora*, of phrases starting
with the words 'Quantes fois'. Within these there are parallel half-line
phrases (in lines 5–6 and line 10). After the repetitive, questioning
'Quantes fois?' the word 'Or' comes as a form of resolution of the
situation, and leads into the paradox of line 12.

Repetition of words and phrases, to which Malherbe was to take
such exception, was an essential part of rhetorical training. There were
not only the repetition of words in successive phrases, as in *Epanaphora*
(*repetitio*), *Antistrophe* (*conversio*), and *Conplexio*, but also the repetitions within the phrase, as in *Traductio*, *Antanaklasis*, and *Gradatio*,
and the emotional repetitions of *Conduplicatio*.

Montchrestien is particularly fond of *epanaphora*, though often he
gives it additional savour by varying the last repetition. In Act IV of
Hector, for example, we find the following passage:

> Dedans moy comme flots s'abisment les malheurs,
> Dedans moy comme traits penetrent les douleurs,
> Comme orages dans moy les tristesses s'émeuvent.[3]

In Act I of *David*, the continual repetition of 'Suis-ie ce grand
David . . .' is resolved by the words 'Sans doute ie le suis', and two
lines later, by: 'Ie suis vrayment David'.[4]

---

[1] *La Cartaginoise*; P. de J., p. 127.   [2] *Rhetorica ad Herennium*, IV. xxvii. 38.
[3] *Hector*; P. de J., p. 45.   [4] *David*; P. de J., p. 204.

Traductio, or the frequent reintroduction of a word within the phrase, was particularly distasteful to Malherbe; yet, particularly when used for the purpose of antithesis, it can be extremely effective. This usage was very common in the Renaissance; and Montchrestien does not neglect it. It is above all useful in rounding off a speech, e.g.:

> Quand s'abstenant de pleurs elle force à pleurer
> Quand ne soupirant point elle fait soupirer.[1]
>
> Et son cours n'est à rien qu'à un rien comparable.[2]
>
> Et qui daigna du Ciel en terre s'abaisser, . . .
> Afin qu'au Ciel la terre il puisse rehausser.[3]

Even more common is the form of antithesis based upon similar words, e.g.:

> Immuables decrets du Ciel tousiours mouvant[4]
>
> Iouissant de la vie a moins d'esiouissance[4]
>
> Fidele executeur d'une infidelité.[5]

Repetitions of these two types are common, but not usually overdone. A rare exception to this moderation is the chorus which ends *La Reine d'Escosse,* where the following repetitions are to be found:

> Mais lors que tu *mourus* elle *mourut* aussi . . .
>
> Car bien que *le Soleil* rayonne sur nostre œil,
> Nostre ame en te perdant a perdu *son Soleil* . . .
>
> S'il te *falloit* mourir naistre il ne *falloit* pas,
> Ou si rien ne peut *vivre immortel* ici-bas,
> Tu devois toute *vive* au Ciel estre ravie.
> *Immortel* ornement des *mortelles* beautez . . .
>
> *Amour* estant luy-mesme *amoureux* de ta grace . . .
>
> Avec *toy* dans les *Cieux* elle alla d'ici bas,
> Comme des *Cieux* en *toy* elle estoit descenduë.[6]

This is somewhat excessive, even though the chorus from which these have been culled consists of 72 lines. On the whole Montchrestien uses these ornaments sparingly and well.

The measure and rhythmical balance which has been described is, of course, to be found in the choruses as well, particularly in those

---

[1] *La Reine d'Escosse; P. de J.,* p. 109.
[2] Ibid., p. 112. (This is strictly speaking antanaklasis.)
[3] Ibid., p. 101.   [4] *Les Lacènes; P. de J.,* p. 192.
[5] *La Reine d'Escosse; P. de J.,* p. 89.   [6] Ibid., pp. 111–12.

which are composed of alexandrines. Excellent examples are the Chorus
to Act III of *Les Lacènes*,[1] and the Chorus to Act II of *La Reine
d'Escosse*.[2]

This is not, however, the only method of expression used by Montchrestien. Where the occasion demands it, the rhythm is broken, and
the tempo becomes more urgent. A good example of this is to be found
in the messenger speech in Act I of *La Cartaginoise*:

> On tire, on pousse, on crie, et sans cesse on appelle;
> Qui s'éveille en sursaut, qui saute brusque et promt,
> Qui plein d'estonnement leve à peine le front,
> Qui se musse de peur. Compagnons, arme, arme, arme,
> Crions nous d'une voix, ià l'ennemi gensdarme   5
> Tient le creux du fossé; desia de toutes parts
> Murmurent les soldats au pied de nos ramparts.[3]

Here, in the swift, curt phrases separated by commas in line I the
hearer feels a sense of haste, of flurry. The same impression is given by
the triple repetition of the word 'arme' in line 4. The haste is still
further marked by the leaving of the phrase 'Crions nous d'une voix'
until the next line; the cry to arms comes suddenly, in the middle of a
line, with no warning.

The two violent enjambments in lines 5–7 add to this over-all
impression of hurry, of fear. The whole passage moves rapidly, with
no pause for breath, except for the gulping breaths of a flustered,
surprised man.

Similarly, the Nurse's speech at the end of *La Cartaginoise* expresses
surprise and grief at Sophonisbe's death. The first eight lines are dis-
jointed and hurried; but then she grows calmer, and the play ends with
a calm decision to die with her mistress. Here are the eight lines in
question:

> Au secours, elle meurt. Helas! Helas! Madame?
> Madame! Elle n'oit plus, son corps est privé d'ame,
> Il est ià froid par tout, ô jour infortuné!
> Mais plustost noire nuict! ô poinct determiné
> Pour ioindre l'Occident de ma triste vieillesse   5
> A ton midi luisant! O ma chere Maistresse
> Ie ne veux ni ne dois plus long temps vivre ici
> Apres toy, toy qui fus mon bien et mon souci . . .[4]

---

[1] *Les Lacènes*; P. de J., pp. 185–6.   [2] *La Reine d'Escosse*; P. de J., pp. 87–8.
[3] *La Cartaginoise*; P. de J., p. 123.   [4] Ibid., p. 155.

Here the disorder of the two first lines, with the repeated exclamations stretching from line to line, points to the shock and surprise felt by the nurse. This impression is supported by the *correctio* in line 4, 'Mais plustost noire nuict', by the enjambments in lines 4–8, and by the repetition of the word 'toy' in line 8.

The rhetorical figure known as *Comma*, or *Articulus*, is very useful for such moments. Hector, when exhorting the Greeks, says:

> Donnez, frappez, tuez, courageux citoyens.[1]

The 'Mégère', calling on the other Furies, says:

> Vous dont les rouges fers, les torches execrables
> Percent, bruslent les cœurs des pauvres criminels . . .[2]

The *Rhetorica ad Herennium* says of this figure: '. . . Crebro et celeri corpus vulnere consauciari videtur',[3] and certainly, although this description of it was meant metaphorically, in these two instances this impression is literally given. A similar effect is found in the messenger speech in Act v of *La Reine d'Escosse*, where the executioner's blade can be felt thudding down on to the block:

> Un, deux, trois, quatre coups sur son col il delasche.[4]

Another kind of repetition, which is very effective in this type of speech, is the figure of *Conduplicatio*, which is described by the *Rhetorica ad Herennium* as 'cum ratione amplificationis aut commiserationis eiusdem unius aut plurium verborum iteratio'.[5] Of this type are the repetitions in Andromache's speech in Act iv of *Hector*:

> Pleurez, Dames, pleurez vos maris et vos freres,
> Pleurez les fers de Troye, et vos propres miseres.[6]

and in Davison's speech in Act iii of *La Reine d'Escosse*:

> Ie vay fraper un coup, mais soudain ie le voy,
> Ie le voy, malheureux, retomber dessus moy.[7]

Montchrestien's style, then, is at most times rhythmically and rationally measured, according to the procedures of rhetorical training; where, however, an impression of haste or of agitation is needed, this measure is deliberately broken according to the same procedures. The

---

[1] *Hector*; P. de J., p. 62.   [2] *La Cartaginoise*; P. de J., p. 133.
[3] *Rhetorica ad Herennium*, IV. xix. 26.   [4] *La Reine d'Escosse*; P. de J., p. 110.
[5] *Rhetorica ad Herennium*, IV. xxviii. 38.   [6] *Hector*; P. de J., p. 45.
[7] *La Reine d'Escosse*; P. de J., p. 88.

use of the rhetorical figures of diction need not necessarily have been deliberate, for they remain at the basis of all good style; but deliberate or not, his employment of them to such an extent shows the far-reaching influence of the rhetorical tradition.

(b) *Imagery*

Like other Renaissance poets, Montchrestien, in his imagery, remains within certain set traditions. His style, varying as it does from character to character and mood to mood, gains its colour in each case from the tradition within which that character is intended to speak, in the mood in which he is being portrayed. Thus we have, at various times, Massinisse and David as Petrarchan lovers, using the full range of Petrarchan imagery; Nathan speaking in the tones of a Biblical prophet (and of a late sixteenth-century religious poet); the Queen of Scotland using the language of Catholic devotion; Aman making a typical 'tyrant-speech'; and many other cases of a specific traditional vocabulary being used.

In the sixteenth century, the originality of an author's approach to imagery lay not in the imagery used, but in the way it was used. To take the example of Petrarchan imagery, poets such as Scève, Jodelle, Ronsard, Papillon, Sponde, could each achieve a different effect from the use of exactly the same vocabulary of imagery.[1]

Montchrestien's imagery, though almost entirely traditional (apart from various Baroque effects typical of his period), stands out through an impression of richness and harmony which is rare even among French Renaissance poets. This impression would appear to stem from several sources, among them: (*a*) A concentration on sound, on melody, part of which is evident in the rhythmical flow which we have already noted, and part in the choice of words for mellifluous effect with much use of alliteration and assonance; (*b*) A concentration on the senses (typical of the late sixteenth and early seventeenth centuries), which would seem to have some basis in the teachings of Ramist rhetoric; (*c*) Above all, a capacity for extending an image, and for making a whole speech revolve around one striking parallel.

The most common form of image employed in these plays is, of course, the extended simile;[2] though not so formally fixed, the extended

[1] See my article, 'Some Uses of Petrarchan Imagery in Sixteenth-Century French Poetry', *F.S.*, xviii, 4 (1964).
[2] A study of the form of the extended simile is to be found in Chapter 6, 'Set Pieces', in the section on the *Récit*.

metaphor can be even more telling, and is used with great skill. The lesser tropes (metonymy, periphrasis, hyperbole, synecdoche, catachresis, etc.) are found in profusion.

It is in the use of the extended simile that Montchrestien's style is most typical of its time. As Scholl says, by the time of Corneille this has been 'durch den einfachen [Vergleich] oder durch die noch kürzere Form der Metaphor ersetzt'.[1]

Though the poet remains within certain traditions, not all his imagery has necessarily to stem directly from the *vocabulary* of that tradition. The poet, searching for a comparison, can look within his own experience for what may seem most apposite. Life itself provides some of the *loci* from which the comparisons may be drawn. The advice of the *Rhetorica ad Herennium* is apposite here: '. . . Inventio similium facilis erit si quis sibi omnes res, animantes et inanimas, mutas et eloquentes, feras et mansuetas, terrestres, caelestes, maritimas, artificio, casu, natura conparatas, usitatas atque inusitatas, frequenter ponere ante oculos poterit, et ex his aliquam venari similitudinem quae aut ornare aut docere aut apertiorem rem facere aut ponere ante oculos possit.'[2]

This 'universality' of imagery, with the whole of nature at its disposal, is quoted by Scholl[3] as one of the main differences between the poetry of the sixteenth century and that of the seventeenth, so bound by rules and regulations of a negative nature.

Most of Montchrestien's images, nevertheless, are variations on traditional themes, e.g. the torrent descending from the mountains, the lion descending on the flock. But all are chosen for their capability of 'embellishing, proving, clarifying, or vivifying'; and all are made real by a vividness, a sensuous originality, which can possibly be traced to the growing emphasis on the senses, and especially on vision, which is to be traced to Ramist rhetoric. Abraham Fraunce, in his *Arcadian Rhetorike*, which is to a great extent based on Talon's *Rhetorica*, states this point very clearly: 'There is no trope more flourishing than a Metaphore, especially if it be applied to the senses, and among the senses chiefly to the eie, which is the quickest of all the senses.'[4]

Montchrestien seems to see everything with a new eye; his imagery

---

[1] Scholl, *Die Vergleiche in Montchrestiens Tragödien*. This thesis is very good, but devotes itself almost entirely to the subject-matter of the images rather than to their treatment.

[2] *Rhetorica ad Herennium*, iv. xlviii. 61.

[3] Op. cit.

[4] Abraham Fraunce, *Arcadian Rhetorike*, book i, chap. 7.

is at all times reinforced by a sensuous awareness. The images are not just commonplace comparisons; one sees and feels what the author describes. For example, when David sees Bethsabée, he says (describing her as the sun):

> Il esclairoit dans l'eau, et d'un esclat glissant
> La pointe de ma veuë alloit esblouïssant,
> Comme l'œil le plus ferme estant surpris s'estonne
> A l'esclair tremoussant qui sur les eaux rayonne.[1]

In the description of the narrow path to heaven, the adjectives which are used make the experience real and painful, and not just a conventional metaphor:

> La croix est sans cesse attachée
> Sur l'espaule toute *escorchée*
> De ceux que Dieu cherit le mieux;
> Et le chemin qui méne aux Cieux
> Est semé de *ronces mordantes*,
> De cailloux, d'espines *poignantes*.[2]

The description of two bulls fighting is dominated by an impression of sound:

> Comme on voit au Printemps deux toreaux fort puissans
> Apres une genisse a l'envi *mugissans*
> De colere, d'amour, de ialousie ardente;
> Celuy qui veut iouir en *ronflant* se presente . . .[3]

But above all it is the sense of sight which is most frequently invoked:

> Combien de fois encor' Simoïs et Scamandre,
> Voyans à gros torrens le sang Gregeois s'espandre
> Dans leurs flots estonnez de perdre leur couleur . . .[4]

> L'amour des Rois ressemble au feu pront et volage,
> Qu'on apperçoit la nuict dans le Ciel flamboyer
>   Aupres d'un gras rivage;
> Si le passant le suit il le mene noyer
> Esblouy des rayons qu'il darde à son visage.[5]

> Pan, si tes plumes t'orgueillissent,
> Pour y voir tant de beaux miroirs;
> Qu'au moins tes yeux se reflechissent
> Dessus tes pieds sales et noirs.[6]

---

[1] *David; P. de J.*, p. 205.   [2] *Aman*, A 1155–60.
[3] *Hector; P. de J.*, p. 53.   [4] Ibid., p. 34.
[5] *David; P. de J.*, p. 226.   [6] *Aman; P. de J.*, p. 251.

The vivid and novel view with which Montchrestien comes to his images can be seen from various small details. For example, the image of a wolf attacking an unguarded herd is a common one, yet Montchrestien's version of it shows that he is envisaging the scene anew; he mentions the reasons for the herdsman's absence:

> Comme loups attaquans les bœufs gras d'un herbage,
> Tandis que le Pasteur cause au proche village.[1]

This realism is to be found everywhere, even amidst the commonplace images of the vicissitudes of fortune, e.g.:

> La vie est un air chaud sortant par la narine
> Qu'un pepin de raisin peut soudain estouffer.[2]

If we compare Montchrestien's treatment of an image with, for example, Garnier's statement of the same image, we see even more clearly the new eye with which Montchrestien approaches a conventional word-picture.

For example, let us take the image of a fire starting from a small beginning, which Garnier uses in *La Troade* in the following form:

> Ainsi d'un gran brasier qu'on pensoit amorti,
> Un simple mécheron de la cendre sorti
> Dans la paille s'accroist, si que telle scintille
> En peu d'heures pourra dévorer une ville.[3]

Montchrestien's image is far more evocative. The smallness of the original spark is stressed by the words 'foible' and 'recelle':

> Car comme en la forest cette *foible* estincelle,
> Qu'une souche creusee en la cendre *recelle* . . .

We see its gradual growth, among the brushwood:

> . . . Rampant de *peu a peu* par le plus *menu* bois . . .

And then comes the immense destruction, stressed by the words 'mille', 'tout à la fois', 'bruyant ravage', 'flots enflammez', 'fourrage',

> *Mille* arbres de cent ans brusle *tout à la fois*;
> *Un seul n'est point sauvé* de ce *bruyant ravage*,
> Qui de *flots enflammez* deça delà *fourrage*.

---

[1] *Hector*; *P. de J.*, p. 38.   [2] *La Reine d'Escosse*; *P. de J.*, p. 87.
[3] Pinvert, ii. 35.

Finally, the moral is drawn:

> Où si comme il naissoit quelqu'un l'eust fait mourir,
> On n'eust veu sa fureur par les branches courir.[1]

Montchrestien's vision has made of the image something new and startling; the contrast between the small spark and the vast destruction caused by it has been pointed; and the whole scene becomes vivid to our eyes.

The concentration, in Montchrestien's plays, upon images drawn from nature, and the Ramist stress upon the senses, serve to explain the comparative lack of mythological references in these plays. This lack is not necessarily due to a desire for clarity, as Lebègue would suggest. The explanation for this lack would seem to lie with the new trend in imagery which we have observed. The most common use to which mythology had been put in the plays of the Renaissance was that of providing examples or comparisons; Montchrestien and his contemporaries, in their desire to provide concrete evidence to the senses of their audience, tend to avoid non-sensuous images, among which must be included many of those taken from mythology. Where Montchrestien does use a mythological image, it is usually bound up with some other more concrete picture, e.g.:

> ... Niobe devenuë à la mort de ma race:
> Si ie ne suis rocher, au moins que ie sois glace
> Pour faire decouler au feu de mes douleurs
> Mon ame languissante en un ruisseau de pleurs.[2]

Montchrestien's poetry is at times enriched by a series of connected images which dominate a particular passage, or at times a whole speech, and which give it a particular atmosphere derived from their own being. Such a passage is to be found in the Queen of Scotland's farewell to her companions (which is reported in a messenger speech):

> Ie vous pri' que ma mort ne soit point poursuivie
> De larmes et sanglots; me portez-vous envie,
> Si pour perdre le corps ie m'aquiers un tel bien,
> Que tout le monde entier aupres de luy n'est rien?
> Puis qu'il faut tous mourir suis-ie pas bien-heureuse
> D'aller revivre au Ciel par cette mort honteuse?
> Si la fleur de mes iours se flestrit en ce temps,
> Elle va refleurir à l'éternel Printemps,

---

[1] *Aman*, B 433–40.   [2] *Les Lacènes*; *P. de J.*, p. 191.

Et la grace de Dieu comme une alme rosée,
Distilera dessus sa faveur plus prisée,
Pour en faire sortir un air si gratieux,
Qu'elle parfumera le saint pourpris des Cieux.
Les esprits bien-heureux sont des celestes Roses
Au Soleil de Iustice incessamment escloses;
Celles-là des iardins durent moins qu'un matin,
Mais pour ces fleurs du Ciel elles n'ont point de fin.[1]

This passage is formed by the intertwining of various images connected with flowers and with dew. The basic image is a common one, that of life being short, like the life of a rose. This commonplace image is, however, transformed by the idea of the immortal soul being an eternal flower. In the springtime of redemption, God's grace, likened to dew, descends upon the soul, and produces from it a heavenly scent.

This procedure is followed in many other speeches. Commonplace images, including the conventional Petrarchan love-images, are transformed as they mingle with other, related metaphors, until a whole passage appears to be one continuous image. The opening monologue of *David*[2] is a very good example of this: the whole speech is built upon the traditional image of love as both ice and fire:

Un volage Demon qui possede mon ame
Or me glace de crainte, or de desir m'enflame.

The lover's condition is contrasted with that of the sun, which does at least come to rest at evening-time:

Au poinct que le Soleil ses rais nouveaux desserre
Sur les nouvelles fleurs qui tapissent la terre,
Ie sens mille soucis s'esclorre dans mon cœur
Au seul obiet d'un œil trop doux en sa rigueur.
Quand la chaleur du iour à midi se r'enflame,
De mesme croist aussi la chaleur de mon ame;
Mais l'une sur le soir va tousiours finissant;
Et l'autre par sa fin va sans fin renaissant.
    O Phebus, di-ie alors, tu vas finir ta tasche,
Ià tes chevaux lassez vont prendre leur relasche,
Où mon travail n'a cesse . . .

Soon we are given details of the lover's condition; again the emphasis is on fire:

Mes yeux tous embrasez d'ardantes estincelles
Font voir que mon cœur brusle en des flames cruelles;

---

[1] *La Reine d'Escosse*; P. de J., pp. 108–9.   [2] *David*; P. de J., pp. 203–6.

Mon teint terni, livide et iaunastrement blanc
Montre que ie nourri du souffre dans le sang;
Et que l'esprit mouvant au creux de mes arteres
Languit comme privé de ses forces legeres;
Que ma cervelle est cuite, et que mes os cavez
Ne sont comme ils souloient, de mouëlle abreuvez . . .

After a short digression on David's glorious past, we come to a description of Bethsabée, his beloved. Here, the image of the sun is transferred to her, with the conventional comparison between the loved one and the sun. The sun is setting as David, walking on his roof, sees Bethsabée in her bath:

. . . Où comme de mes yeux s'esloignoit le Soleil,
Un autre s'y presente en beauté nompareil,
Bref tout semblable à luy quand il tire de l'onde
Son ieune front orné d'une perruque blonde.

Naturally, the stress in this case is more upon the light of the sun than on its heat:

Il esclairoit dans l'eau, et d'un esclat glissant
La pointe de ma veuë alloit esbloüissant,
Comme l'œil le plus ferme estant surpris s'estonne
A l'esclair tremoussant qui sur les eaux rayonne.
Dans le cristal coulant ores il s'allongeoit,
Or sous les flots d'argent sa beauté se plongeoit;
Telle qu'en Orient on void la belle Aurore . . .

The brightness is further stressed by the Petrarchan image of her eyes as 'astres iumeaux' and her 'teint aussi clair qu'un miroir radieux / Qui par trop de clarté perd la force des yeux'.

But the whole passage is drawn together by two final comparisons, both of which stress once more the heat of the sun. Bethsabée, who has been compared to the brightness of the sun and the stars, is shown to have their heat as well, and to have imparted it to her lover (so we return once more to the opening of the speech):

Lors ie devins Amant de cette belle Amante;
Et comme au doux Printemps sur le haut Erimante,
Ou sur le froid Riphee on void dissoudre en eaux
Les neges que l'Hiver y tasse par monceaux;
Ie senti s'escouler la glace de mon ame,
Sous le feu doux-cuisant de sa iumelle flame . . .

The last comparison is a paradox; the flame has remained alight even when under water:

> ... Sa iumelle flame,
> Qui demeurant tousiours dans les flots allumé
> Iallissant hors des flots m'a le cœur consommé.

This extended use of imagery is not peculiar to Montchrestien; it is, indeed, one of the advantages of the Renaissance form of tragedy that it provides the opportunity for such studies in mood. Dr. Odette de Mourgues has, in lectures and in talks, drawn attention to Garnier's use of contrasting moods throughout a whole play such as *Hippolyte*, so that this play becomes orchestrated, as it were, in shades of light and dark, most of this effect being achieved by the recurrent use of specific kinds of imagery. The last act of *Hippolyte* she has shown to be skilfully balanced by the insertion of a sad but graceful chorus between two *tirades* of grief. While Montchrestien's over-all 'orchestration' is perhaps not always as skilful as this, he nevertheless manages to sustain a specific atmosphere not only through a single speech, but also through a whole act at a time, by the skilful use of imagery. The 'Mary' scenes in *La Reine d'Escosse*, the erotic overtones throughout most of *David*,[1] are good examples of this. Montchrestien and Garnier are the two great exponents of this technique in Renaissance tragedy.

The rich effect of Montchrestien's imagery stems from several causes: First, from the opportunities for expansion offered by the Renaissance conception of tragedy. Second, from the melodious sound of his verse. Third, from the stress upon the senses, above all the sight, which was inculcated by Ramist rhetoric. Fourth, from freedom from the constraints of seventeenth-century poetic with regard to imagery. This imagery is the main element in the excitement of Montchrestien's verse, whether in the long extended simile or metaphor, or in the sudden, revealing word-picture. In comparisons, as in descriptions, the visual element gives a three-dimensional effect to the writing.

Montchrestien's style is not as powerful as that of Garnier; yet in its own way it is as impressive. In the measured rhythm, the flowing sound, the rational progression of its speeches of persuasion or of calm resignation; in the richness, the vividness of the images which ornament this basic structure, Montchrestien's poetry can be seen as the most perfect expression of the poetic language and style of its time, and as a poetical fulfilment of the rhetorical training of the Renaissance.

[1] See Appendix I 'Malberbe Correcteur de Trágedie'.

APPENDIX I

'Malherbe Correcteur de Tragédie'

OF Montchrestien's play *Sophonisbe* there are three widely differing versions which appeared during the lifetime of the author—those of 1596, 1601, and 1604.[1]

One can see, in Ludwig Fries's edition of *Sophonisbe*,[2] the three main editions placed side by side. This edition, however, makes very little in the way of judgement upon the variants, apart from marking those lines which appear to correspond to each other; the introduction deals almost entirely with the sources to the play.

The first person to deal critically with these three editions was Eugène Rigal, in his book *De Jodelle à Molière* (Paris 1911). His interest was mainly directed upon the question of *mise en scène*, though he also mentions one or two advances in the language.

The most serious study of the editions is that of M. Raymond Lebègue, in his three articles *Malherbe Correcteur de Tragédie*.[3] Here he develops the theory that between the publication of the 1596 and the 1601 editions, Montchrestien placed the text of his play before Malherbe, who pointed out to him the errors in language and style; and it is chiefly the merits of this theory which I shall be discussing in the course of this appendix.

This theory has been questioned by G. O. Seiver, firstly in a paragraph of the introduction to his edition of Montchrestien's *Aman*,[4] and later in an article entitled *Did Malherbe Correct Montchrestien?*[5] In this article, however, he bases his argument entirely upon the variants in *Aman*, i.e. between the 1601 and 1604 editions, and thus, while proving that there was no appreciable influence of Malherbe at this point, he does not necessarily prove the lack of influence on the other play and the earlier edition. In fact, in a recent

---

[1] After the first edition, the play is known as *La Cartaginoise*. The other editions, those of 1603, 1606, and 1607, are merely copies of one or other of the editions of 1601 and 1604. The edition of 1601 also includes all the other plays except *Hector*, which appears for the first time in the 1604 edition.

[2] 'Montchrestien's Sophonisbe, Paralleldruck der drei davon erschienenen Bearbeitungen', in Stengel's *Ausgaben und Abhandlungen*, t. 85, Marburg 1889.

[3] *R.H.L.F.* (1934).　　　　　　　　　　　　　　　　[4] Philadelphia 1939.

[5] *P.M.L.A.* (Sept. 1940), pp. 968–78.

edition of *David* Mr. Lancaster E. Dabney has found it possible to agree with both M. Lebègue and Mr. Seiver. He claims that 'Lebègue does make a case for *Sophonisbe–La Cartaginoise*', but then agrees with Mr. Seiver that Montchrestien 'nevertheless asserted his linguistic independence shortly thereafter.'[1]

Certainly this distinction has already been used, to defend M. Lebègue, by his pupil M. René Fromilhague, in his book *Vie de Malherbe*.[2] Here M. Fromilhague, in order to support M. Lebègue's view, slightly changed it to fit in with Seiver's discoveries, by suggesting that the influence of Malherbe was only temporary.

M. Lebègue's theory is as much believed now as when it was first stated; the influence of Malherbe is taught as a definite fact in the career of Montchrestien, and is referred to in books of all kinds.[3]

One of the results of this widely-held theory has been for critics to see in Montchrestien an author already strongly under the influence of seventeenth-century theories and methods of poetic construction. Such a view is, however, as we have seen in our discussion of Montchrestien's style, very much mistaken. Lanson's description of Montchrestien as 'un de nos derniers et plus exquis lyriques, avant le règne du bon sens eloquent',[4] holds good; and it is in an attempt to explain this, and to re-establish Montchrestien's freedom as a late Renaissance lyric poet, that we must here re-examine the whole question of the possibility of Malherbe's influence.

M. Lebègue bases his theory on two main points: firstly, on the multitude of changes in the second edition, the majority of which have little effect on the dramatic structure of the play, but are concerned with language and style (however, as I hope to show later, other reasons independent of Malherbe's influence can be found for these changes in almost every case); and secondly, on the fact that an acquaintanceship with Montchrestien is mentioned twice by Malherbe in his letters, once in 1618 and once in 1621.

Let us deal first with the letters, on the evidence of which M. Lebègue suggests that on his second visit from Provence to Caen, in the years 1598 and 1599, Malherbe personally corrected the tragedy of Montchrestien. These are (*a*) a letter from Malherbe to M. du Bouillon Malherbe, his cousin, dated 2 August 1618, 'à Paris': a letter full of his genealogical interests, in which he says:

J'ai reçu votre lettre du 24ᵉ. passé, et avec elle celle de M. de Cagny. Ce n'a pas été sans m'étonner de ce que vous m'écrivez que par une de mes lettres je vous avois assuré que je tenois de lui-même ce que je vous mandois, qu'il avoit un livre

---

[1] L. E. Dabney, *David*, Texas 1963, p. 10.
[2] Paris 1954.
[3] In 1944 (that is to say, four years after Seiver's article), M. Lebègue writes: 'Cette opinion . . . n'a pas été admise par tous les spécialistes; *mais on ne m'a pas encore opposé d'argument probant.*' (*Tragédie française de la Renaissance*, p. 67.) This he still maintains.
[4] *Revue des Deux Mondes*, 15 Sept. 1891.

de la noblesse de Normandie qui avoit passé avec le duc Guillaume. Je vous supplie, mon cousin, de revoir ma lettre, et vous trouverez que c'est chose dont je ne vous parlai jamais. M. de Cagny a grande raison de dire qu'il ne me connoissoit point, pource que c'est un homme que je n'ai point l'honneur d'avoir jamais vu. *Un nommé M. de Montchrestien est celui de qui je le tenois, et qui le m'a dit, non une fois ou deux, mais une douzaine.*

(*b*) A letter from Malherbe to Peiresc, written from Caen on Thursday, 14th October 1621, just after the death of Montchrestien, and the burning of his body as that of a rebel leader. He mentions the main facts of Montchrestien's life, as far as they were known to him, and then adds: 'Il a fait un livre de tragédies en vers françois; je crois que c'étoit ce qui lui avoit donné sujet de me venir voir deux ou trois fois.'[1]

These letters constitute the whole *historical* basis upon which M. Lebègue's theory rests; let us consider their value.

(1) In both letters (not merely in that of 1621) Montchrestien is referred to in the indefinite term of a slight acquaintance: 'Un nommé M. de Montchrestien' and 'un nommé Montchrestien'.

(2) The letters were written twenty years after the time M. Lebègue suggests for the meeting:

Nous, nous en retiendrons que Montchrestien est venu le voir souvent, et que leurs conversations avaient trait surtout à ses tragédies. Or le dernier texte de celles-ci a paru en 1604, et de 1599 à 1605 Malherbe résida en Provence; peut-on imaginer que Montchrestien alla le retrouver à Aix? Non. Par conséquent, les entretiens qu'ils eurent au sujet de ses pièces remontent au plus tard au mois de novembre 1599, ce qui apporte à mon hypothèse une nouvelle confirmation.

But to start from the assumption that they discussed the plays in the time between the editions seems to be putting the cart before the horse. Mr. Seiver, in his preface to *Aman*, states: 'This letter is dated October 14th, 1621. Since Montchrestien made no changes in his plays after 1604, we may only conjecture as to the actual date of meeting between the two compatriots.'

M. Fromilhague, in support of M. Lebègue, produces a series of very questionable statements:

Nous pensons pourtant que M. Lebègue a raison. La rencontre entre les deux poètes nous semble bien remonter au séjour de Malherbe à Caen en 1598–1599. Où situer ces visites renouvelées que le jeune poète rend à son aîné? Certainement pas à Paris, où rien ne permet de croire que Montchrestien ait pu être, même pendant une courte période, l'assidu des réunions qui se tenaient en la chambre de Malherbe.[2]

---

[1] M. Lebègue follows, for this second letter, the theory of Petit de Julleville, who says in the introduction to his 1891 edition of the plays: 'Trois années plus tard, Malherbe . . . se croira obligé de désavouer la fréquence de leurs relations.' Montchrestien was a condemned rebel, and as such a dangerous acquaintance.

[2] *Vie de Malherbe*, p. 152.

Why should Montchrestien not have met Malherbe in Paris? We know very little about Montchrestien's life, but some things we do know: 'S'estant retiré vers la forest d'Orleans, et puis à Chastillon sur Loire, il trauailla à faire de l'acier et en faire faire des lancettes, couteaux, canivets, et autres instruments *qu'il venoit vendre à Paris: et pource se logea en la ruë de la Harpe chez un taillandier, et demeura quelques années en cest estat . . .*'[1]

He thus came to Paris during this period of his life (somewhere between 1611 and 1621)[2] and we also learn from the letter to Peiresc, 14 octobre 1621: 'Vous le pouvez avoir vu à la suite du conseil, il y a, ce me semble, deux ou trois ans.'

From this statement it would seem that Malherbe had had opportunities of meeting Montchrestien in these later years. Malherbe had obviously seen Montchrestien 'il y a . . . deux ou trois ans', i.e. about 1618, the time of his letter to M. du Bouillon Malherbe; the tone in this letter of 1618 seems to point to a recent acquaintanceship, rather than one of twenty years ago: 'Un nommé M. de Montchrestien est celui de qui je le tenois, et qui le m'a dit, non une fois ou deux, mais une douzaine.' Added to this, we must mention the fact that Montchrestien was living in Paris in 1618, at the time of his wedding. M. Fromilhague continues:

La conversation des deux poètes porte avec insistance sur un livre concernant la plus ancienne noblesse de Normandie. Certes ce sujet a toujours intéressé notre poète. Mais n'était-il pas d'une brûlante actualité en 1598–9, au moment où la 'recherche' de M. de Mesmes devait mettre en ébullition la plupart des familles nobles de la province? Au cours de ses deux séjours à Caen de juin–juillet 1606 et septembre–octobre 1611, Malherbe aura des préoccupations d'un autre ordre.

This may be so, but he was also vitally interested in this subject about 1618, as his letters to his cousin du Bouillon Malherbe show.

Upon the question of time, I would thus suggest (*a*) that Malherbe had opportunities of meeting Montchrestien later than 1604; (*b*) that from the letters I have quoted it seems more probable that their acquaintanceship does date from after this time.

(3) What did they discuss at their meetings? From the two letters we gather (*a*) that genealogy was mentioned 'une douzaine de fois' and that Montchrestien came to see Malherbe 'deux ou trois fois' about his tragedies. It should be noted that whereas Malherbe may for obvious reasons be playing down his acquaintanceship with Montchrestien in the second statement, yet, before any danger threatened, he mentions only the genealogical interest as a subject of their discussion.

---

[1] *M.F.*, t. vii, p. 815.

[2] 1611 is the first date we hear of him living at Oussune-sur-Loire, near Châtillon, where he made his factory. (See Acte de procuration, Rouen, 23 juillet 1611, in the *Bulletin de la Commission des antiquités de la Seine-Inférieure*, vol. 7 (1888), p. 369.) It was presumably just before this time that he returned from his exile. It was in 1621 that he left Châtillon, of which he was governor, in order to take part in the Huguenot uprising.

It would seem that the meetings mentioned are capable of many other plausible explanations.

For example, the two authors may have discussed Montchrestien's tragedies, but long after the publication of the 1604 edition. Montchrestien may have used them as a means of getting to know Malherbe, perhaps because he was an influential figure, perhaps because of their common interest in genealogy.

Another possibility could be snobbery upon Malherbe's part. He was willing to admit that 'un nommé M. de Montchrestien' had the same genealogical interests as himself, but when he discovered that this man was Mauchrestien, the son of an apothecary, he may have felt that doubt might also be laid on his own claims to nobility. For though Malherbe had an avid interest in genealogy, his own family background was by no means assured. It was suggested that 'les Malherbe dont estoit le poète si fameux viennent de paysans de Missy dont l'un d'eux s'establit à Caen et y fut tanneur, dont on voit encore la maison en la paroisse St-Etienne.'[1] M. Fromilhague has supported Malherbe's claims to nobility, which are great, yet the fact remains that his position in his lifetime seems to have been very uncertain, and people noticed 'la volonté ferme et arrêtée qu'il avait de faire connaître à tous, Provençaux ou Normands, courtisans ou conseillers du Roi, l'antiquité de sa noblesse.'[1]

Now at the time of Montchrestien's uprising in 1621, loyal subjects of the king were spreading the story of his low birth, that story which we hear in Malherbe's letter and in the *Mercure François*. The truth or falsehood of the story has no bearing on our argument; what matters is that it was believed. Malherbe may have picked on the tragedies as a good explanation for his acquaintanceship with Montchrestien.

I do not claim that either of these theories is necessarily correct, but I suggest that as conjectures they are just as plausible as M. Lebègue's contention, on the evidence of these letters, that the two men met twenty years before, that one corrected in detail the tragedy of the other, and that they never met again in later years.

If M. Lebègue's theory were supported by the internal evidence provided by the play it would obviously be far more plausible. Let us examine the play to see if it provides such evidence.

Before we do so, however, there is one point that needs to be made. M. Lebègue says: 'En outre, Malherbe n'attachait pas un grand prix à des pièces dont le succès avait été restreint et dont le style devait lui sembler souvent médiocre.' Now Montchrestien's greatest enemy, the *Mercure François*, while running him down in every other way, is forced to admit, in 1621: 'Il a esté un des bons Poètes Tragiques de son temps: il fit imprimer plusieurs tragédies qu'il auoit composees, lesquelles furent bien receues . . .'

[1] Abbé V. Bourrienne, *Malherbe, points obscurs et nouveaux de sa vie normande*, Paris, 1895; quoted in Fromilhague, op. cit., p. 19.

The fact that there is also a posthumous edition (1627) of the works of an author who had such an ignominious end, shows that his works must still have been quite popular. He was still recognized as a good tragic poet. Though Malherbe might disapprove of Montchrestien's style, if he had made improvements to this he would surely not disapprove of them, but rather point to them as redeeming features. His silence on the subject of his work would seem very hard to understand.

The Corrections

M. Lebègue and M. Fromilhague are the first to admit that it is extremely difficult in any particular case to prove the positive influence of Malherbe. M. Fromilhague says: 'Nombreux sont les progrès de l'auteur qui reflètent l'évolution générale de la poésie française à cette époque, et il est difficile d'en distinguer ceux qui peuvent être attribués à l'influence particulière de Malherbe.' As M. Lebègue himself admits, many of the changes conform with the ideas of earlier authors; Garnier no longer used *mots composés* after 1580, and had already started cutting out repetitions of words. Many of Montchrestien's predecessors were far more concerned about the *bienséances* than he is in any of his plays. Ronsard condemned the hiatus and the 'e non élidé qui suit une voyelle' in his *Abrégé de l'art poétique*. Audacious inversions are condemned in the Preface to *La Franciade*. 'Il ne faut pas exagérer la nouveauté de la doctrine de Malherbe.... Ce qui le distingue de ses prédécesseurs, c'est la rigueur avec laquelle il les applique et la forme qu'il leur donne d'une doctrine logique et cohérente.' (Lebègue.)

But it is this very rigour of application which seems to be lacking in the changes in *Sophonisbe*. Phrases which, M. Lebègue informs us, are being cut out, do reappear in the second edition, and also in the third. It is hard to find anything that is completely cut out between the first and second editions.

As for the third edition, our critics seem in two minds upon the subject. M. Lebègue says: 'Montchrestien garda le souvenir des conseils de Malherbe. En effet, les changements effectués entre 1601 et 1604 m'ont semblé conformes aux principes de son Mentor, et ... il ne revint presque jamais à son premier texte.' M. Fromilhague says: 'L'influence du réformateur n'ayant pu être que passagère, il est impossible que Montchrestien ait eu le temps d'assimiler sa doctrine, et à plus forte raison, qu'il y ait conformé l'ensemble de ses écrits.'

It is ludicrous to imagine that, as M. Fromilhague suggests, someone of Montchrestien's intelligence would accept corrections to his text without accepting or understanding the reasons for these changes, and would then fail to make similar changes in later editions of this and the other plays.

If, on the other hand, as M. Lebègue suggests, the influence continued, the 1604 edition of all the plays should show this influence, and not just *La Cartaginoise* alone. Thus we can make use of the other plays for our research into M. Lebègue's theory; these all fail to show any particular influence of Malherbe or of anyone else, as we shall see.

The corrections themselves rarely seem to have been made for any positive reason. There are innumerable retentions, and even additions, in both second and third editions; and the reasons for most of the actual suppressions, if suppressions they be, seem very uncertain. First of all, there is the question of long suppressed passages. The main reason one could find for these would be the matter of length; the play is successively cut down from 2237 lines to 1822 and then to 1663. M. Lebègue himself admits: 'Mais comme il est improbable qu'à cause d'un seul mot l'auteur de *Sophonisbe* ait supprimé plusieurs vers on pourra ne tenir aucun compte de ces exemples', and puts after many of his examples the phrase 'pass. supp.' to show that they appear in such passages. But there are many other cases in which he does not put this phrase in places where it should appear, and a great many of his arguments are invalidated when examined closely upon this point. It is surely reasonable to count as suppressed passages not only those which completely disappear from the play, but also those which disappear to be replaced by completely different passages. Also, where a single word or a small phrase is in question, I would regard a suppressed passage of only four lines as requiring the explanation 'pass. supp.'.

For an example, let us take Massinisse's monologue (Act v). M. Lebègue admits that it is cut down for reasons of length, and indeed, from 234 lines in 1596 it drops to 134 in 1601. Throughout the speech there are very few lines which even faintly correspond with each other in both editions. In the passages counted as suppressed according to the definition above, we find the following reasons attached by M. Lebègue to the suppression of individual words and phrases:

v. 1822 (s'amie: Morph.), 1827 (le mourir: Vocab.), 1831 (brandiler: Vocab.), 1834 (povre: Biens.), 1835 (adj. app.: Synt.), 1838 (titre: Morph.), 1840–1 (rime), 1847 (fiel: Biens.), 1852 (povre: Biens.), 1853 (lairrois: Morph.), 1855 (Voies voies: Rép.), 1857 (à notre dam: Vocab.), 1858 (vie de: e muet. Also eclerans yeux: Ordre), 1859 (serenes: Vocab.), 1861 (darde: Vocab.), 1862 (Absconsera, rais: Vocab.), 1863 (és: Morph.), 1865 (baisoter: Vocab.), 1867 (Biens.), 1869 (Jupin: Biens.), 1871 (coléré: adj. app.: Synt., also vocab.), 1872 (tretif, bessonnes: Vocab.), 1872–3 (rime), 1873 (à tous cous, ie décœuures: Morph.), 1876 (Ains: Morph.), 1879 (alentir: Vocab.), 1880 (frétillarde: Vocab.), 1883 (les cœurs plus marbrins:'les' left out. Also Vocab.), 1884 (absente: Vocab.), 1890 (sus: Morph.), 1893 (lors: Morph.), 1894 (tout-pouvant: Vocab. Jupin: Biens.), 1895 (M'amour: Morph.), 1896 (Lame: Vocab.), 1913 (adj. app.: Synt.), 1916–17 (rime), 1918 (conquests: Vocab.), 1921 (traieté: Vocab.), 1923 (ma bien aimée: Biens.), 1924 (Je n'eusses eu: Morph.), 1929 (Biens.), 1930 (nopcier: Vocab.), 1939 (povre: Biens.), 1950 (Biens.), 1952 (Morph.), 1956 (Rép.), 1957 (qui en: Hiatus), 1965 (obscure mythology), 1967 (redonde: Vocab.), 1972 (emmiellé: Vocab., Ordre), 1973 (doux-amer: Vocab.), 1976 (Rép.), 1978 (Jupin: Biens.), 1980 (sus: Morph.), 1981 (cendroya terre-nés: Vocab.),

1982 (Rép., obscure mythology), 1993 (ie faux: Morph.), 2000 (Rép.,
Biens.), 2001 (aréneux: Vocab.), 2006 (Rép., Biens.), 2010 (Biens. Also
sucçoter: Vocab.), 2013 (le vague: Vocab.), 2015 (Metaphor. Also porte-voiles:
Vocab.), 2018 (Morph.), 2024 (roule-univers: Vocab.), 2026 (raiz: Vocab.),
2026–7 (Biens.), 2028–9 (Métaphore bizarre), 2030 (Métaphore bizarre),
2032 (Chere ame: Biens. Also respiter: Vocab.), 2034 (Synt.), 2039 (Porte-
brandon: Vocab.), 2043 (nues épaisses: e mute), 2044 (Neptun' qui: elision of e
mute), 2048 (Sus: Morph.), 2049 (un qui: Morph. Also ça bas: Biens.).

Besides this difficulty, there is also that of accurately assessing the reasons
for a change, even when this change occurs in only one or two changed lines.
There are very often many conflicting possibilities; enjambment, cacophony,
etc., appear in many cases to be the most likely. If the mere changing of one
word or phrase always meant that the author intended to suppress a particular phrase, one could imagine that line 258 'Premier qu'avec plaisir la
liqueur douce on hume' was changed to 'Ains qu'une liqueur douce avec
plaisir on hume' because 'Ains que' seemed preferable to 'Premier que'!
(Whereas Lücken informs us that 'premier que' was in usage in the seventeenth century.)

The fact is that there are only about 110 identical or closely similar lines
in texts A and B, about 280 in B and C, while over the whole three editions
there are only about 29 (see Fries). Amidst so much change, it is hard to
point to any reasons, and it seems a strange thing when a line is not changed.
For this reason, it is hard to regard a single example of change or suppression
as providing sufficient evidence of intention.

One can find other reasons for alteration just as likely as that given by M.
Lebègue. For example, a great many of the changes may have been caused
by the fact that Montchrestien had witnessed a performance of his work at
Caen. The shortening of the play would point to this, for a production brings
out *longueurs* more than any reading could.

Admittedly, the shape of the play is hardly altered; but Montchrestien,
though in the Preface he denies knowledge of Saint-Gelays's translation of
Trissino's play, obviously knows the Italian original;[1] and he keeps fairly
close to Trissino's plan, a plan which caters well for the sixteenth-century
requirements of tragedy, in that it gives great opportunities for stylized 'set
pieces' suitable for rhetorical expansion: 'Quand à ce que les personnages
introduits en la mienne parlent longuement, sans entrerompre le fil de leurs
discours; sçache que ie ne l'ay fait sans exemple.'

As far as the composition of the play is concerned, however, there are
various small improvements which show that Montchrestien is thinking of
performance.[2]

[1] See Chapter 3, 'Imitation'.
[2] See Chapter 7, 'Stage Representation'. Entrances of characters, changes of place,
are dealt with in a much more convincing way.

The main changes in the play, as I have said, are in the field of style and language. Montchrestien has closely followed the advice of Ronsard, du Bellay, and other Pléiade theorists, carefully to emend his verse, 'corriger et limer',[1] 'ajouter, oter, ou muer à loysir ce que cete premiere impetuosité et ardeur d'ecrire n'avoit permis de faire'.[2] The aim, in the majority of cases, has obviously been to improve the sound of the verse, to suppress cacophony, and to lessen the familiarity of conversational speech. There has also been a slight decrease in the number of hiatuses, and in the number of enjambments which would hold up the flow of the declamation and destroy the rhetorical balance of Montchrestien's verse. All these changes point to an overwhelming interest, on Montchrestien's part, in the *sound* of his verse, rather than in the observance of any kind of strict grammatical and poetic ruling.

Where, on the other hand, the changes do occasionally seem to point to grammatical intention, this intention seems to be typical of the mood of the time, rather than indicative of any positive influence of Malherbe (e.g. the suppression of compound adjectives). In many cases, Montchrestien must have felt he had made the mistakes of youth: in the preface to the 1596 edition he laid stress on the inadequacy of his efforts, of which he was aware even then: 'Amy lecteur, ce me seroit une chose longue et presque impossible, de m'excuser de toutes les fautes que i'ay faites en la composition de céte tragedie. . . . Au reste, i'ourdis céte tragedie en un âge qui peut à peine receuoir aucun iugement, qui doit accompagner telles compositions.'

So, as possible reasons for the changes, we have improvement of sound, natural developments of the time, and correction of youthful errors. These seem as plausible as M. Lebègue's theory, if not more so.

Two points must be cleared up. First, when M. Lebègue says that the corrections 'nous révèlent que, dès 1599, sept ans avant l'annotation de Desportes, la doctrine de Malherbe était constituée', he again seems to be putting the cart before the horse. This was another thing that should have been proved before trying to blame the corrections upon Malherbe. Secondly, both M. Lebègue's and M. Fromilhague's mention of the influence of Malherbe's published poems on Montchrestien is a theory which (*a*) seems to rest on very slight evidence, and (*b*) proves very little, in that the works in question were open for everyone to read, and also contained at the time very little of the later doctrine of Malherbe.

A. L'ORTHOGRAPHE

Le plus souvent, quand B rétablit une consonne ou qu'il remplace une voyelle par une diphthongue, il nous est impossible d'attribuer ce changement de lettre à Malherbe plutôt qu'à l'imprimeur ou à Montchrestien; à cette époque l'orthographe variait selon les ateliers d'imprimerie . . .

[1] Ronsard, *Abrégé de l'art poëtique françois.*
[2] Du Bellay, *Deffence et illustration de la langue françoyse.*

On the whole, the spelling seems to take a step backward in B, as M. Lebègue points out.

Where elision, etc., affects the.metre, I shall deal with it under the heading 'Versification'.

B. MORPHOLOGIE

The summary of this section, on page 162 of M. Lebègue's article, runs as follows: 'Les pronoms et adjectifs maint, maint et maint, cil, cetuy, les adverbes et conjonctions ainçois, ains, ains que, ja, ja déjà, si que, disparaissent.'

Let us examine more closely the examples given of the disappearance of these words:

Maint et maint: 'Au vers 587 "maint et maint" . . . n'a pas été conservé dans la 2e édition.' It does not occur even in the first edition at this point, and it must be presumed that a printing error has occurred in the numbering. However the phrase 'maint et maint' is *introduced* into edition B at line 357:

> Quand nous aperceuons que mainte et mainte troupe.

In edition C this becomes 'mainte effroyable troupe', which brings us to the previous phrase mentioned by M. Lebègue:

Maint: 'Au vers 1067 "maints alarmes" a peut-être été supprimé à cause du genre d'alarme, mais au vers 1631 c'est certainement le mot "maint" qui a motivé la correction.' This may seem so; but how does one then explain the introduction of the word into B 1339 'maint perilleux danger', and also into text C at the point mentioned above?

'Lücken a relevé trois exemples dans les tragédies de Montchrestien[1] . . . (éd. P. de J., pp. 73, 76, 268).' Merely by scanning this edition, however, one can find several other examples of this word, which Montchrestien is still using in 1604 (e.g. *David*, pp. 204, 218 (twice), 211 (mainte et mainte), and *Aman*, pp. 243, 269, 275).

Cil: 'Cil . . . ne disparaîtra complètement que dans l'édition C.' This is false, in that it is restored in C 781, after having been cut out from A 1055. Let us take, however, the examples of A–B changes which M. Lebègue gives:

Of the seven suppressions he mentions, two are in long suppressed passages (1551 and 2185), two are converted into a similar fault (1627–8 become 'un qui'), and one is restored in C (A 1055). 'Mais, *par mégarde*, il le conserve une fois (A 1788), et l'ajoute trois fois (B 105, 247, 1255).' Why, when the suppressions and additions are so equal (if one ignores the examples in suppressed passages, the ratio is 5 to 3, with one example of retention), should one thing have been done with intention, the other 'par mégarde'?

---

[1] M. Lebègue is here, as elsewhere, making the mistake pointed out by Seiver, in presuming Lücken to have listed all the examples illustrative of the item treated, which he does not do.

Admittedly, in edition C 'cil' is cut out in four places, and only added in one; but surely if he had intended to suppress the word, the author would have cut it out from the 1604 edition of all his plays? Lücken notes five examples of it in the Petit de Julleville edition.

He also mentions the interesting fact that this form was not to be found in the works of Garnier nor in those of Montaigne; it was already obsolescent, if not obsolete.

Cetuy: There is but one example of this in text A; as M. Lebègue points out, this has been cut out; to what extent, however, can one example be held to prove intention of suppression?

Lücken mentions eleven examples of the use of 'cestui-ci' in the works of Montchrestien, but only two of them in the plays, the rest being in his prose.

Ainçois: One example only in A; this disappears. We find this word, however, in C 621, and it is used twice in the 1601 edition of *Aman* (408, 1663), and once in the 1604 edition of that play.

Ains: Of the four examples given, three are in long suppressed passages (1182, 1526, 1876). This leaves one example of suppression (557) and one of retention (289). This word is used quite often in the other plays. Lücken says of it: 'Ains = mais, das um die Mitte des XVII. Jahrhunderts verschwindet, findet sich bei Montchrestien *häufig*.'[1]

Ains que: The one example of suppression (1224) is part of four suppressed lines; with no proved example of intentional suppression, we are left with one example of introduction of the word in 1601 (B 189). Admittedly, as M. Lebègue says, this is cut out in 1604, but we find it in the 1604 edition of the other plays (e.g. *Aman*, B 550, 1434).

ja: Of the six examples given of suppression, two are in suppressed passages (219, 832). In B there are the five additions mentioned by M. Lebègue, also a retention of the word from A 450. In C there are many examples (though M. Lebègue says there are only two, 750 and 1282). Additional ones are C 813, 346, and 1628 (retentions of B) and C 438 and 848. The word is also very common in the 1604 edition of the other plays (in *David* alone, *P. de J.* pp. 203, 204 (twice), 205, 221, 222, 223, 233). Lücken notes a great many examples (p. 47.)

Ja déjà: As M. Lebègue admits, one example is in a suppressed passage. This leaves us with one only.

si que: Again, one suppressed passage (1536), leaving us with one example only.

To sum up our inquiry into M. Lebègue's initial statement; it is true only of 'cetuy', 'ja déjà', and 'si que' that they 'disparaissent'; and in each case

---

[1] Op. cit., p. 63, para. 3.

there is only one definite suppression of the word. However, the fact that they were used so sparingly in the 1596 edition suggests that Montchrestien may have been wary of these words even before the time suggested for his meeting with Malherbe. As for the other words, they are far from disappearing, either in this play or in the others.

Let us now scan quickly the rest of this section:

Es: Of the five examples, two are in suppressed passages (772, 1863); one is restored in C (A 1070), and one is very uncertain, having almost certainly been changed to avoid an awkward enjambment by cutting down the phrase:

A 696–8   Je ne logé iamais és détours de mon ame
             Aucune cruauté: l'homme en toute saison,
             Doit mesurer ses faits du compas de raison.

B 588–90   La rigueur n'eut iamais de puissance en mon Ame.
             Un Prince vertueux doit en toute saison,
             Régler ses actions au compas de raison.

The word is retained in B 625 and introduced in C 479. Mr. Seiver's examination of *Aman* shows two examples in 1601, both kept in 1604 (A 1742, 692), and two further examples introduced in 1604 (B 90, 812).

Noms et adjectifs qualificatifs: As M. Lebègue says, 'artisane de gloire' disappears because of an enjambment, while 'ta vainqueresse teste' is introduced in B and C. He does not mention, however, that 'soldade' is cut out in the middle of a long passage. He admits that nothing can be proved about the feminine 'grand', and so this whole section is uncertain.

Pronoms et adjectifs: M. Lebègue would appear to be right about the suppression of 'Mamie' and 'm'amie' (A 1336, 1326). However, 'm'amour' and 's'amie' are both cut out in suppressed passages. For 'un qui', the three examples of suppression all occur in suppressed passages, and we are left with one certainty, the introduction of the phrase in 1601 instead of 'cil qui' (A 1627–8).

Le verbe: actif, passif, pronominal: Of the four examples of 'Élancer', three are in long passages (772, 1011, 1643). There is only one example of 'moquer' being intentionally cut out, because A 2050 is in a suppressed passage; and, on the other hand, it returns, as is pointed out, in C 70. Of 'accroistre' there is only one example; and the reflexive may have been added for the sake of scansion in a completely altered line:

A 734–5   Quoy? que par ma prison sa gloire doive accroistre?
B 630–1   Pourrois-ie voir sa gloire en ma honte s'acroistre?

Of 'se (dis) paroistre' there is one example only, because A 909 is in a suppressed passage; 'alterer' also provides only one example.

Conjugaison interrogative: M. Lebègue seems justified in his statement here, although one finds examples of this construction in the later edition. This suppression is a sign of the times, though, rather than of the influence of Malherbe.

Radicaux: There is only one example each for 'fleurissant' and 'épardre'; 'Elle oit' is kept; 'je faux' and 'disse' are in suppressed passages; 'me deult' and 'se deule' are in completely changed lines:

{ A 203	Mais ce qui plus me deult, c'ét de vous voir, helas!
{ B 147	Mais lors que de pleurer et de plaindre on est las.

{ A 293–4	Endurés donc un peu, car vous n'estes pas seule,
	Qui pour les maux venus amérement se deule.
{ B 221–2	Madame endurés donc: car la fortune aduerse
	A vous seule n'en veut, vous seule ne trauerse.

'Me deult' can be found in the 1604 edition of *Hector* (P. de J., p. 5), also in the 1601 edition of *Aman*, 'se deult' (A 1018).

Désinences: Both examples of the 's' being cut out are in suppressed passages; of the examples of 's' in the first person, five are in suppressed passages, leav- us with one other example (163). Against this we must place B's addition, 'je l'eusses allaitée' (1789), added 'par mégarde' (!). For the extra 's' in the imperative, we are informed of one example of suppression, one of intro- duction.

Tistre: Both examples are in suppressed passages, as are 'Decheute', 'cheute'.

Que+Subjonctif: 'Je meure' is in a suppressed passage, 'périsse' is retained.

Futurs et conditionnels: 'Donra' and 'lairrois' are both suppressed in long passages. 'Cueillirons' is introduced in 1601.

Formes périphrastiques: As M. Lebègue says, expressions using 'aller' and the present participle are common through all the editions.

Prépositions: For 'amont' and 'aval', 699 is uncertain (Lebègue) and 1558 is retained; we thus have one example on each side. Though two of the six examples of 'dessur' are in suppressed passages, and one is completely changed, I can find no trace of this word in the other editions, and agree that it must have been completely avoided.

Of the two examples of 'Fors', one is in a suppressed passage (924). Lücken says that this word was still quite common in the 1604 edition, and gives six examples, three of them from *La Cartaginoise* (*Sophonisbe*).

Of the eleven examples given of the preposition 'sus', four are in suppressed passages (1643, 1890, 1980, 2048), and two are in lines that are completely changed:

{ A 386	Fait errer sus le dos du triquétre Neptune.
{ B 314	Tous les Dieux de la mer par ses vœux importune.

$\left\{\begin{array}{l}\end{array}\right.$

A446–7   Demandant quelle peur a la palleur emprainte
          Qu'on lit sus notre front,

B 368–9   Quel morne estonnement vous fait pallir le front,
          Dit-il demy troublé?

It is introduced in 1601 in B 665, as well as in B 1594. Lücken notes that
Haase can find no example of this word in the seventeenth century; Lücken
himself, however, finds five examples in the 1604 edition of these plays.

Adverbes et conjonctions: 'A tous cous' and 'Lon-tens a que' are both suppressed in long passages; 'lors' may have been removed for diverse reasons,
as M. Lebègue admits. Lücken notes many examples of 'lors' in the other
plays.

    'Lon-tens-a', far from being 'sûr', is in a line which is completely changed:

A 2194–5   Pour voir finir le cours de ma triste vieillesse,
           Qui vers son occident lon-tens-a se rabbaisse.

B 1785–6   Pour ioindre l'occident de ma triste vieillesse,
           Au midy le plus clair de ma belle Princesse.

The same is true of 'Ne . . . ne':

A 203–4   Mais ce qui plus me deult, c'ét de vous voir, helas!
           Ne prendre en votre mal, ne confort ne soulas.

B147–8   Mais lors que de pleurer et de plaindre on est las,
           Encor est-on contraint de chercher du soulas.

There is only one example each of 'à tous les coups', 'n'y a gueres', and
'tant loin que', while 'B conserve ores, jaçoit que et du depuis que'.

Conclusion. Altogether it is impossible to come to any general conclusion
about Montchrestien's intentions with regard to the changes dealt with in
this section. Here and there one finds a single word (e.g. 'dessur') which
seems to be being avoided, but this could be explained by the gradual progress
of the language.

C. LA SYNTAXE

L'article: Lücken remarks (p. 18): 'Bei Montchrestien ist *wie bei seinen Zeit-
genossen* die Setzung des Artikels im Gegensatze zum Altfranzösischen im
allgemeinen zur Regel geworden.' The use of the article would thus seem to
be part of the general progress of the language. Close examination of the
examples given shows once more, however, that there is little evidence of
much change in this situation between the various editions of the play. On
certain items M. Lebègue himself admits this.

    Lücken says that in common with the authors of the seventeenth century,
Montchrestien often leaves out the article in the superlative. He gives
eighteen examples of this usage.

On the whole, however, it would be difficult to agree that 'l'article est employé un peu plus souvent'.

Le substantif: ('Alarme' I cannot find at line 1061.) 'B. n'admet que le féminin' for 'poison' because the other examples of the word have been left out, while C again uses both genders. The rest of the examples seem to point to no definite conclusion.

L'adjectif: One example only of the 'emploi adverbial de l'adjectif' being cut out (apart from the examples with which M. Lebègue deals under the heading 'Apposition'). Lücken[1] notes many examples of this adverbial use of the adjective in the 1604 edition.

There is but one example of the archaic use of the 'complément du comparatif' being cut out, and this is in a completely refashioned passage.

Le pronom: personnel, sujet (omission): It would certainly seem that Montchrestien attempts to correct this fault; of the ten examples of suppression, at least six are fully valid, and there is but one example of addition in B. Lücken finds several similar omissions in the other tragedies, however,[2] so this once more brings uncertainty upon the subject.

Pronom réfléchi: One finds examples of 'soi' referring to a person in all three editions; the one example of a correction is changed back in C. Lücken notes that the usage is uncertain with Montchrestien, as with his contemporaries.[3]

Pronom explétif: One example only, which may have been changed for another reason, as M. Lebègue admits.

Pronoms et adjectifs possessifs: There are two examples of suppression of 'mien' as an adjective. 'Cet emploi de mien et de tien commençait à disparaître',[4] however, so the suppressions would seem a sign of the times rather than of the influence of Malherbe. What is more, there are examples of this usage in Malherbe's works, as M. Lebègue states.

There seems to be one example, on each side, of the next point: Replacement of the possessive adjective by the article and the personal pronoun, and vice versa.

Pronoms démonstratifs: The one example of 'celle', used as an adjective, being cut out, occurs in a suppressed passage of four lines. Lücken finds no examples of this usage in Montchrestien (1604) or in Garnier, but finds one example in Malherbe! He says that it was a usage which was dying out.[5]

One of the three examples of suppression of 'cela qui' might easily have been caused by an avoidance of enjambment, and of lines split between

[1] Lücken, p. 46.
[2] Ibid., pp. 8–9, para. 7.
[3] Ibid., p. 12, para. 21.
[4] Lebègue, op. cit.
[5] Lücken, pp. 15–16.

speakers. The passage in question is one of stichomythia, which is almost entirely regularized in B; our phrase appears in the middle of it:

A 1746–8   *Ma.* Nous dirons que voulant courir à la mort bléme
                    Elle a prins un poignard.
              Sci.   Mais c'est un mal extréme
                    De frustrer un état de cela qu'on lui doit.

B 1477–8   *Ma.* Nous dirons que sa mort elle a causé soy-mesme.
              Sci. Vouloir tromper l'Estat est un danger extresme.

There are still two valid examples of suppression; but the phrase returns in 1604, in lines C 587 and 659. Lücken notes it as a fairly common phrase, and gives six examples of it.[1]

In the case of 'celuy là qui', there is only one valid example of suppression (M. Lebègue admits that the other is in a suppressed passage), one of retention, and one of addition. Even if there is no example of it in the 1604 edition of this play, there are examples in the same edition of the other plays. Lücken notes that it is very common in Montchrestien's works, as with all sixteenth-century authors and many early seventeenth-century ones.[2]

Le verbe: impersonnel: Two valid examples of suppression of the 'passif impersonnel', one of retention, one of addition.

Verbes intransitifs employés transitivement: Montchrestien would seem, from these few examples, to be avoiding this usage. (Though none of these words are actually criticized by Malherbe.)

Verbes transitifs employés sans complément: Though the one example of 'esclairer' is corrected in B, the fault reappears in C.

Attoucher à: Both examples of this phrase may have been suppressed for different reasons:

(*a*) Enjambment (874)

A 873–4   Qu'à nul autre qu'à vous mon plus chaste côté
              N'attouchera jamais.

B 733   Qu'à vous tant seulement se ioindra mon costé.

(*b*) The suppression of a rather ridiculous phrase (1579)

A 1578–9 (of horses):
                         Qui d'un pied superbe,
              Marchent dessus les fleurs sans attoucher à l'herbe,

which is changed to the more simple (B 1369–70)

                         Dont le pied superbe
              N'imprime point ses pas en marchant dessus l'herbe.

[1] Op. cit., p. 17, para. 7.   [2] Ibid., para. 9.

Songer, in the sense of 'voir en songe': as M. Lebègue says, this construction is found in writers of the seventeenth century.

La proposition infinitive: Montchrestien does cut out the article from the Greek construction 'L'avoir des maux d'un Roy quelque compassion est bien digne de toi'; also he changes 'l'œil découvre . . . s'écarter un heraut' to 'nous avisons . . .'.

The two examples of suppression of the 'proposition infinitive dépendant d'un verbe passif' are very uncertain, as M. Lebègue admits. One is in a suppressed passage, the other has been completely changed.

'Le sujet non exprimé de la proposition infinitive'—M. Lebègue cites two examples of suppression, one of them possibly for other reasons, and one example of retention.

'Pronom réfléchi sujet de la proposition infinitive'—One of the two examples is in a suppressed passage, the other is completely changed.

Le participe: Ablatif absolu: Two examples of suppression, one of retention, one of addition. Lücken notes its rarity (five examples only). Corneille used it a great deal.

Accord du participe passé avec 'avoir' quand le régime précède le verbe. The examples seem to show no particular trend.

Accord du participe passé avec 'être'.—One example of correction. Lücken finds no example of this fault in the 1604 edition of the plays.[1]

Adverbes de négation: 'Ne' sans 'pas'. In both examples, B is the only edition in which this construction appears; the phrases are thus in a perpetual state of flux. Lücken notes innumerable examples of this construction in the 1604 edition of the plays. (See in *Sophonisbe* alone, *P. de J.*, pp. 116, 122, 124, 129, 130, 132, 134, 138, 145, 153, 156.) Lücken says: 'Montchrestien weicht trotz der gegenteiligen Behauptung Wenzels hierin von der Sprache des sechzehnten Jahrhunderts nicht ab.'[2]

Ellipse de 'ne' dans l'interrogation directe: As M. Lebègue says, this construction is common in edition B, and in the 1604 edition of all the tragedies. Lücken gives innumerable examples.[3]

'Non' suivi d'un verbe: One example of suppression. This phrase, at any rate, 'tombe en désuétude'.[4]

Adverbes et prépositions: All three editions contain the prepositions 'dedans' and 'dessous'. This use of 'dessus' can be found in all three: e.g. B 316 C, C 765, C 791, C 792, B 119, B 1370. It appears also in the other plays, e.g. *Aman*, A 58 B, A 287 B, A 622 B, A 743, A 919 B, B 1328, A 1491, A 1644 B, A 1712 B. Lücken gives innumerable examples of all three words in the 1604 edition.[5]

---

[1] Ibid., p. 45, para. 5. [2] Ibid., p. 50, para. 2. [3] Ibid., p. 51, para. 4.
[4] Lebègue, op. cit. [5] Op. cit.., p. 56, para 1(a); p. 57, para. 3(a).

Prépositions: 'Parler avec luy' is uncertain as far as the cause of suppression is concerned, and 'mal-gré de' is in a suppressed passage, as M. Lebègue admits.

L'ordre des mots — l'inversion: Of the five examples given, two are in suppressed passages (198, 2067), one is an enjambment (623–4). However, it is surely natural that any author, especially a dramatic author, whose words, if his play is performed, have to be understood at a first hearing, should clear up obscurities of any kind caused by his wording—and these passages are indeed obscure. (M. Lebègue informs us that audacious inversions were condemned by Ronsard in the Preface to *La Franciade*.) Seiver notices a similar attempt to clear up obscurities in *Aman* between 1601 and 1604.

Participes transposés: Of the twelve examples of suppression of the past participle before the noun, all except A 850 and A 1582 are in suppressed passages (in the case of A 754, four lines). As for A 1582, just as likely a reason for suppression would seem to be avoidance of the enjambment:

A 1581–2   Ils vont où les conduit l'industrieuse main
               Du pratiqué cocher.

B 1372   Ils vont où les conduit de ton Cocher la main.

In B, I find two examples of this construction, B 205, 'un asseuré courage', and B 1236, 'Infortuné Siphax', and in C there are three examples, consisting of a retention of B 1236, and the introduction of C 796, 'Les serrez bataillons', and C 1474, 'des fortunez Amans'. (This last is changed from B 1627, 'des Amans fortunés'.)

In the case of the present participle, M. Lebègue says: 'On peut discuter sur la cause de quelques-unes de ces corrections.' Of the fourteen examples of suppression, four are in suppressed passages (430, 1086, 1653, 1858), one is in a two-line 'sentence' which is cut out (701), one is probably cut out in the changes caused by avoiding two rather awkward enjambments:

A 2198–2200   Que i'aimois plus que moy, non pour l'auoir portée
                Dans mon fertille flanc, mais l'ayant allaitée
                De mes propres tétins, dès le branlant berceau.

B 1789–90   Car bien que seulement ie l'eusses allaitée
              Je l'aimois tout autant comme l'ayant portée.

'Les volans etendars' becomes 'les sanglans estendars', which is merely another version of the same fault. In B, there is B 837, 'ta sanglante colère', B 857, 'la sanglante Bellone', B 1151, 'sur la bruyante mer'; in C we find a retention of B 837, plus the introduction of C 803, 'un grondant tonnerre'.

L'apposition: Substantifs apposés au sujet: Of the three examples of suppression, one is in a long passage (1683). In the other plays we find several examples of this construction, e.g. *David*; *P. de J.*, p. 205: 'Alors qu'Aigles d'amour ils tournent la paupière'; p. 210: 'Tes braues soldars, Vrais foudres de Bellonne et tempestes de Mars, sont tous plus ravis d'aise . . .'; and *Hector*, p. 8: 'Nous aveugles mortels . . .'; p. 9: 'Je veux avant la nuict vainqueur de ceste armee / Reduire son espoir et sa flotte en fumee'. It also occurs in the third edition of *Sophonisbe*:

C 1400–1   Deux yeux Soleils ardens de claire et vive flame
             Ont amassé leurs rais au centre de mon ame.

This was changed from B 1551: 'Deux beaux soleils d'Amour . . .'.

Adjectifs apposés au complément: Of the five examples of suppression, one is in a long passage (1087). I find one example in B (53):

             Pour seule m'affliger r'ammassés tout ensemble.

It also occurs on occasion in the other plays, e.g. *Aman*, B 1045–6:

             Le guide de sa main,
             Tout écumeux de fougue alentour de son frein.

But on the whole this is an unusual and ungrammatical construction, leading to obscurity; and this may well be the reason for its gradual suppression.

Adjectifs apposés au sujet: Of the twenty-five examples of suppression, eleven are in long passages (664, 765, 1084, 1115, 1169, 1313, 1637, 1835, 1871, 1913, 2131). In B we have the five examples given by M. Lebègue, plus B 379 (from A 467):

             Mais hélas! malheureux nous ne fusmes sitost
             Arriués en ce lieu.

In C we have 1027, 'Qu'infidele ie manque . . .', and also the example given by M. Lebègue. Examples still remain in the other plays, e.g. *Aman*, B 816, 'regner glorieuse au thrône d'Assuere', and

B 1453–4   Qui de longtemps captif en ces lieux estrangers
             Y court iournellement mille et mille dangers.

The use of this construction has been cut down, but has not disappeared.

La construction de la phrase: Only one example is given of correction of the fault of co-ordinating two different complements.

Conclusion: The only things which seem at all certain in this section are the gradual suppression of awkward inversions, and of adjectives in apposition to the complement; both of these constructions lead to obscurity, and would thus be cut out by an author who intended his play for performance. The one or two examples of proved suppression could be a result of the gradual changing of the language.

Lücken, in the conclusion of his *Zur Syntax Montchrestiens*, can make a definite statement only about the prose work, which, he says, follows in much greater measure the rules of modern French than does the poetry. He gives the impression that the poetry, written between ten and fifteen years before the prose, belongs much more to the sixteenth century.

D. LE VOCABULAIRE

Substantifs: formés par dérivation:

'*L'infinitif substantivé* est fréquemment employé par Montchrestien, Malherbe et leurs contemporains. Mais Malherbe blâme chez Desportes le substantif *espérer*.'

'Le crier' is the only positive example that M. Lebègue finds of this construction being cut out: 'd'autres infinitifs ont disparu, *peut-être pour d'autres motifs*'. A 15, 1827, and 1358 are in suppressed passages. Of 'le vouloir' he mentions one example of suppression, one of introduction. Wenzel[1] and Lücken[2] give many examples of Montchrestien's use of the 'infinitif subsubstantivé'.

Adjectifs substantivés: 'Un privé' is certainly cut out, and only one of the three examples of 'ses haineux' is uncertain, as A 2154 is in two completely changed lines; but the word seems quite common in the other plays (e.g. *Aman*, A 1034, B 1102). Both examples of the word 'le chaut' are changed to 'l'ardeur', while 'le sensuel' becomes 'l'apetit'; but the example for suppression of 'le plus froid' is in a long suppressed passage. Montchrestien would seem to be avoiding the adjectival noun to a certain extent, though he still uses it in the other plays, e.g. 'le sur-abondant' (*Aman*, v. 405), 'l'honneste utile' (*Aman*, B 334), 'le commun' (*Aman*, A 1267), 'le populaire' (passim).

The case of 'le vague' seems very uncertain. Both examples of disappearance are in suppressed passages, and it is kept at 532, also appearing in *Aman*; *P. de J.*, p. 253.

Substantifs formés par dérivation propre: 'Charton' is cut out, but there is only one example of this suppression. The same applies to 'enfançon' which we find again in *Hector* in 1604 (*P. de J.*, p. 11), and 'archerot', which is also introduced into the 1601 text of *Sophonisbe* (B 949).

Synonymes et mots ayant plusieurs formes: The one example of 'renom' is in a suppressed passage. The same is true of one of the two examples of 'rais', as M. Lebègue mentions; what is more, it is introduced three times in B (B 374 and 1552 (both mentioned by Lebègue) and B 478). Of the two examples of 'rais' ('des yeux d'une femme'), again, one is in a suppressed passage (1862): this word, used both of eyes and of the sun, is very common in the other plays (e.g. *Aman*, A 3 B, A 721 B, A 1233 B, A 1306 B, B 1600, A 1725 B).

The sole examples of 'conquests' and 'la darde' are in suppressed passages, as is one of the two examples of 'épouzés' (1063). There is only one example of each of the two words 'nuaux' and 'le pâme'. 'Oppresse' still exists in 1601.

---

[1] Wenzel, *Aesthetische und sprachliche Studien über Antoine de Montchrestien*, Weimar, 1885, pp. 79–80.   [2] Op. cit, p. 42.

While it is cut out once in the 1604 edition, 'naux' is also restored once in the same edition, showing how little method there is in the changes. (See also *Hector*; *P. de J.*, p. 62, and *Aman*; *P. de J.*, p. 264.)

As M. Lebègue remarks, 'scadron', while cut out twice from the 1596 edition, is introduced once in 1601 (and kept in 1604), and introduced once in 1604.

In the case of 'soudart' and 'soldart', I agree with M. Lebègue; both have been changed to 'soldat', except when they are at the end of a line, where the word 'soldart' is used for the rhyme.

Autres substantifs: The only examples of 'arroi', 'arretail', 'étorce', 'pard', and 'randon' are cut out in long passages, or in lines that have been completely refashioned:

A 123–4   Te voila donc décheu de ton premier arroi!
            Te voila serviteur qui fus n'agueres Roi!

B 91–2   Ton front couvert de honte, et ton cœur plein d'esmoy,
            Monstrent qu'à la fortune il ne faut auoir foy.

'Arroi' is also introduced in 1604, in C 335.

Both examples of 'guerdon' are in suppressed passages, while M. Lebègue notes that the word is introduced in B 1568, and also retained from A 1281 in both B and C. Two of the three examples of 'los' are also in suppressed passages (Not 1724. See also *Aman*; *P. de J.*, p. 268), as are one of the two examples of 'Austres' (136), of 'diffame' (2066), and of 'à mon dam' (1857) (the other example of the last returns in C. See also *Hector*; *P. de J.*, p. 41). M. Lebègue states that though 'lame' (pierre tombale) is twice cut out, B keeps it from A 1896, and that it is then cut out in a passage of a few lines before 1604. He also notes a suppression in B of 'lame' in its other sense (glaive).

One of the three examples of 'soulas' is cut out in a passage of four lines, and as M. Lebègue points out, the example in A 204 is kept in both 1601 and 1604, though this may be because of the rhyme.

'La gent romaine' is probably not avoided, we are told; as for 'fère', in one case it is kept in B and cut out in C, and in the other it is cut out in a suppressed passage between 1596 and 1601. (It also appears in *Aman*, A 702.) 'Nef' has one example of retention, one of introduction, two of suppression.

Among other nouns that Malherbe condemned, but which are kept in the second edition by Montchrestien, are 'ost' or 'hot', 'chef', and 'liesse' (B 178), 'spasme' (introduced in B 1687).

Adjectifs: (1) *Verbaux*: As M. Lebègue admits, 'coléré', 'embesogné', 'emmiellé', and 'ensouffré' are cut out only once each, and this in a suppressed passage. One of the two examples of 'mignardé' is a similar case, cut out in a passage of four lines. All the other words, except 'bouffans étendars' (which occurs in 1604 in *David*; *P. de J.*, p. 224), have only one example each of suppression.

(2) *Dérivés avec suffixe*: In the first paragraph, M. Lebègue says that 'deceuable', 'nuital', 'fretillard', and 'astré' are cut out in suppressed passages. 'Gazouillard' is in a line that has been completely changed—

A 48	Orrai-ie auec plaisir les gazouillardes eaux?
B 44	Mon esprit ne conçoit que des tristes tombeaux—

and 'sein viellard' is in a single line that has been completely cut out, together with the idea expressed. This leaves 'fuiart' and 'rongeart', both of which have only one example of suppression.

As for the adjectives in '-eux', the only examples of suppression of 'aréneux', 'chagrineux', 'nuiteux', 'menteux', 'odoreux', and 'vagueux' are in the middle of suppressed passages, as is true of one of the two examples of 'angoisseux' (1685) and 'naufrageux' (1600). 'Rayonneux' is in one line that has been completely left out:

A 2212   Ton beau front rayonneux, rougi n'en a-t-il point?

We are left with eight valid examples of adjectives in '-eux' being cut out; on the other hand, we find in B the 'vergoigneux' mentioned by M. Lebègue (B 292), and also 'nerveuses', though this becomes 'guerrieres' in C. We also find 'oublieux' (A 439 B).[1] In the other plays such adjectives are common; in *Aman*, there is one example of 'angoisseux' in each edition (A 632, B 634). The same is true of 'haineux' (A 1034, B 1102). 'Piteux' has one example of introduction in B, and also two examples in A, one of which is repeated in B (A 237, A 773 B). 'Pompeux' has one in A, one in B (A 1401, B 825). Then there are examples of 'perleux' (A 91), 'chatouilleux' (A 175 B), 'fumeux' (A 229 B), 'radieux' (A 528 B), 'fastueux' (B 627), 'dépiteux' (A 725), 'dédagneux' (A 1420), 'écumeux' (B 1406), etc.

'Blédier', 'nez trétif', and 'cœur marbrin' occur, as we are told, in suppressed passages in *Sophonisbe*; but so are both examples of 'nopcier', and the one example of 'coléric'. We are left with one example of 'terrien', one of 'maisonnier'. As far as adjectives ending in '-ier' are concerned, a note states that 'sorcier' is kept in; and in the case of those ending in '-in', B keeps 'ebenin' (953), while 'benin', condemned by Malherbe, is found throughout the plays.

(3) *Diminutifs*: Two examples of suppression, one of conservation (A 545). (See also *Aman*, A 1445, 'Pauvret'.)

(4) *Tirés de noms propres*: The only examples of 'numidien' and 'itaquois', and one of the two examples of 'letheane', are cut out in suppressed passages. This leaves one example of suppression of 'letheane', one of 'ausonien', and one of 'getulois', but in B we find 'argolides' (from A 1134), 'numidique' (from A 1024), 'libien' (from A 363), and 'thracienne'

---

[1] For Malherbe's views on this word, see *Doctrine*, p. 317.

(from A 518), all kept from A, and 'ciprienne' introduced (B. 429). Of these, 'argolides' and 'libien' are kept in C, while 'ciprienne' is converted into ciprine'.

Such adjectives seem quite common in the other plays, e.g. the use of 'argien', 'argive' in *Hector*, of 'memphien' in *Aman*.

(5) *Composés*: Though fifteen of the twenty-seven examples are in suppressed passages (429, 2176, 242 (4 lines), 89, 1582 (4 lines), 89 (bis), 2039, 2015, 2024, 608 (five lines), 1894, 1981, 1089, 650 (4 lines) and 1973), and though there are infrequent examples of such words in 1601 and 1604, in this and the other plays (C 277 'aspre louche', A 1130, kept in B and C, 'douce-amere'; and *David*; *P. de J.*, p. 205, 'doux-cuisant'), it must be admitted that the sudden drop in the use of such words after 1596 seems to point to intention of suppression upon Montchrestien's part.

However, as we are informed in the introduction to M. Lebègue's articles, such suppression had already been practised by Garnier, long before the time of Malherbe.

(6) *Formés irrégulièrement*: Eugène Rigal draws our attention to the suppression of 'fanfa-fan-farant' and 'flo-flotant', in his book *De Jodelle à Molière*. There are no similar constructions in any of the later plays. However, a growing maturity of taste, and a respect for the sound of words upon the stage, could quite easily have inspired this change.

(7) *Tirés du latin*: Two of these, as M. Lebègue admits, are in suppressed passages; the third is in a line that has been completely changed:

A 386	Fait errer sus le dos du triquétre Neptune.
B 314	Tous les Dieux de la mer par ses vœux importune.

(8) *Autres adjectifs*: 'Besson', 'gloute', and 'ocieux' are in suppressed passages; M. Lebègue himself is unsure of the reason for cutting out 'adextre'. 'Bonace' has but one example of suppression, and is found, we are told, in the 1604 edition of two other plays. 'Vive' has two examples of suppression, and one of introduction in B (47). This leaves one example each of 'asseur', 'have', and 'bravache'.

Verbes: The only examples of 'absconser', 'absenter', 'accallir', 'accouardir', 'brandiler', 'se contre-balancer', 'contr'imiter', 'culebuter', 'déjoins', 'emmenotter', 'enceptrer', 'engraver', 'enjoncher', 'oreiller', 'rebruler', 'redonder', 'rentrôner', 'respiter', 'ribler', 'tourne-bouler', and 'trajeter' (which appears in *Hector*; *P. de J.*, p. 13), are in suppressed passages, as are both examples of 's'absenter' (2115 in 4 lines), of 'nouer', and of 'allentir'. One of the two examples of each of the following is in a suppressed passage: 'béqueter' (1115), 'cendroyer' (1981), 'conjoint' (1546), 'diffame' (1207), 's'éjouir' (1384), 'entre-rompus' (2076), 'martirer' (1683), and 'serener' (1859): in the case of this last word, the other example is changed into 'rasserener', and 'serener' is used in B 219 of this play, and in the 1604 edition of *Aman* (*P. de J.*, p. 210). 'Arranger', in its only example of suppression in B, is returned in C. 'S'entrelivrer le choc' is changed into 's'entredonnent l'assaut'. 'S'entredevancer' and 's'entrepousser' are cut out in four lines, as is 'déchasser', of which we find an example in B 862, and also in the *Reine d'Escosse* (*P. de J.*, p. 88). As M. Lebègue says, Malherbe himself used 'atterré'. There is one example only of the suppression of 'attoucher', 'béer', 'se contrister', 'créper', 'enaigrit', 'enceindre', 'ensucrer', 'homicider', 'hor-ribler', 'juzer', 'oppresser', 'se paoner', 'plomber', 'postillonner', 'raccoiser' (which is also retained in 1601 from A 291), 'raualer', 'recouru' (which is used in the form 'recourir' at the beginning of Act IV of *Aman*), 'repurge', 'rouer', and 'vaguer'.

There are two examples of the suppression of 'consommer', but one of its retention from A 334. On the other hand, as we are told by M. Lebègue, it is spelt correctly in B 1398, so all is very uncertain.

We are now left with 'darder', 'obtemperer', and 'point'. Of the four examples of the first, two are in suppressed passages (236, 591 (4 lines)), while a third is in two completely changed lines (709). This word is common in the other plays (e.g. *David*; *P. de J.*, pp. 222, 226, 230). Of the four examples of 'obtemperer', two are in suppressed passages (1107, 2131). However, we have two valid examples of the suppression of this word, as we have of 'point'.

'Œillader', though condemned by Malherbe, remains intact in most cases in the plays. M. Lebègue can find no reason for 'dévaler' being cut out, nor 'brasser sa ruine'.

As for the diminutives, one example of 'baisoter', and both of 'sucçoter', are in suppressed passages. This leaves us with three examples of diminutive verbs being cut out, against which one must place the introduction of 'frisotté' in B 952.

Adverbes: Only one example of each of the two mentioned.

Conclusion: In this section it is almost impossible to prove any planned intention on the part of Montchrestien, except in one or two small instances: (*a*) He seems to be avoiding 'adjectifs composés' (but so did Garnier twenty years before). (*b*) He seems, to a certain extent, to be avoiding 'adjectifs substantivés'. (*c*) He has cut out two unsightly and unwieldy words, 'fanfa-fan-farant' and 'flo-flotant'.

One or two words, here and there, seem to be being avoided, but no pattern forms, and many words of which Malherbe disapproves are used in all editions of the play.

E. LE STYLE

Les Bienséances: 'Il a le culte des bienséances? Mais plusieurs de ses prédéces-seurs ont eu des scrupules analogues.'[1]

[1] Lebègue, 'Malherbe correcteur de tragédie', p. 168.

(1) *Parties du corps humain*: The word 'tétins' is certainly cut out, but the word 'sein' is introduced in the same passage in 1604: 'car bien que seulement mon sein t'eust allaitée'. Sophonisbe's 'poitrine' also returns in C (1030). The word is also used in 1601, e.g. B 701, B 309 (this time the nurse's, which was referred to in A as 'ta vieille poitrine'), etc. 'Estomac' is cut out from A 1073, but is still used by Montchrestien in 1601 and 1604, e.g. *Aman*, A 232: 'L'estomac glouton des chiens et des corbeaux', B. 744: 'l'estomac deschiré', A 788 B: 'Son palle estomach se montrant tout ouvert'.

'Délié coton' (of beard) and 'poil frisé' are cut out in a long passage.

Together with these examples we must place the use, in the other plays, of 'les enfançons pendans à la mamelle' (*Aman*, A 987 B), 'ce ventre enflé de son germe royal' (*David*; *P. de J.*, p. 207), 'leurs boyaux' (*Aman*, A 906), etc.

(2) *Termes qui ont trait à l'amour physique*: 'Mon fertile flanc' and 'porté des flancs d'une paillarde' are indeed cut out, but, as M. Lebègue points out, 'au sortir du ventre de sa mère' has been kept, both in B and C. 'Étraignant ton mari dans le tour de tes bras' and 'Languir entre vos bras, et sucçoter ses roses' both occur in suppressed passages.

The description of Sophonisbe may have been cut out for reasons of length, as it neither furthers the action, nor adds very much to our knowledge of the characters. (However, taking into account the cutting of the description of Bethsabée in her bath in *David*, Montchrestien may indeed have been bowing to the *bienséances*.)

'Charnelles delices' become 'molles delices' (not 'mignardes blandices', which exists in both editions). 'Impudique' appears three times in A (1096, 1206, 1412), once in B (from A 1412), twice in C (from A 1096, and 1412). 'Cet amour lascif' disappears completely, in the suppression of an enjambment.

'Mais son triomphe fut passager',[1] if one can call such an imperfect, uncertain picture a triumph; the exceptions are almost as many as the examples. As M. Lebègue says, the later editions are full of terms of physical love, especially David, whose very plot demands it. This play is full of lines ending in the rhyme 'couche–bouche', e.g.

p. 205   Coniure son amour par la secrette couche
         Complice des baisers qu'il reçoit de ma bouche.

p. 210   J'ateste sa grandeur que iamais en ma couche,
         Ie n'iray receuoir les baisers de sa bouche.

p. 218   Cette impudique bouche,
         Qu'un autre a mignardee au milieu de ma couche.

p. 221   Nul ne me gardera de venir dans ta couche
         Gouster cent fois le iour les douceurs de ta bouche.

---

[1] Lebègue, op. cit.

David wonders if anyone can have told Urie 'Que mes bras ont pressé sa femme toute nuë?' and whether he knows of 'mes esbats secrets pris avec son espouse'. Urie threatens his wife:

> De te crever le flanc sous mes roides genoux,
> De planter ce poignard dans ce sein miserable.

The whole play ends on the prophecy of Nathan (p. 231):

> Puisque contre ma loy ton execrable flamme
> D'un espoux innocent a desbauché la femme,
> J'iray ton lict royal d'incestes emplissant;
> Tes fils denaturez, toute honte chassant,
> Coucheront sans respect avec tes concubines,
> Et ne cacheront pas leurs lubriques rapines . . .

Such passages, though most common in *David*, are to be found also, for example, in *Aman*, A 221 B: 'Qu'ils soyent arrachés du ventre de leurs meres'; A 225–6 (B is slightly different, but just as much against the bienséances):

> Qu'aux yeux de leurs Maris les femmes soient souillees,
> Et que les filles soient des Bourreaux violees.

(3) *Ton familier*: The large passage which is mentioned as being changed, becomes much more poetic in style, more beautiful, and the reason for the change is obvious.

Though the phrases M. Lebègue mentions have, in some cases, been part of large suppressed passages, nevertheless he does seem to be trying to avoid them. Altogether, it would appear that the 1601 edition is aiming for a more poetic style in the conversation of the lovers; it also replaces conversations made up of short replies by monologues of greeting.

Though these phrases do return, as M. Lebègue states, in the other plays, especially in *Aman*, they are used there much more poetically, and seem much more acceptable, e.g. 1604, B 1188: 'Qu'as-tu ma chere amour, mon petit œil, mon ame', which is a definite improvement poetically on the 1601 edition, A 1264: 'Ha ma fille qu'as-tu! qu'as-tu ma petite ame.' This would seem to point to the fact that Montchrestien did not object to the phrases for their familiarity, but rather for their unpoetical use, both in the 1596 *Sophonisbe* and in the 1601 *Aman*.

(4) *'Mon' before name of friend*: This is kept, as is 'o gentil Massinisse' and the phrase 'mon soucy'.

(5) *Termes de commisération*: 'Pauvre' is the only such term referred to here. Of the eleven examples, five are in long suppressed passages (833, 1834, 1852, 1939, 1950), and one in two lines that are cut out (1357). There are three examples in B, and it is *not* entirely suppressed in C (see 1544).

Admittedly, it is not an adjective entirely suitable for the noble sentiments of tragedy. It has a certain banality about it. One can see the reasons for its gradually dwindling use.

(6) *Dialogues ou répliques prosaïques*: Most of the short passages of conversation at the entrance of a character are converted into short monologues of welcome, at the end of the previous speech made by the character already on the stage. This speech is usually rather more in the noble style.

(*a*) The first of M. Lebègue's examples is converted into:

B 973–6　　Et bien, mon grand Amy, ceste heureuse iournée,
　　　　　　Semble avoir à peu pres la guerre terminée,
　　　　　　Les Dieux en soient loüés; mais qui vous peut ainsi,
　　　　　　Obscurcir le visage et troubler le sourci?

(*b*) The second example, part of which is the passage M. Lebègue has mentioned under *ton familier*, becomes a Petrarchan praise of the lady. Moreover, the entrance is prepared by a short passage, so that there is no longer the abrupt, unprepared entrance, of which the first words were:

A 1314　　*Soph.*: Bon-iour mon grand ami.
　　　　　　Mass.: Bon-iour ma petite ame.

Instead we have:

B 1117–20　Mais la voicy venir, bons Dieux quelle merveille!
　　　　　　L'Afrique n'eut iamais une beauté pareille,
　　　　　　Je croy que si l'Amour defaisoit son bandeau,
　　　　　　Il deuiendroit rauy d'un visage si beau.

This is followed by the speech of welcome:

B 1121–5　Doux objet de mon cœur, belle ame de mon Ame,
　　　　　　Qui nourrissés ma vie en l'amoureuse flame,
　　　　　　Comme pourray-ie helas! abandonner vos yeux,
　　　　　　Puisque par leur clarté ie voy celle des Cieux:
　　　　　　Si ie vous laisse, helas! moy mesme ie me laisse.

which again runs smoothly into Sophonisbe's first line:

B 1126　　Si vous m'abandonnés ie mourray de tristesse.

(*c*) The other large passage mentioned, A 1542–5, is similarly handled, but gradually, from edition to edition. In A, we had a long speech by Siphax, followed, without warning, by Scipion saying:

　　　　　Vous venés fort a tens. Bon-iour mon Massinisse:
　　　　　Comme vous portés vous.

No explanation is given of what what happens to Siphax, and Massinisse's entry is not led up to in any way.

In B we have a short speech by Siphax, followed by a *tirade* against women by Scipion. During the course of this speech (while we must presume Siphax being led away), he touches on the subject of Massinisse; he then says:

> Qu'il survient à propos. Ça ça mon Massinisse,
> Qui fais incessamment quelque nouueau seruice
> Aux Romains tes amis, tu sois le bien venu:
> Grand Roy de qui les bras . . . etc.

The author thus avoids Massinisse's one lame line, and Scipion's long speech to Massinisse continues straight away.

In C the matter is dealt with even more carefully, because between Siphax's speech and Scipion's *tirade* on women, Scipion speaks these lines:

C 1210–13   Remene le soldat et sans luy faire tort.
> Infortuné Siphax! certes ie plains ton sort
> Mais helas! c'est un mal, ie ne puis que le plaindre,
> De nos seueres loix je me sen trop contraindre.

Thus, (i) we know that Siphax is being led off, (ii) we are naturally led into the *tirade* upon women, because Siphax's fate was caused by a woman. (In the course of this *tirade* in both B and C, we are given full details of Scipion's reasons for his treatment of Massinisse and Sophonisbe: 'O qu'il vient à propos . . .', etc.)

'Hola di' is changed to 'dy le moy', which seems very little different, but perhaps more fitting to the style of tragedy. 'Baste, ce m'est tout un', is cut out, but 'mais baste' recurs in C 1452, and the whole phrase 'Mais baste, c'est tout un', comes into *Aman*, A 15 B.

There are still examples of prosaic expression in the other plays: e.g. in *David*, a short conversation between David and Nadab, upon the latter's entrance (*P. de J.*, p. 206):

David: Ie vay parler à luy. Et qui te mene icy?
Nadab: C'est vostre Bethsabée; elle a bien du souci.
David: Au comble de son heur est-elle mescontente?
Nadab: Elle est grosse sans doute, et ce poinct la tourmente.

In *Aman* there is the famous 'Mais cesson de parler et commençon à faire' (A 565), and also such phrases as: 'Il sembloit en ses dents quelques mots remascher' (A 1426), and 'Ie m'en vay depescher le paquet à mon homme' (B 558), etc.

(7) *Vulgarité*: 'Jupin' is cut out. (But we find him in *Aman*, B 381.) One of the three examples of 'ça bas' is in a suppressed passage (2049). B and C keep 'femelle', 'galant', and B uses 'homme' in the sense of husband.

(8) *Vulgarité* (contd.): All the words except 'bons Dieux' and 'Sus' have only one example each of suppression, and in the case of 'ta vieille poitrine' the phrase recurs in C.

Of the three examples of suppression of 'bons Dieux', one (1902) is in a suppressed passage of four lines.

The interjection *'Sus'* is a very peculiar case. Malherbe uses the construction himself, we are told. Four of the six examples of suppression are in long passages (932, 939, 1040, 1058). It appears in B at line 871, 'Sus donc, mes cheres sœurs', right between two suspected suppressions. It also occurs in C 647, and throughout the other plays, e.g. *Aman*, A 539 B, 'sus sus', B 1155, 'Sus donc', A 1560, A 1607, B 1577, 'Sus'.

(9) *Objects vulgaires ou malpropres, actions basses ou comiques*: Of all the examples, 653, 934, 283, 1617, 1568, 1847, 1584 (4 lines), 1684, 1637, 2026, and 1867 are in suppressed passages. 'Fourneaux' (A 376) returns in C. Of the other words, there is only one example of each. The two long passages mentioned could have been cut out for reasons of length.

In *Aman* we find Mardochée 'défiguré de crasse' in 1601, 'difforme de crasse' in 1604. In *Hector* we hear of 'le crasseux Nocher' (*P. de J.*, p. 13).

In *Aman*, the word 'puante', which would seem to come under the same heading as these other phrases, appears in 1601 (A 724, 'une puante herbe', A 50, 'charongnes puantes'). The word 'charongne' occurs in both texts of this play (A 50 B, A 909 B). In 1604 we find 'suans avec moy sous le fardeau des armes' (B 94), 'squelet' (B 890). The word 'fiel' occurs in both texts (A 1535 B, B 1452).

(10) *Conclusion on the Bienséances*: Mr. Seiver says of the two texts of *Aman*: 'It will be readily apparent when reading the two versions that from the point of view of improving the style by elevating it, Montchrestien has made very little advance from one text to the other.' I would submit that it is also, on the whole, very hard to prove any decisive change in this matter in *Sophonisbe* or in the other plays, except in the case of the improvement of prosaic conversation and style. What changes there are to be seen in the case of vulgarity or indecency, which are few, can be traced to the sixteenth-century ideas on the *bienséances*,[1] while the elevation to the 'style noble' of tragedy from the prosaic tone of conversation is in accordance with sixteenth-century ideas of the tone suitable for tragedy.[2]

La mythologie: Naturally, if Montchrestien found that one of his examples of mythology was inexact, he would change it. Use of mythology is rare in Montchrestien.[3]

---

[1] See the quotation from M. Lebègue at the head of this section (p. 198).

[2] Jodocus Badius Ascensius, 1502: '. . . Tragoedia semper est de altissimis personis et *in altisono stilo* conscripta.' Jean de la Taille, 1572: '. . . une espece et un genre de Poësie non vulgaire, mais autant elegant, beau et excellent qu'il est possible.' Pierre Matthieu, 1589: '. . . la Tragedie, dont les vers doivent estre haults, grands et plains de majesté, non effrenez ny enervez comme ceux des Comiques . . .'

[3] See Chapter 8, 'Style'.

Obscure mythology does remain to a certain extent in the later editions: for example, B 1174:

> Son Dioscure aussi luit mieux en la tempeste.

But few of the mythological examples quoted by M. Lebègue (few, indeed, of all the mythological figures used by Montchrestien) would have been obscure to the educated audiences of the time. 'Les Dires', 'Atropos', 'Erynne', 'Tisiphone', 'Alecton', 'Mégère', would have caused no one any trouble. We are far from the wilful obscurity of the earliest outpourings of the Pléiade. Montchrestien is, however, well in line with the development of poetry in his age. Indeed, within the later work of Ronsard and Du Bellay there had been a great development towards clarity of allusion.

Les comparaisons homériques: Where some of these are cut out, and others cut down, it could easily be because of length. Such comparisons are essentially adornments, and not absolutely necessary in most cases.[1]

Les métaphores: Scholl, in his thesis *Die Vergleiche in Montchrestiens Tragödien*, suggests the following reasons for the changes in metaphors between 1601 and 1604: first, rhythm and expression; then, clarity and logic (including the avoidance of mixed metaphors). These reasons appear to hold good for the changes made between 1596 and 1601 as well; these changes owe nothing to Malherbe, but are on the contrary the natural emendations of a conscientious poet, and a sign of growing maturity and mastery of poetic form.

(1) *Images hyperboliques*: 'Mes yeux, debordez-vous en deux larges ruisseaux' (35) is kept in, while 'Je nage sur les flots d'un torrent fait de pleur' (72) is cut out, and 'Asséchés les ruisseaux de ces larmes contraintes' (182) is altered.

In B, however, we find such phrases as 'Cent deluges de maux ayant sur moy passé' (39) and 'Du vent de vos soupirs vous allumés le feu' (127).

In 1601, in *Aman*, we find 'Deux ruisseaux s'escouloient de ses moites paupieres' (A 775); also:

> Arrozent leur beau sein d'une pluye de pleurs,

which becomes in 1604 (B 840–1):

> Quoy? leurs moites prunelles
> Font encore ondoyer un gros fleuue de pleurs?

This section is thus inconclusive. Hyperbolic images such as these are typical of the period, and are to be found in profusion in Malherbe's early work *Les Larmes de Saint Pierre*.

(2) *Métaphores incohérentes*: Mr. Seiver says in his introduction to *Aman*: 'In a few instances there is what appears to be a definite attempt on the part

---

[1] See Chapter 8, 'Style'.

of Montchrestien to clarify and simplify the text.'[1] This agrees with Scholl's view on the later editions of *Sophonisbe*, and seems also to hold true of the changes between 1596 and 1601, thus explaining much of the cutting of mixed, incoherent, and absurd metaphors.

Montchrestien's growing maturity of taste, however, is not faultless. Some bizarre images are kept, e.g.:

A 2160   Sans qu'un cordeau servil face rougir son front,

which remains in B and in C becomes:

Sans que des fers honteux me rougissent le front.

Other bizarre metaphors are added in B. (See M. Lebègue's examples on page 485.)

Both editions of *Aman* are full of mixed metaphors. Mr. Seiver mentions some of them on pages 10–11 of his edition.

I agree, on the whole, that the next list of suppressed metaphors is a loss rather than a gain to the play. But those I most regret are in suppressed passages (1682, 40 (4 lines), 88, 1599, 2030), or cut out possibly for another reason, e.g. enjambment:

A 1560–1   Que nulle passion hors des bornes n'emporte
                Le char de son esprit.

B 1354   Que nulle passion hors de soy ne l'emporte.

Most of those which are changed by only one word or so seem as good as before, or even improved. For example, A 1120–B 927: 'Par le canal de ses yeux' is as poetic as 'par la porte de ses yeux'. A 1051–B 876: 'S'allument' seems as good as 'se coulent' in this context. A 102–B 70: 'Toute cette rondeur de la mer enlacée' becomes 'Ceste basse rondeur sur la mer balancée' (just as unusual a metaphor; and no more prosaic). A 1586 seems just as pleasing in its new form, while A 103 flows much more easily in 1601:

A 103–4   Sans songer que nature a dedans l'homme enté,
               Le desir du repos . . .

B 71–2   Et songe que Nature en chacun a formé
               Le desir du repos . . .

Thus it would seem that, far from spoiling his text for the sake of a rule, he is here changing his text for the better, while most of the actual suppressions occur in long passages.

Of the four examples of the metaphor 'dos' being cut out, two are in suppressed passages (2015, 1598 (four lines)), one is probably to avoid an enjambment (646), one returns in C (A 633).

The metaphors of dramatic art are, as M. Lebègue says, preserved.

[1] i.e. between the 1601 and 1604 texts of *Aman*.

From A 540, 'caressé de fortune', the phrase becomes in C an even more striking metaphor, 'Comme allaité dans le sein de fortune'.

All the rest of this section is admitted to be uncertain or is supported by only one example in each case.

Les périphrases: In *Aman* we find exactly the opposite of the change recorded here. Montchrestien changes 'Les poissons escailleux' to 'les peuples escaillez'. (Here, in *Sophonisbe*, the same change is made between 1601 and 1604.)

Descriptions, narrations et amplifications: As M. Lebègue suggests, many of these have been cut out or cut down because of length.

Les répétitions de mots: Mr. Seiver says, in his introduction to *Aman*: 'The device of repeating the same word or a like-sounding word within the same line, which so rattled Malherbe . . . is used quite extensively in both texts.' This, I should say, was true of all three texts of *Sophonisbe*. *Répétition* was one of the main rhetorical devices of the day, and Montchrestien makes much use of it throughout his plays.[1] For the sixteenth century, this device was an ornament rather than a drawback. It took the seventeenth century, and Malherbe, to be 'rattled' by it.

Antithesis apart, there are plenty of examples of repetition in the 1601 *Sophonisbe*. For example:

B 1757   Trionfés du trionfe.

B 139   Qui parmy ses tourmens n'auroit plus grand tourment.

B 633–4   Et choisirois plustost de mourir mille fois,
               Si mille fois mourir au monde ie pouois.

B 1102   Ceste belle Beauté.

B 420–2   Tous pour le bienveigner courent de toutes pars;
               Tous monstrent tout deuoir, tous offrent leur service,
               Tous de bouche et de cœur benissent Massinisse.

B 283–4   Le Coq se resueillant à l'approche du iour,
               Deffioit à chanter les coqs qui tour à tour . . .

B 215–16   Sans que des Aquilons les souffles redoublés,
               Ni les flots ondoyants des Aquilons troublés . . .

Les répétitions oratoires: There is more cause to believe that Montchrestien is suppressing this type of *répétition*. Against the innumerable examples of suppression, however, we can place those examples which M. Lebègue gives of retention and introduction, plus B 1695–6, C 654, C 459–61, C 127–30.

In the three successive editions, as in both editions of the other plays, the examples of this type of repetition are cut down. Twenty years before, however, Garnier had been doing the same kind of pruning in his plays, as such exclamatory repetitions are often a sign of metrical weakness (see Jodelle).

[1] See Chapter 8, 'Style'.

Les antithèses: These were popular both in the sixteenth and seventeenth centuries. The number seems to grow larger in the later editions, and antithesis of this kind is an important part of Montchrestien's stylistic stock-in-trade.

Les stichomythies:[1] Where they are regularized, this is rather more in accordance with sixteenth-century usage than with anything else. (See the plays of Montreux.) Where they are shortened, it might easily be part of the general shortening of the play.

Conclusion on Style (apart from the Bienséances): Inexactitudes, obscurities, and lengthy comparisons, descriptions, and narrations are cut out or cut down for obvious reasons. Metaphors are improved from the point of view of clarity and logic, but also from the point of view of poetry, rhyme, and expression. Apart from these changes, *répétitions oratoires* seem the only obvious suppressions, and in this Montchrestien is following the example of Garnier. Stylistically, Montchrestien remains typical of the late sixteenth century, in his use of repetition and antithesis, and in his use of metaphors.

G. LA VERSIFICATION

La prosodie: e muet: To start with, a slight misunderstanding must be cleared up. In the list of examples of suppression, 'ayes de moi pitié' (A 1273) is mentioned. A little later, we are told: 'B garde . . . "aye" (A 1273), et il ajoute "aye de moy pitie" (B 1084).' Now all three examples are the same phrase, and the fact is that it is retained in B, in a slightly different form which makes no difference to the point in question.

Of the twelve other examples of suppression, six are in long passages (1174, 1284 (4 lines), 1858, 197, 1248, 2043). I have found one more example of retention in B than the three that are listed (A 820, 1054, and 1273). This is A 1809, 'Son foye, qui renaissant', which is in a stanza requiring lines of seven syllables. It is retained in exactly the same form in B. In C it becomes 'De son foye renaissant'; this appears to refute the statement 'C supprime tout cela'. 'Vraiement digne' is cut out in a long passage.

Though the other plays have examples of this usage, e.g. *Aman* (*P. de J.*, p. 254, 'ie l'aye mesprisé', and p. 243, 'n'aye point'), it does seem to be gradually being suppressed; the signs of this are, however, more decisive between 1601 and 1604 than between 1596 and 1601.

Lotz, in his book *Der Versbau Antoine de Montchrestiens*, also notes this gradual suppression. In the 1604 edition of all the plays he can only find ten examples of this usage. 'Hieraus folgt, daß im Gegensatz zu Jodelle (Herting S.5) und Ronsard (Bücher S.24), Montchrestien hier auf dem Malherbeschen

---

[1] See section on *stichomythia*. In *Hector*, Montchrestien's last play, such passages are far more common than in the earlier plays.

Standpunkt steht.' But he adds a point which is of vital importance to our present inquiry: '*Dasselbe gilt, wenn auch in geringerem Maße, von Garnier* (Körner S.19).' This change had already begun to take place before Montchrestien and before Malherbe.

Lotz also notes that Montchrestien seems to be avoiding a mute 'e' after a diphthong, in the same way as Desportes.

Plurals in '-ent': The examples cited seem to point to no definite conclusion.

Elision of e mute: Of the seventeen examples of suppression, eight are in long passages (787, 788, 993, 837, 932, 1212, 2044, 332). Then in B we find seven examples of the same fault (A 2160, 1802, 2106 kept; B 403, 204, 270, 657 added 'sans le faire exprès'). Also in C, we find some examples, C 1534, C 1577, which are not exactly 'conforme à la doctrine de Malherbe'.

If Montchrestien had been intending to cut this usage out from the later editions, he could hardly have done worse than in *Aman*, where we find the following examples: A 386 B 'remu'ments', B 677 'm'essay'rois', B 749 'ie vous pri'', A 959 'ie te pri' et repri'', (which becomes in B 'Mais en fin, ie te pri''), A 1016 'ie te pri'', B 1157 'ie vous pri'', B 1358 'le pay'ment': not to mention the examples of 'grand'' in the feminine (A 820, B 811, A 1106, A 1080). Lotz lists, in the plays, eleven examples of 'grand'', four of the feminine 'grand'.

Elision of 'si': There are two examples of suppression, and two of addition 'par inadvertance'. One of the examples of suppression is in a long passage (2077), as is one of the two examples from B being cut out in C (B 46). Lotz notes many examples of such elision in both the 1601 and 1604 editions of the plays.[1]

Apocope: 'tu peusse' endurer': As M. Lebègue says, this is in four suppressed lines.

'*Suivrions, vivrions*': Of the two examples given, one becomes the same mistake in B under a different form:

A 1905	Là d'un pas mesuré nous *suivrions* la carole.
B 1626	Où nous nous *meslerions* aux gaillardes paroles.

(In both cases '-ions' is counted as one syllable.) The other is in two lines which have been completely changed:

A 1910–11	Nous *vivrions* en repos et iamais les langueurs,
	Ne feroient leur retraite au milieu de nos cœurs.
B 1631–2	Là sous les myrtes verds tant de nuit que de iour,
	Nous cueillirons les fleurs et les fruits de l'amour.

---

[1] See Lotz, *Der Versbau Antoine de Montchrestiens*, p. 18.

Lotz notes the following examples of '-ions' and '-iez' as one syllable, in the 1604 edition of the plays (in some cases printing errors have caused the wrong line-number to be given; these I have endeavoured to correct): *P. de J.*, p. 4. (32), 10(45), 48(27), 52(24), 102(12), 277(4), 51(41), 57(3), 58(1), 136(16), etc., 43(32), 48(2), 80(1), 192(9), 109(43), 187(29), 198(6), 132(22).

L'hiatus: Of the thirty-two examples of suppression, ten are in suppressed passages (1177, 1393, 1173, 1182, 839, 1169, 660, 1197 (4 lines changed), 671 (same), 1429 (5 lines changed)). One is in a *sententia* that is completely cut out: A 1760, 'Si la loy est mauvaise, il la faut corriger.' This leaves us with twenty-one valid examples, to place against six examples of retention, fifteen of addition in B 'par mégarde'. (Apart from the thirteen examples mentioned, I find B 353, 'a-il', B 562, 'i'en doy encor plus'.) In C, I find six examples, consisting of the four mentioned (B 176, 511, 1280 retained, C 55 added), plus C 831, 'peu à peu', and a retention of B 353, 'a-il'.

Thus, while no real change can be noticed between 1596 and 1601, there does appear to be a cutting-down between 1601 and 1604, at a time when no direct influence of Malherbe was possible. The hiatus was condemned by Ronsard, and a gradual cutting-down like this could point to a preoccupation with the spoken sound on the part of the author.

There is never a wholesale suppression of this fault; in the other plays we find examples of it, e.g. *Aman*, ça et là (B 218, A 429 B, A 646 B, A 1552 B), peu à peu (A 86, A 447 B, A 570, A 1274), et au (A 24), là où (A 457 B), de lieu en lieu (B 637), etc.

La cacophonie: 'Tu antidates ton trépas' and 'ce songe qui vous ronge' certainly seem cut out to good purpose, as, in *Aman* between 1601 and 1604, do 'Puis que jusqu'à ce poinct', 'Comme à ceux-là que l'on caresse', 'Car comme', etc. Mr. Seiver lists many examples of cacophony in the 1604 edition of *Aman*; but this question is not a strictly grammatical one, and in each case the only judge is the author's sensibility; certainly in the successive editions of these plays there is an effort to avoid awkward sounds, and to improve the poetic value of the verse. (Despite the 1604 tongue-twister in *David*, p. 216:

Qui fait faire est fautif comme celuy qui fait.

La rime: This is the aspect upon which M. Fromilhague bases his support for M. Lebègue's theory, so I shall first turn to his proofs:

(1) *La proscription des rimes associant voyelle et diphthongue*: There are ten examples of suppression, three of which are in suppressed passages (1114–15, 1524–5, 321–2 (4 lines)). In the second edition, there are four valid examples of retention ('peine–geisne', 'hemisphere–affaire', 'laisse–tristesse', and 'ordinaire–pere'), plus four examples of introduction ('contraire–misere', 'veines–geines', 'laisse–blesse', and 'pleine–meine').

If Montchrestien then had intended to cut this type of rhyme out of the third edition, surely he would have done so in the other plays? There are a few examples of this usage in this very play (C 230, 1018–19, 1164–5, 29–30, 778–9), and the 1604 edition of *Aman* is full of them: 'Desers–airs' (511–12), 'effet–fait' (547–8, 555–6), 'effet–souhait' (993–4, 1173–4), 'miseres–contraires' (607–8), 'populaire–Assuére' (815–16), 'adversaire–desespere' (1027–8), 'espere–aduersaire' (1415–16), 'destre–maistre' (1159–60), 'delibere–esclaire' (1631–2), 'desplaire–cholere' (1551–2). Lotz notes this as a typical practice of Montchrestien.[1]

(2) *Les rimes d'homonymes*: There are eighteen examples in A, three in B, three in C. M. Lebègue says: 'Je ne sais si c'est exprès.' M. Fromilhague admits that, for most of the examples, 'Leur disparition peut donc s'expliquer, en dehors de toute intervention de Malherbe, par la tendance générale à l'élimination des rimes de mots de même racine.' He goes on, however, to claim that the few examples of suppression of similar-sounding words *not* of the same root, could only have been suggested by Malherbe.

Far from agreeing that this is a 'raffinement d'une telle singularité', however, I would suggest that it would have been even more strange, given the general tendency, not to cut out 'face–face', etc. The words seem so similar, and sound so similar, that it must have seemed just as natural to cut them out as 'point–point', which M. Fromilhague gives us as one example of the 'tendance générale'. For the poet it was a matter of sound, and he probably did not distinguish between similar-sounding words of the same root and similar-sounding words of different roots. 'Plaine–pleine' must have seemed much the same, for 'pleine' was very often spelt 'plaine' at the time.

One must count all these examples together, as *rimes d'homonymes*. As such, their suppression falls in with the general tendency of the time.

To turn now to M. Lebègue's other main example:

(3) *Rime du simple et du composé ou de mots de même racine*: Of the eleven examples of suppression, eight are in suppressed passages (1618, 1547, 1456, 1840, 1656, 1916, 919 (4 lines cut out), 941 (completely changed stanza)). In B I find ten examples: pris–espris (from A 885), cela–là (from A 335–6), combat–abat (from A 1220–1), commande–demande (from A 1321–2), recours–secours (from A 2232), and the additions of semble–resemble (B 595), ensemble–assemble (B 53), ouuerte–couuerte (B 253), reposer–disposer (B 1639), prendre–entreprendre (B 1661). I agree with M. Lebègue when he says 'Je préfère ne rien affirmer', especially as examples are very common in the other plays (though, as Lotz says, they are more common 'dann, wenn die Verwandschaft der Reimwörter nicht leicht erkannt wird'[2]).

(4) To go back to the examples quoted at the beginning of the section on *la rime*, 'memoire–plaire', etc., I would not consider them as necessarily

[1] Op. cit., p. 34.
[2] Ibid., pp. 30–1.

marking any influence from outside, but rather a correction by the poet himself.

(5) *Rimes brèves ou longues*: M. Lebègue himself is uncertain. There are many examples of this usage in Racine. Lotz quotes many examples of it in Montchrestien.[1]

(6) *Rimes léonines*: M. Lebègue is also uncertain of the reasons for the suppression of two examples of these.

La césure et l'enjambement: These two questions must be treated together, because they have some bearing on each other. On the cutting-down of enjambments, M. Lebègue says in his conclusion: 'On doit reconnaître que sur ce point ses conseils [the imaginary reviser's] ont eu l'effet le plus heureux: grâce à lui, la rédaction de 1601 s'éloigne plus que la première de la prose rimée.'[2] Not that the enjambment is done away with altogether. As Lotz says, 'Enjambements begegnen sich häufig', but by the last edition it can be said of them: 'wodurch jedoch im allgemeinen der Wohlklang der Verse nicht gestört wird'.[3] Wenzel says: 'Seine Verse sind im Übrigen recht glatt, fließend und wohlklingend, und das Enjambement bringt keine Störung im Rhythmus hervor.'[4]

The fact is that, as M. Lebègue says, many enjambments are cut out from the 1596 edition; and these enjambments were of the kind which did bring 'Störung im Rhythmus hervor'. The enjambments that remain, and those that are introduced, are of the kind which do not harm the poetry, but rather enhance it. I would suggest that the suppressions were a product of the poet's own maturity. Montchrestien's verse is written for sound; his aim was to produce flowing poetry, suitable for rhetorical declamation. Now some enjambments would tend to hold up the flow of such a declamation. Only those which did not destroy the rhythm could be allowed, except in moments of great emotion.

As for lines divided between speakers, these do not entirely disappear in this or in the other plays, but they tend to break up the line of the alexandrine, and may thus have been suppressed for poetic reasons. (Such splittings of lines were still used very much by the seventeenth-century writers. In one scene alone of Racine's *Athalie* (II. 7), there are the following 6–6 divisions between speakers: ll. 625, 627, 633, 637, 638, 643, 665, 670, 673, 682, 685, 689, 737.)

Conclusion on Versification: The changes in hiatus, cacophony, caesura, and enjambment could all be based upon a preoccupation with sound, and a desire to write poetry rather than *prose rimée*. Apart from this, the uses of mute e after a vowel (suppression uncertain until after 1601) and of the hiatus were both condemned by Ronsard, while the suppression of *rimes d'homonymes*

---

[1] Lotz, pp. 34–6.   [2] Lebègue, op. cit., p. 496.
[3] Lotz, p. 46.   [4] Wenzel, p. 65.

can be explained by 'la tendance générale à l'élimination de mots de même racine'.[1] None of the other examples given of suppression are at all certain.

H. CONCLUSION

In the course of this close study of the three texts of *Sophonisbe*, the only changes or suppressions that I have been able fully to substantiate seem to point rather to the other alternatives given in my introduction, than to the influence of Malherbe.

(*a*) A preoccupation with sound, and a desire to write flowing verse based on rhetorical principles, would seem to be shown by the changes with regard to hiatus, cacophony, caesura, and enjambment, also by the suppression of the words 'fanfa-fan-farant' and 'flo-flotant'. This preoccupation with the sound of the spoken word could have been caused by the poet's listening to the first performance of the play, at Caen. It is, at any rate, an established characteristic of his verse.

(*b*) A desire to avoid obscurity, by suppressing awkward inversions, adjectives in apposition to the complement, and inexactitudes.

(*c*) The tremendous shortening of the play at each successive edition could have caused many things to be cut out because of length.

(*d*) There are the changes which are symptomatic of the gradual development of the language.

(*e*) There are the changes which are in accordance with the views of Montchrestien's predecessors (e.g. *bienséances, style noble,* etc.).

(*f*) And finally, there is the fact that the poet himself was more mature, and could see many of the faults in his youthful first edition (e.g. too many *répétitions oratoires*). He mentions, in 1596, his dissatisfaction with the play. Jodelle had been full of such faults, but by the time French tragedy had progressed to Garnier, many of them had been cut out. Montchrestien's development is thus in some ways a microcosm of the development of sixteenth-century tragedy.

Malherbe's influence is belied by various facts:

(*a*) Apart from the examples given above, any suppressions are very hard to prove.

(*b*) M. Lebègue tells us that what distinguishes Malherbe's doctrine from that of his predecessors is 'la rigueur avec laquelle il les [les règles] applique.' A glance over the examples given throughout this essay will show that rigour of application is completely lacking: phrases reappear in 1601, and there is no definite suppression of any usage.

(*c*) Study of the 1604 edition of this and the other plays shows that the faults supposedly suppressed are still as rife. M. Lebègue maintains, however, that 'Montchrestien garde le souvenir des conseils de Malherbe'.

[1] Lebègue, op. cit.

To add to the complete lack of internal evidence to support the theory of Malherbe's influence, there is the tremendous uncertainty of the historical facts. The main points of doubt are (*a*) the time when the two authors met, and (*b*) what they discussed. The unlikelihood of the letters referring to an event which occurred twenty years before could only be counterbalanced by certainty in the internal evidence.

Without further evidence, either historical or textual, however, this theory does not come within the bounds of probability.

M. Lebègue does not force his theory upon the reader; he says: 'Si mon hypothèse était fausse, il suffirait de remplacer son nom, dans les pages qui suivent, par celui d'un mystérieux X.' It is only because of the widespread acceptance of this theory, which I believe to be false, that this study has been undertaken, with no idea of disrespect for the work of a great critic.

Finally, I might quote a sentence from Montchrestien's Preface to the first edition:

Nous sommes plus clair-voyans aux fautes d'autruy qu'aux nôtres.

Additional Evidence based on the 1599 edition of
'Les Derniers Propos'

⚜

THIS edition, previously unknown, appears to corroborate the results of the inquiry in *Appendix I*. For the purposes of this study, I shall number the poems as follows:

(*a*) 'Les Derniers Propos'—Discours
(*b*) 'Tombeau' (in prose)
(*c*) 'Stances'
(*d*) 'Complainte de la ville de Rouen'
(*e*) 'Sonnet'
(*f*) 'A Monseigneur le premier President'
(*g*) 'A mes Demoiselles ses filles'

These poems must have been written some time late in 1599. Barbe Guiffart died on 4 January 1599.[1] In his dedication to her husband, Montchrestien says:

Ce sont des vers que ie vous offre. Ie ne leur voudrois donner change de r'ouvrir les playes de vostre esprit s'elles estoyent sur le poinct de se cicatrizer: Mais tant s'en faut, n'estant encor en voye de consolation, et *la longueur du temps au lieu de les guarir en ayant fait des ulceres incurables,* ie les viens apliquer dessus comme un cataplasme pour seruir de lenitif à la vehemence de leurs douleurs.

At this time, more than any other, if M. Lebègue's theory were correct, Montchrestien should have been fully under the influence of Malherbe. And yet we find throughout this collection of poems many of the faults of which Malherbe would have complained, e.g.:

(1) *Rimes associant voyelle et diphtongue*: estre–naistre (c., ll. 42–4), taire–mere (e., ll. 12–13), fidelles–aisles (a., ll. 125–6).

(2) *Repetitions of the same word*: This occurs throughout but especially a. 11–13, 63, 70, 72, 83, 92, 100, 113, 217, 240; c. 5, 7, 8, 16, 22, 36; d. 28; f. 3, 4, 7, 11, 27, 48, 50, 51–2, 57, 58, 64, 72, 78–9, 96; g. 18, 71, 72.

[1] See Petitot, *Mémoires sur l'histoire de France*, vol. 49.

(3) *Apposition to the object, complicated inversions, and other things liable to lead to obscurity*:

a. 30–31	Nul n'eut recours à moy qui ne m'eust secourable, Luy fournissant d'argent, et de vin et de pain
a. 95	Bien qu'en mourant de vous ie vienne m'absenter . . .
a. 177–8	Aussi le doit-il bien, car sa prochaine perte Ceste couche luy rend solitaire et deserte.
f. 24	La departant à tous elle luy reste entiere.
a. 187–8	Lors se tenant tout coy, se presente à ses yeux, Ie ne sçay quoy plus clair que le Soleil des cieux.
a. 230	Apres auoir vescu, place t'est assignee.
f 29–32	Ie ne m'ébahy donc, grand Magistrat, de voir Tant d'hommes renommez en vie, et en sçauoir, Rapporter à toy seul leur plus grande excellence, *Comme faisant leur centre*, eux ta circonference.
g 40–2	Dont le merite eut tel credit Que toute seule il la rendit, Digne d'espouzer vostre pere.

(4) *Emute after vowel*: a. 133, 'disoyant', a. 216, 'Voyent', a. 233, 'rient'.

(5) *Prosaic expressions*:

a. 19–20	Ie suis preste à partir, et ne remporte rien En terre qu'un limon que d'elle aussi ie tien.
a. 138	Alors prenant au Ciel sa gaillarde volee.
a. 206	Le Nectar dans les cieux à longs traits ie puis boire.
a. 231–2	. . . Les bienheurez Qui se font un plancher des cercles etherez.
f. 82	Dis luy que ie l'honore, et que ie n'en dis mot.
f. 85	Hé! ne vaut-il pas mieux . . .

(6) *Vocabulary, morphology, etc.*: a. 15 'celle là qui', a. 55 'lors', a. 83 'hastif', a. 87 'le vivre et le mourir', a. 101 'son vouloir', a. 130 'dessus', a. 195 'stigieux', a. 205 'chef', a. 207 'dessous', a. 212 'dessus', a. 238 'Ia', c. 11 'rays', c. 27 'Ores que', d. 6 'dessus', f. 4 'rays', f. 13 'œillader', f. 42 'rays', f. 61 'Jupin', f. 76 'ores', f. 83 'ores', g. 7 'vostre leuer', g. 8 'son arriuer', g. 12 'le plain de vos clartez'.

(7) *Hiatus, cacophony*:

a. 190	peu a peu,
f. 71	Aussi l'a-elle pris,

g. 65–6   Puisque pour rendre le bois droit,
                 Il faut que la ligne soit droite.

f. 58   Esprit viuant du droit, droit des Esprits viuans.

(8) Aller+present participle:

a. 152   Un seul mot ils ne vont de leur bouche tirant.

a. 159   Tous la vont regretant.

a. 172   . . . et s'y va tourmentant.

c. 47   Fasché qu'un corps mortel l'allast ainsi cachant.

e. 1   Rouen, tu vas perdant ton plus riche ornement.

e. 11   Il a gaigné ceste Ame, il en va triomphant.

f. 42   Que les rays du Soleil n'aillent sa bouche ouurant.

f. 43   Si tes belles raisons tu ne vas decouurant.

g. 17   Iront à l'enui r'allumans.

(9) Hyperbole:

a. 52   Ainsi comme torrens ces larmes s'espandoyent.

a. 149–50   Leurs yeux ne sont plus que des larges fontaines,
                 Fecondes en ruisseaux.

(10) Rimes d'homonymes, rime de simple et du composé de mots de la même racine:

a. 163–4   Aussi le ciel ialoux leur rauit un tel bien,
                 Qu'il ne le pourroit rendre et le voulut-il bien.

f. 41–4   L'Oracle de Memnon ses secrets ne découure,
                 Que les rays du Soleil n'aillent sa bouche ouurant.
                 Si tes belles raisons tu ne vas découurant,
                 Le Parlement aussi ses Decrets ne nous ouure.

(11) Elision of mute e: f. 18 'Infini'ment'.

The changes between this 1599 edition and that of 1601 seem to conform to the conclusions formed in Appendix I. No influence of Malherbe can be seen between these two editions, the only definite changes being a lessening of obscurity, a very slight cutting of repetitions, and of prosaic expressions.[1]

Obscurity (inversions, apposition to object, etc.):

⎰ a. 30–1   Nul n'eut recours à moy qui ne m'eust secourable,
                 Luy fournissant d'argent, et de vin et de pain . . .
⎱ becomes   Tandis que ie vesqui le pauure miserable
                 Ayant recours à moy me trouua secourable;
                 Et ie fournis d'argent de bruuage et de pain . . .

---

[1] For this examination, of course, only the first five poems can be used, as the other two do not appear in the 1601 edition.

a. 95	Bien qu'en mourant de vous ie vienne m'absenter
becomes	Si de vous en mourant il me faut absenter

a. 177–8	Aussi le doit-il bien, car sa prochaine perte,
	Ceste couche luy rend solitaire et deserte.
becomes	Plus il va repensant à sa prochaine perte,
	Plus son âme attristée est aux douleurs ouuerte.

a. 187–8	Lors se tenant tout coy, se presente à ses yeux,
	Ie ne sçay quoy plus clair que le Soleil des cieux.
becomes	Lors se tenant tout coy, il void deuant ses yeux . . . etc.

a. 230	Apres auoir vescu, place t'est assignée.
becomes	Ton cours estant fini, place t'est assignée.

Repetitions: These are cut down slightly when used to excess:

a. 11–13 is slightly cut down,	
	Plus elle me flattoit, plus ie la méprisois,
	Plus ie la méprisois, plus ie la métrisois,
	Plus ie la métrisois, et plus i'auois d'ennuie . . .
becoming	Plus elle me flattoit, plus ie la méprisois,
	Plus ie la méprisois, plus ie la métrisois,
	Gardant diligemment et le soin et l'ennuie . . .

c. 5	Mondains, viuez au monde autant que vous pourrez.
becomes	Viués, pauures Mondains, autant que vous pourrés.

c. 8	Le songe ne seront que de l'ombre d'un songe.
becomes	Ne seront toutefois que l'ombre d'un court songe.

c. 36	Et pour vous plaire encor me plaist de me deplaire.
becomes	Et pour plaire à vous seul ie veux bien me deplaire.

All the other repetitions I have mentioned remain in 1601.

Prosaic expressions:

a. 19–20	Ie suis preste à partir, et ne remporte rien
	En terre qu'un limon que d'elle aussi ie tien.
becomes	Ie suis preste à partir et ie n'emporte rien
	Sinon ce que i'ay fait ou voulu faire bien.

a. 138	Alors prenant au Ciel sa gaillarde volee.
becomes	Alors volant au Ciel, de prison relaschée.

a. 206	Le Nectar dans les cieux à longs traits ie puis boire.
becomes	En la coupe de Dieu le Nectar ie puis boire.

All the other faults that I have mentioned remain on the whole, with occasional suppressions or re-introductions which, point to no definite purpose.

These poems, then, written at a time when, if at all, Montchrestien should have been most under the influence of Malherbe, i.e. towards the end of 1599, and thus towards the end of Malherbe's stay in Caen, show no direct influence of this poet. Added to this, the changes in the 1601 edition, presumably made between late 1599 and late 1600 (the first privilège for the 1601 edition is 12 December 1600, the second 9 January 1601) conform to my findings as to the changes between the 1596 and the 1601 editions of *Sophonisbe* and show merely a desire for greater clarity and nobility of style.

Bibliography

In the case of works which are rare, details of the libraries in which they are to be found are given. For Montchrestien himself, all known editions are listed. For other authors, on the whole the most available of reliable editions is listed.

(a) *Works by Montchrestien*

1. *Sophonisbe, Tragédie*, Caen, Vve. Jacques le Bas, 1596, pet. in-8°.
Arsenal B.L. 14,057 (only copy)

2. *Les Derniers Propos, avec le Tombeau de feu noble dame Barbe Guiffart, femme de messire Claude Groulart* . . ., Rouen, Raphael du Petit Val, 1599, in-8°.
B.Nat. Rés. p. z. 1578 (only copy)

3. *Bergerie*, Rouen, ?1600, in-8°. (Part of a collection: pp. 370–469; incomplete.)
B.M. 163. d. 8 (only copy)

4. *Les Tragedies de Ant. de Montchrestien, sieur de Vasteville, plus une Bergerie et un poème de Susan* . . ., Rouen, Jean Petit, s.d. [1601] in-8°, deux parties en 1 vol. (Contains the tragedies *L'Escossoise*, *La Cartaginoise* (i.e. *Sophonisbe*), *Les Lacènes*, *David*, *Aman*. Also the *Bergerie* and the long poem *Susane ou la chasteté*. Also many shorter poems.)
B.M. 11735. bbb
B.Nat. Yf. 2083–4
Arsenal B.L. 13,610

5. *Les Tragedies de Ant. de Montchrestien, sieur de Vasteville, plus une Bergerie et un poëme de Susan* . . ., Rouen, Jean Petit, 1603, in-12° (reprint of 1601 edition).
Arsenal B.L. 12,622 (only copy)

6. *Escossoise, ou le desastre, tragedie. Seconde édition*, Rouen, Jean Petit, 1603, in-12°.
B.M. 1073 d. 7(1)

7. *Les Tragédies d'Antoine de Montchrestien, sieur de Vasteville* . . . *Edition nouvelle augmentée par l'auteur*, Rouen, Jean Osmont, 1604. (Contains new versions of the five previous tragedies (the title of *L'Escossoise* being

changed to *La Reine d'Escosse*), and a new tragedy, *Hector*. It also includes the poem *Susane*, but not the *Bergerie* or the *poésies diverses*.)

> B.M. 240. a. 34
> B.Nat. Rés. p. Yf. 90
> Arsenal B.L. 12,623
> Institut Q. 561. b

8. *Au Roy* (poem, signed: Montchrestien), s.l.n.d., in-4°.

> B.Nat. Rés. Ye. 835 (only copy)

9. *Les Tragédies d'Anthoine de Montchrestien, sieur de Vasteville* . . . *Dernière édition, reveüe et augmentée par l'autheur*, Nyort, Jacques Vaultier, 1606, in-12°. (Reproduction of 1604 edition, but a bad one.)

> B.Nat. Yf. 2085

10. *Au Roy*, in *Le Parnasse des plus excellens poètes de ce temps*, collected by d'Espinelle, Paris, Mathieu Guillemot, 1607, in-12°.

> Inst. Q. 314A

11. *Traicté de l'œconomie politique, dédié au Roy et à la Reyne mère du Roy, par Antoyne de Montchrétien* [sic], *sieur de Vateville*, s.l.n.d. [Priv. 1615], in-fo.

> B.Nat. Rés. *E. 244

12. *Les Tragédies d'Anthoine de Montchrestien, sieur de Vasteville* . . . *Edition nouvelle, augmentée par l'autheur*, Rouen, Pierre de la Motte, 1627, in-8°. (Reproduction of 1601 edition, thus without *Hector*. Misses out also some of the *poésies diverses*.)

> B.Nat. Rés. p. Yf. 91
> Arsenal B.L. 12,624

13. *L'Économie politique patronale, traicté de l'œconomie politique dédié en 1615 au Roy et à la Reyne mère du Roy, par Antoyne de Montchrétien, avec introduction et notes par Th. Funck-Brentano*, Paris, Plon, Nourrit et Cie., 1889, in-8°.

14. *Montchrestiens Sophonisbe, Paralleldruck der drei davon erschienenen Bearbeitungen, besorgt von Ludwig Fries*, Ausgaben und Abhandlungen, t. lxxxv, Marburg, 1889, in-8°.

15. *Les Tragédies de Montchrestien, nouvelle edition, d'après l'édition de 1604, avec notice et commentaire, par L. Petit de Julleville*, Paris, Plon, Nourrit et Cie., 1889, in-16°.

16. *La Reine d'Escosse, tragédie. Texte critique établi d'après les quatre éditions de 1601, 1604, 1606, 1627, par les élèves de seconde année de l'École Normale, sous la direction de G. Michaut*, Paris, A. Fontemoing, 1905, in-16°.

> B.Nat. Yth. 31310

17. *Aman*, a critical edition by G. O. Seiver, Philadelphia, 1939, in-8°.

18. *Les Lacènes*, a critical edition, by G. E. Calkins, Philadelphia, 1943, in-8°.

> B.Nat. 8°. Z. 31132 (8)

19. *David; édition critique*, by Lancaster E. Dabney. The University Co-operative Society, Austin, Texas, 1963.

(b) *Works attributed to Montchrestien*

1. Stances (signed A. de Mont.), and Élégie, 'Si David revivoit', in *Sonets spirituels de feüe tres-vertueuse et tres-docte Dame Sr. Anne de Marquets Religieuse à Poissi, sur les dimanches et principales solennitez de l'Année. à Mme. de Fresnes*, Paris, Claude Morel, 1605, in-8°.

B.Nat. Rés. Ye. 2058

2. Sonnet (signed Mon Chrestien) in *Œuvres poétiques du sieur Daudiguier*, Paris, Toussainct du Bray, 1614, in-8°.

B.Nat. Ye. 11450–1
B.M. 240. f. 6

(c) *Works by other authors (up to the end of the 17th century)*

AESCHYLUS: *Tragedies*, Loeb edition, 2 vols.

APHTHONIUS: *Progymnasmata, partim a Rodolpho Agricola, partim a Ioanne Maria Cataneo Latinitate donata: cum luculentis et utilibus in eadem Scholiis Reinhardi Lorichii Hadamarii*, London, 1583.

APPIEN ALEXANDRIN: *Des guerres des Romains, livres XI, traduicts en françois par feu maistre Claude de Seyssel . . . plus y sont adjoutez deux livres nouvellement traduicts de grec en françoys par le seigneur d'Avenelles . . .*, Paris, B. Prevost, 1560, 3 tomes en 1 vol., in-8°.

B.Nat. 8°. J. 6700

—— *Des guerres des Romains, traduit de grec en françois par M. Odet Philippe, sieur Des Mares . . .*, Paris, A. de Sommaville, 1659. in-fo.

B.Nat. Fol. J. 187

D'AUBIGNAC, ABBÉ: *Pratique du théâtre* (ed. Martino), Alger, 1927.

BELLAUD, J.-B.: *Phaéton, Bergerie tragique des guerres et tumultes civiles . . .*, Lyon, 1574, in-8°.

Mazarine 35,270

BÈZE, THÉODORE DE: *Abraham sacrifiant, tragédie françoise*, Genève, 1550, in-8°.

BILLARD, CLAUDE: *Tragédies*, Paris, F. Huby, 1612.

B.Nat. Rés. Yf. 2972

BRINON, PIERRE DE: Buchanan's *Baptistes*, a translation from the Latin, Rouen, Jean Osmont, 1613, in-16°.

B.Nat. Rés. p. Yc. 1556

—— *La Tragédie des rebelles*, Paris, Vve. Ducarroy, 1622, in-12°.

B.Nat. Yf. 12023

BUCHANAN, GEORGE: *Jephthes, Baptistes, Alcestis*, and *Medea* (in complete works), Amstelaedami, 1687.

CHANTELOUVE, J.-F. G. DE: *La Tragédie de feu Gaspar de Colligni . . .*, s.l., 1575, in-8°.

B.Nat. Yf. 6359

CHRESTIEN, FLORENT: *Jephté ou le veu: tragédie tirée du latin de George Buchanan,* L. Rabier, Orléans, 1567, in-4°.

                                                                        B.Nat. Rés. m. Yc. 885 (1)

COIGNAC, JOACHIM DE: *La déconfiture de Goliath, tragédie,* s.l.n.d., in-8°.

                                                                        B.Nat. Rés. Yf. 4349

DARÈS DE PHRYGIE: *L'Histoire véritable de la guerre des Grecs et des Troyens . . . Ensemble les effigies des Grecs et Troyens plus signalez . . . Escrite premierement en grec par Darès de Phrygie, depuis traduite en latin par Corneille Nepueu et faite françoise par Charles de Bourgueville,* Caen, 1893. (Facsimile of original 1572 edition, printed in 136 copies. Original destroyed in Normandy landings, 1944.)

DES MASURES, LOUIS: (see also PHILONE) *Tragédies sainctes,* Geneve, 1566, in-8°.

——*Tragédies sainctes,* Paris, Droz, 1933.

DIODORE DE SICILE: *Histoire de Diodore Sicilien, traduite de grec en françois, les premiers livres par M. Robert Macault . . . et les autres sont traduits par M. Jacques Amyot . . . Reveüe et enrichie de table et annotations en marge, par M. Loys de Roy, dit Regius,* Paris, M. Guillemot, 1585, in-fo.

                                                                        B.Nat. J. 681

DION CASSIUS: *Des faictz et gestes insignes des Romains . . . premièrement traduict de grec en italien par messire Nicolas Leonicene, ferrarois, et depuis de italien en vulgaire françois, par Claude Deroziers,* Paris, les Angeliers, 1542, in-fo.

                                                                        B.Nat. J. 960

DU BARTAS, GUILLAUME DE SALUSTE: *Œuvres,* Paris, J. Febvrier, 1580, in-12°.

                                                                        B.Nat. Rés. 1956–7

DU BELLAY, JOACHIM: *Deffense et illustration de la langue françoyse,* Paris, 1549, in-8°.

DU RYER, PIERRE: *Esther, Saül,* in *Théâtre françois,* t. iii, Paris, 1737, in-8°.

ERASMUS: *Opera Omnia . . .* Lugduni Batavorum, 1703, 10 vols. (*Parabolae,* tom. i. Translations of *Hecuba* and *Iphigeneia,* tom. i. *Adagia,* tom. ii. *Apophthegmata,* tom. iv.)

EURIPIDES: *Tragedies,* Loeb edition, 4 vols.

FENNER, DUDLEY: *The artes of logike and rethorike, plainlie set foorth in the Englishe tongue . . .,* (Middelburg), 1584.

FONTENY, JACQUES DE: *Cleophon,* Paris, 1600, in-8°.

                                                                        B.Nat. Rés. Yf. 3888

FRAUNCE, ABRAHAM: *The Arcadian rhetorike,* ed. from the edition of 1588 by E. Seaton, Oxford, 1950.

—— *The lawiers logike,* London, 1588.

GARNIER, ROBERT: *Les Tragédies,* Paris, 1585, in-12°.

—— *Œuvres complètes* (ed. Pinvert), Paris, 1923.

—— *La Troade, Antigone* (ed. Lebègue), Paris, 1952.

——— *Les Juifves, Bradamante* (ed. Lebègue), Paris, 1949.

GRÉVIN, JACQUES: *Le Théâtre de J.G.*, Paris, 1561, in-8°.

—— *Théâtre complet et Poésies choisies* (ed. Pinvert), Paris, 1922.

HOMÈRE: *Les XXIV livres de l'Iliade . . . traduicts du grec en vers françois, les XI premiers par M. Hugues Salel . . . et les XIII derniers par Amadis Jamyn*, Paris, Breyer, 1580, in-8°.

B.Nat. Yb. 1121

JODELLE, ESTIENNE: *Les Œuvres et meslanges poétiques*, Paris, 1574, in-4°.

—— *Cléopâtre, Didon*, in *Ancien Théâtre françois*, vol. 4, Paris, Jannet, 1855.

JOSEPHUS: *Jewish Antiquities, Book vi*, Loeb edition, London, 1950.

LA CROIX, ANTOINE DE: *Tragi-Comédie*, s.l.n.d. [1561].

B.Nat. Rés. p. Yc. 1198 (2)

LA PÉRUSE, JEAN BASTIER DE: *La Médée, tragedie*, Poitiers, 1556, in-4°.

—— *Œuvres*, ed. E. Gellibert des Seguins, Paris, 1867, in-8°.

LA TAILLE, JEAN DE: *Saül le furieux*, Paris, Morel, 1572, in-8°.

—— *Saül le furieux* (in *Münchener Beiträge*, t. 40), Leipzig, 1908.

—— *La Famine, ou les Gabéonites . . .*, Paris, Morel, 1573, in-8°.

B.Nat. 8°. Yf. 467

—— *De l'art de la tragédie* (ed. F. West), Manchester, 1939.

LAUDUN DAIGALIERS, PIERRE DE: *Art poëtique françois*, Paris, du Brueil, 1597, in-16°.

LIBANIUS: *Praeludia Oratoria LXXII, Declamationes XLV et Dissertationes Morales, Federicus Morellus . . . nunc primum edidit; idemque Latine vertit*, Paris, 1606.

MAIRET, JEAN DE: *Sophonisbe* (ed. Dédéyan), Paris, 1945.

MALHERBE, FRANÇOIS DE: *Corrections de Desportes*, in Lalanne edition, Paris, 1862–9, 5 vols., in-8°.

MATTHIEU, PIERRE: *Esther, tragédie*, Lyon, 1585, in-8°.

—— *Vasthi, tragédie*, Lyon, B. Rigaud, 1589, in-12°.

B.M. 840. a. 9. (1)

—— *Aman, tragédie*, Lyon, B. Rigaud, 1589, in-12°.

B.M. 840. a. 9. (2)

—— *Clytemnestre, tragédie*, Lyon, B. Rigaud, 1589, in-12°.

B.M. 840. a. 9. (3)

—— *Troisiesme édition de 'la Guisiade'*, I. Roussin, Lyon, 1589, in-8°.

B.M. 1073. d. 35

—— *Histoire des derniers troubles de France . . .*, Lyon, 1594–5, in-8°.

—— *Histoire des derniers troubles de France*, s.l., 1600, in-8°.

MERMET, CLAUDE: *Sophonisbe*, Lyon, 1584, in-8°.

Arsenal Re 3565
B.Nat. Rés. p. Yd. 11

MIRANDULA: *Illustrium poetarum flores*, Lugduni, 1553.

MONTREUX, NICHOLAS DE: *Sophonisbe*, Rouen, 1601, in-8°.

Arsenal B.L. 14592

MURET, M.-A.: *Julius Caesar* (in *Delitiae C. Poetarum Gallorum . . . Collectore Ranutio Ghero . . . Prostant in officina Jonae Rosae*, 1609 . . ., vol. 2).

Mystere du Viel Testament, ed. Rothschild.

NAOGEORGUS: *Hamanus* (in Oporin's *Dramata sacra*), Bâle, 1547.

NÉRÉE, R.-J.: *Le Triomphe de la Ligue*, Leyde, 1607, in-8°.

B.Nat. Yf. 6527

PELETIER DU MANS, JACQUES: *Art poëtique*, Lyon, 1555, in-8°.

—— *Art poëtique* (ed. Boulanger), Paris, 1930.

PETRARCH: *Africa*, Paris, 1872, in-8°.

B.Nat. Yc. 11692

PHILONE: *Josias, tragédie*, Genève, Perrin, 1566, in-8°.

B.Nat. Yf. 6508

—— *Adonias, tragédie*, Lausanne, Chiquelle, 1586, in-8°.

B.Nat. Rés. m. Yf. 10

PLUTARQUE: *Vies des hommes illustres* (tr. Amyot), N.R.F., Paris, 1951.

—— *Les Vies de Hannibal et Scipion l'Africain* (tr. Charles de l'Ecluse), Paris, Vascosan, 1567, in-8°.

B.Nat. Rés. J. 2095–2100

POLYBE: *Histoires* , tr. Louis Maigret, Lyon, J. de Tournes, 1558, in-fo.

B.Nat. J. 932

PRISCIANUS: *De praeexercitamentis Rhetoricae ex Hermogene* (in Priscian's complete works), Florentiae, 1525.

PUTTENHAM: *The arte of English poesie*, 1589.

RAINOLDE, RICHARD: *A booke called the foundacion of rhetorike . . .*, London, 1563.

RAMUS, PETRUS: *Dialecticae libri duo*, Francofurti, 1579.

Rhetorica ad Herennium: (*Ad. C. Herennium de Ratione Dicendi*), Loeb edition.

RIVAUDEAU, ANDRÉ DE: *Œuvres*, Poitiers, 1566, in-8°.

—— *Œuvres*, ed. C. Mourain de Sourdeval, Paris, Aubry, 1859, in-8°.

ROILLET, CLAUDE: *Varia Poemata*, Paris, 1556, in-16°.

—— *Philanire* (translated into French by the author), Paris, Th. Richard, 1563, in-4°.

Inst. Q. 147a

RONSARD, PIERRE DE: *Abrégé de l'art poëtique françois*.

SAINT-GELAIS, MELLIN DE: *Sophonisba*, Paris, 1559, in-8°.

B.Nat. Rés. Yf. 3972

Scaligerana, Coloniae Agrippinae, apud Gerbrandum Scagen, 1667.

SEBILLET, THOMAS: *Art poëtique françoys*, Paris, 1548, in-8°.

—— *Art poëtique françoys*, ed. Gaiffe, Paris, 1910.

SENECA: *Tragedies*, Loeb edition, 2 vols.

SHERRY, RICHARD: *A treatise of schemes and tropes*, London, 1550.

—— *A treatise of the figures of grammar and rhetorike*, London, 1555.

SOPHOCLES: *Tragedies*, Loeb edition, 2 vols.

TALAEUS, AUDOMARUS: *Rhetorica, e P. Rami . . . praelectionibus observata*, Francofurti, 1601.

TEISSIER, A.: *Les Éloges des hommes savans, tirez de l'histoire de M. de Thou*, 2 vols., Genève, Widerhold, 1683.

TRISSINO: *Sofonisba*, Vicenza, 1529, in-4°.

B.M. 82 k. 3

VAUQUELIN DE LA FRESNAYE, JEAN: *Art poëtique françois*, Caen, 1605.

—— *Art poëtique* (ed. G. Pellissier), Paris, 1885.

WILSON, THOMAS: *The arte of rhetorique . . .*, London, 1553.

(d) Critical works

ANDRAE, A.: 'Sophonisbe in der französischen Tragödie', *Zeitschrift Französischer Sprache und Literatur*, Supplementheft (1891), Oppeln, 1891.

AXELRAD, A. J.: *Le Thème de Sophonisbe dans les principales tragédies de la littérature occidentale — France, Angleterre, Allemagne*, Lille, 1956.

BALMAS, ENEA: *Un poeta del rinascimento francese, Étienne Jodelle, — la sua vita — il suo tempo*, Con una premessa di Marcel Raymond, Firenze, Olschki, 1962.

BANACHÉVITCH, N.: *Jean Bastier de la Péruse (1529–1554)*: *Étude biographique et littéraire*, Paris, 1923.

BARBIER, R.: 'Le Théâtre militant au XVIᵉ siecle', *Vierteljahrschrift*, 1872, pp. 176–204.

BÖHM, KARL: *Beiträge zur Kenntnis des Einflusses Senecas auf die in der Zeit von 1552 bis 1562 erschienenen französischen Tragödien*, Münchener Beiträge, t. 24, Leipzig, 1902.

BOLGAR, DR. R. R.: *The Classical heritage and its beneficiaries*, Cambridge, 1954.

BRAY, RENÉ: *La Formation de la doctrine classique en France*, Paris, 1957.

BREITINGER: *Les Unités d'Aristote avant 'Le Cid' de Corneille*, Genève, 1879.

BRUNEAU: *La Langue française*, Paris, 1955.

BRUNET, J. C.: *Manuel du libraire*, Paris, 1860–80.

BRUNOT: *La Doctrine de Malherbe*, Paris, 1891.

CASTOR, G. G.: *Pléiade poetics*, Cambridge.

CHARLTON, H. B.: *Senecan tradition in Renaissance tragedy*, Manchester, 1946.

CHARPENTIER, F.: 'La Tragédie précornélienne à Rouen: Montchrestien et la notion de clémence', *Bibliothèque d'Humanisme et Renaissance*, tome xxix. 2 (1967), pp. 305–38.

CLARK, DONALD LEMEN: *Rhetoric and poetry in the Renaissance*, New York, 1922.

—— *John Milton at St. Paul's School: a study of ancient rhetoric in English Renaissance education*, New York, 1948.

—— *Rhetoric in Greco-Roman education*, New York, 1957.

COLLISCHONN, G.: *Jacques Grévin's Tragödie 'César' in ihrem Verhältniß zu Muret, Voltaire und Shakespeare*, Ausgaben und Abhandlungen, 52, Marburg, 1886.

DABNEY, LANCASTER E.: *French dramatic literature in the reign of Henry IV*, Austin, Texas, 1952.

DAELE, ROSE MARIE: *Nicholas de Montreux—Ollenix du Montsacré, arbiter of European literary vogues of the late Renaissance*, New York, 1946.

DALEY, T. A.: *Jean de la Taille, 1533–1608. Étude historique et littéraire*, Paris, 1934.

DANNHEISSER, E.: 'Zur Geschichte der Einheiten in Frankreich', *Z. Fr. Spr. L.* (1892).

DELCOURT, MARIE: *Études sur les traducteurs des tragiques grecs et latins en France depuis la Renaissance*, Bruxelles, 1925.

DUVAL, JULES: *Mémoire sur Antoine de Montchrestien, Sieur de Vasteville . . . Lu en séance de l'Académie des sciences morales et politiques*, Paris, 1868.

EBNER, DR. J.: *Beitrag zu einer Geschichte der dramatischen Einheiten in Italien*, Münchener Beiträge, t. 15, Leipzig, 1898.

FAGUET, É: *La Tragédie en France au XVIe siecle*, Paris, 1883.

FISCHER, K.: *Über Montchrestiens Tragödien*, 1. Teil, 1893.

FORSYTH, ELLIOTT: *La Tragédie française de Jodelle à Corneille (1553–1640), le thème de la vengeance*, Paris, Nizet, 1962.

FRIES, L.: *Montchrestiens Sophonisbe, seine Vorgänger und Quellen*, Ausgaben und Abhandlungen, 85, Marburg, 1886.

GRAS, MAURICE, *Robert Garnier, son art et sa méthode*, Travaux d'Humanisme et Renaissance, lxxii, Genève, Droz, 1965.

HARASZTI, J.: Communication in *R.H.L.F.* (1904), 690 ff.

HOLL, F.: *Das politische und religiöse Tendenzdrama des 16. Jahrhunderts in Frankreich*, Münchener Beiträge, t. 26, Erlangen, 1903.

HOWELL, W. S.: *Logic and rhetoric in England, 1500–1700*, Princeton, 1956.

JONDORF, GILLIAN, 'Robert Garnier and the techniques of political tragedy in the 16th century' (unpublished Ph.D. Thesis, Cambridge, 1964).

KAHNT, P.: *Gedankenkreis der Sentenzen in Jodelle's und Garnier's Tragödien und Seneca's Einfluß auf denselben*, Ausgaben und Abhandlungen, 66, Marburg, 1887.

KIPKA, K.: *Maria Stuart im Drama der Weltliteratur, vornehmlich des XVII. und XVIII. Jahrhunderts*, Breslauer Beiträge, 9, Leipzig, 1907.

KLEIN, DR. FRIEDRICH: *Der Chor in den wichtigsten Tragödien der französischen Renaissance*, Münchener Beiträge, t. 12, Leipzig, 1897.

KOHLER, ERWIN: *Entwicklung des biblischen Dramas des sechzehnten Jahrhunderts*, Leipzig, 1911.

LANCASTER, H. CARRINGTON: *A History of French dramatic literature in the 17th century*, Baltimore, 1929.

LANSON, G.: *Esquisse d'une histoire de la tragédie en France*, New York, 1920.

—— 'Études sur les origines de la tragédie classique en France', *R.H.L.F.* (1903), pp. 177 ff., 413 ff.

—— 'La littérature française sous Henri IV: Antoine de Montchrestien', *Revue des Deux Mondes* 107, Paris, 1891, pp. 369–87. (Also in *Hommes et Livres*.)

—— 'Les sources historiques de *La Reine d'Escosse*', *Revue Universitaire*, May 1905.

LAWTON, H. W.: *Handbook of French Renaissance dramatic theory*, Manchester, 1949.

—— 'The Confidant in and before French classical tragedy', *M.L.R.*, 1943, pp. 18 ff.

—— 'Note sur le décor scénique', *Revue du XVIe siecle*, 1928, pp. 161 ff.

LEBÈGUE, R.: *La Tragédie religieuse en France: les débuts (1514–1573)*, Paris, 1929.

—— *La Tragédie française de la Renaissance*, Brussels, 1944.

—— 'Malherbe correcteur de tragédie', *R.H.L.F.* (1934).

LEROY, J. P.: ' "L'Ampoule venteuse" ou de quelques images baroques dans le théâtre d'Antoine de Montchrestien', *R.H.L.F.* (1964).

LOTZ, H.: *Der Versbau Antoine de Montchrestiens*, Darmstadt, 1905.

LOUKOVITCH, K.: *L'Évolution de la tragédie religieuse classique en France*, Paris, 1933.

LUCAS, D. W.: *The Greek tragic poets*, London, 1959.

LÜCKEN: *Zur Syntax Montchrestiens*, Darmstadt, 1894.

MARQUIGNY: 'Marie Stuart dans l'histoire, dans le drame et dans le roman', *Études Religieuses* (1864).

MOUFLARD, MARIE-MADELEINE: *Robert Garnier, 1545–1590*, 3 vols., La Ferté-Bernard, R. Bellanger, 1961, 1963, 1964.

ONG, W. J., S.J.: *Ramus: Method, and the decay of dialogue*, Harvard, 1958.

OTTO, R.: Introduction to Mairet's *Silvanire*, Bamberg, 1890.

PINVERT, L.: *Jacques Grévin (1538–1570): Étude biographique et littéraire*, Paris, 1899.

PURKIS, HELEN MARY: 'Les écrits théoriques sur le théâtre en France', unpublished Thèse de Doctorat d'Université, Paris, 1952.

RASHDALL, HASTINGS: *The universities of Europe in the Middle Ages* (edited by Powicke and Emden), 3 vols., Oxford, 1936.

RICCI, C.: *Sophonisbe dans la tragédie italienne et française*, Grenoble, 1904.

RIGAL, E.: *De Jodelle à Molière*, Paris, 1911.

—— *Le Théâtre français avant la période classique*, Paris, 1901.

ROATEN, DARNELL: *Structural forms in the French theater, 1500–1700*, Philadelphia, 1960.

SCHÉRER, J.: *La Dramaturgie classique en France*, Paris, 1950.

SCHOLL, S.: *Die Vergleiche in Montchrestiens Tragödien*, Munich, 1894.

SCHWARTZ, R.: *Esther im deutschen und neulateinischen Drama des Reformationszeitalters*, Oldenburg, 1894.

SCHWARTZ AND OLSEN: *The sententiae in the dramas of Corneille*, San Francisco, 1939.

SEARLES, COLBERT: 'The Stageability of Garnier's Tragedies', *M.L.N.* xxii.

SEIDMANN, A. D.: 'La Bible dans les tragédies religieuses de Garnier et de Montchrestien', unpublished Thèse de Doctorat d'Université, Paris, 1953.

SEIVER, G. O.: 'Did Malherbe Correct Montchrestien?', *P.M.L.A.* 55 (1940), pp. 968–78.

SPORLEDER, CARL: *Über Montchrestiens 'Escossoise'* (Diss.), Marburg, 1893.

TITMUS, C. J.: 'The Influence of Montchrestien's *Écossoise* upon French classical tragedies with subjects from English History', *French Studies* (1956), pp. 224–30.

TUVE, ROSEMOND: *Elizabethan and Metaphysical imagery*, Chicago, 1947.

VAUDICHON, G. DE: *Montchrestien (1575–1621)*, Amiens, 1882.

WENZEL, G.: *Aesthetische und sprachliche Studien über Antoine de Montchrestien*, Weimar, 1885.

WILLNER, DR. KURT: *Montchrestiens Tragödien und die stoische Lebensweisheit*, Romanische Studien, 32, Berlin, 1932.

YARROW, P. J.: 'Montchrestien: a Sixteenth- or Seventeenth-Century Dramatist?' *Australian Journal of French Studies*, vol. iv., no. 2 (1967), pp. 140–9.

(e) *Works used for Montchrestien's biography*

(I mark with an asterisk books not previously used by biographers of Montchrestien.)

ANON.: **La Prise et réduction de la ville de Gergeau à l'obéissance du roi, fait par MM. les comte de Sainct Paul et maréchal de Vitry, le dimanche 23 mai, 1621*, Paris, C. Chappellain, 1621, in-8°.

B.Nat. Lb. 36. 1649

—— *La Prise et réduction de la ville de Sancerre à l'obéissance du Roy par Mgr. le prince de Condé le samedy 29 may 1620*, Paris, Pierre Rocolet, 1621, in-8°.

B.Nat. Lb. 36. 1652

—— *La Prise de la ville et chasteau de Sancerre par Mgr. le prince de Condé*, Paris, Nicolas Alexandre, 1621, in-8°.

B.Nat. Lb. 36. 1653

—— *La Memorable Execution des rebelles à Sa Majesté; faite par arrest du parlement de Rouen, suivant le commandement du Roy, ensemble la deffaicte des Bandoliers courans la Normandie, par le sieur de Tourailles-Turgot* . . ., Paris, Abraham Saugrain, 1621, in-8°.

B.Nat. Lb. 36. 1767

—— *Discours véritable de ce qui s'est passé en Normandie, en la deffaicte de Vatteville et de ses bandoliers* . . . *Ensemble la condamnation et exécution dudit Vatteville* . . ., Paris, Abraham Saugrain, 1621, in-8°.

B.Nat. Lb. 36. 1766

AUVRAY, L.: '*L'Escossaise* de Montchrestien représentée à Orléans en 1603', *R.H.L.F.* (1897), pp. 89–91.

BEAUREPAIRE, CHARLES DE ROBILLARD DE, Actes communiqués par, *Bulletin de la commission des antiquités de la Seine-Inférieure*, 7 (1888), pp. 369–71.

*CAHAIGNES, JACQUES DE: *Éloges des citoyens de la ville de Caen. Traduction d'un curieux*, Caen, Le Blanc-Hardel, 1880 (printed in 225 copies).

*CHATEL, EUGÈNE: *Liste des recteurs de l'Université de Caen, dressée d'après leurs signatures sur les registres des rectories, et autres documents conservés aux Archives du Calvados*, Caen, 1882.

FLOQUET, P. A.: *Histoire du Parlement de Normandie*, Rouen, 1840–2, t. iv.

FROMILHAGUE, R.: *La Vie de Malherbe; apprentissages et luttes, 1555–1610*, Paris, 1954.

*FRONDEVILLE, HENRI DE: *Les Présidents du Parlement de Normandie (1499–1790). Recueil généalogique (établi sur la base du Manuscrit Bigot, de la bibliothèque de Rouen)*, Rouen and Paris, 1953.

*FIERVILLE, CHARLES DE: 'Histoire généalogique de la maison et de la baronnie de Tournebu', *Mémoires de la Société des Antiquaires de Normandie*, 3e série, 6e vol.

HAAG FRÈRES: *La France protestante*, Paris, 1847–58, vol. 7.

HÉRON, A.: *Documents concernant la Normandie* . . . (taken from *Mercure François*), Rouen, 1883.

JOLY, A.: *Antoine de Montchrestien, poète et économiste normand*, Caen, 1865.

LACHÈVRE, F.: 'Antoine de Montchrestien. Sa religion, son mariage', *R.H.L.F.* (1918).

LA FERRIÈRE: *Histoire du Canton d'Athis*, Paris, 1858.

LEBOITTEUX: *Les Huguenots des Isles*, Condé-sur-Noireau, 1907. (Contains documents connected with death of Montchrestien and capture of his companions.)

MALHERBE: *Letters* of 16 June and 2 August 1618 (to M. du Bouillon-Malherbe); *Letters* of 14 October and 2 November 1621 (to M. de Peiresc), ed. Lalanne, vols. 3 and 4.

MALINGRE, CLAUDE: *Histoire de la rébellion excitée en France par les rebelles de la religion prétendue réformee*, vol. i, Paris, 1622.

B.Nat. 8°. Lb. 36. 14

—— *Histoires tragiques de nostre temps*, Paris, C. Collet, 1635, in-8°.

B.Nat. G. 26240

Mercure François: 1621 (t. 7) and 1624 (t. 10).

*PETITOT: *Mémoires sur l'histoire de France*, vol. 49: (*Memoirs of Claude Groulart*).

B.Nat. L. 45. 19

YATES, F. A.: 'Some new light on *L'Écossaise* de Montchrestien', *M.L.R.* (1927), pp. 285–97.

INDEX

PRINTED IN GREAT BRITAIN
AT THE UNIVERSITY PRESS, OXFORD
BY VIVIAN RIDLER
PRINTER TO THE UNIVERSITY